Fifteen Lectures on Showa Japan

JAPAN LIBRARY

Fifteen Lectures on Showa Japan

Road to the Pacific War in
Recent Historiography

Edited by
Tsutsui Kiyotada

Translated by
Noda Makito and Paul Narum

Japan Publishing Industry Foundation for Culture

Note on Japanese names

The Hepburn system of romanization is used for Japanese terms, including the names of persons and places. All Japanese names appearing in this book are given in Japanese order, with family name first. Chinese words are romanized using the pinyin system. The romanization of Korean words follows the Revised Romanization of Korea. The local custom of placing the family name first has been followed for the names of Chinese and Korean persons as well as Japanese persons.

Fifteen Lectures on Showa Japan:
Road to the Pacific War in Recent Historiography
Edited by Tsutsui Kiyotada
Translated by Noda Makito and Paul Narum

Published by Japan Publishing Industry Foundation for Culture (JPIC)
3-12-3 Kanda-Jinbocho, Chiyoda-ku, Tokyo 101-0051, Japan

First edition: March 2016

Originally published in the Japanese language as *Showa-shi kogi: Saishin kenkyu de miru senso e no michi* by Chikumashobo Ltd. in 2015.

Jacket and cover design by Niizuma Hisanori
Front and cover photos © Kyodo News; Bettmann/CORBIS/amanaimages; Kyodo News/amanaimages

As this book is published primarily to be donated to overseas universities, research institutions, public libraries and other organizations, commercial publication rights are available. For all enquiries regarding those rights, please contact the publisher of the English edition at the following address: japanlibrary@jpic.or.jp

Printed in Japan
ISBN 978-4-916055-60-6
http://www.jpic.or.jp/japanlibrary/

Contents

LECTURE 14:
Emperor Hirohito's "Sacred Decisions" and the
Political Process of Japan's Surrender.....257
SUZUKI TAMON

LECTURE 15:
The Occupation of Japan: The International
Background behind the Policy of the
United States toward Japan.....277
IGUCHI HARUO

Editor's Note to the English Version

Seeing as there is no other book composed of contributions by the leading experts on each of the important issues in Showa history, it would not be an overstatement to say that the current volume is an invaluable addition to the literature. And the English translation of this book for the benefit of global readers is highly significant because it can not only let the world know the academically accurate Showa history but also help remedy any misunderstandings about Japan.

I seem to remember that there were many books like the current volume when I was young, but nowadays they have become almost extinct. This phenomenon might be attributable to a decline of the liberal arts, which has had the effect of diminishing learned people's sense of mission to inherit the fruits of hitherto accumulated knowledge and add new fruits of their own. While this may be a worldwide phenomenon, it is particularly conspicuous in Japan where the pressure from the masses is stronger than anywhere else.

Today, when the liberal arts are on the wane, one speaks something without knowing what is new in it oneself, and what was said is magnified by mass media with a poor sense of judgment owing to the dearth of awareness for such a thing as the accumulative development of knowledge. And in my judgment, the history of Showa has also been toyed with by this trend.

This book is a humble attempt at retaliation for this trend, and it is our sincere hope that we are not a complete minority. I am convinced that, with the help of this English version, our aspiration will be understood and shared by thoughtful readers of the world.

Although I have offered advice to contributors of chapters included in this volume as need be, it is needless to say that each chapter is independent and the views expressed in it are strictly those of its author.

Allow me to take this opportunity to express our gratitude to Mr. Matsuda Ken of the editorial department of Chikumashobo Ltd., for understanding the significance of publishing this kind of book at the juncture of the 70th anniversary of the end of World War II and for coordinating among the editor and authors to enable the publication. My gratitude also goes to the translation team, particularly Messrs. Noda Makito and Paul Narum and who took up the challenge of translating all of fifteen lectures contained in this volume in a very limited period of time. Last but not least, publication of this book from the Japan Publishing Industry Foundation for Culture (JPIC) would not have been possible without painstaking efforts by Ms. Asonuma Futsuki.

Tsutsui Kiyotada

January 2016

Foreword

In recent years, I have detected an upsurge of intellectual desire among the Japanese people to know more about the history of the Showa period. At times when friction caused by differences in perceptions of history has become a major diplomatic issue with countries such as China, Korea, and the United States, it may be only natural for the people's quest for what the truth is regarding Showa history to intensify.

While there have been such changes on the readers' side, what about the writers' side? Recently, I organized several seminars on Showa history among first-rate mid-career and young scholars. To my surprise, I discovered that the study of Showa history has been so fragmented and compartmentalized that a common perception hardly exists among the scholars.

Readers might be surprised to hear that, nowadays, even among the Showa historians—for instance, specialists on domestic politics in the early Showa period and specialists on Japan's diplomacy toward the end of World War II—communicating about their recent studies has become practically impossible. This goes to show that it has become difficult even for many researchers to accurately grasp the overall picture of this era called Showa.

In the world of academia, it often happens that the most advanced scholars have a hard time understanding the works of their colleagues studying a sub-genre in what, in the eyes of a layman, appears to be the same discipline. But it is problematic if this happens among specialists of such a limited topic as the history of Showa. While this experience has forced me to be keenly aware of the role of catalyst that we the older generations, including myself, should play for the benefit of younger scholars, the more serious problem is the impact that this academic tendency has on general readers who are increasingly interested in Showa history.

Although a strong desire to learn more about Showa is detected among general readers, they hardly benefit from the outcomes of the most advanced studies on specific issues in Showa history because such studies defy easy access by non-experts. Experts on Showa history, for their part, are so specialized in a compartmentalized segment of the history that they have no idea about the findings of their colleagues whose focus years are only slightly different from their own. And this is the background of the recent proliferation of handy, easy-to-understand books on Showa history by authors who are eager to meet the demand of general readers.

In other words, around the time the debate on historical perceptions became boisterous in around 2000, thus raising people's interest in Showa history, inaccurate popular readings on the subject proliferated.

Because outcomes of recent studies are hardly reflected in those books, they tend to inherit past errors unrevised and perpetuate lay views and hearsays unchecked. They are basically nothing but specious narratives of Showa history, unsubstantiated by empirical evidence, which are convenient and comfortable for the authors to write. From the viewpoint of experts of Showa history, these books are so fantastic that they are more objects of folklore studies than anything else.

To take an example from my field of specialization, several books recently appeared on the controversial *Showa Tenno jitsuroku* [The Chronicles of Showa Emperor], which was published at long last. I was amazed to find in those books a decades-old argument that Ishihara Kanji, a staff officer of the martial law headquarters who played a pivotal role in the February 26 Incident in 1936, "had embarked on the suppression of the mutinied troops from an early stage." This argument has long been rejected by experts.

It is an established view among experts today that it was Ishihara whom the rebel officers had trusted and relied on until the very end because he had been consistently sympathetic with the mutiny and had repeatedly proposed solutions that were in favor of the mutinied troops.

This sympathetic attitude toward the rebels by Ishihara, Chief of Operations of the Imperial Japanese Army General Staff and the staff officer in charge of the martial law headquarters, was a crucial factor in the February 26 Incident. Ishihara's attitude was one of the causes that possibly delayed the settlement. As long as these misperceptions on matters that fundamentally affect the interpretation of the incident persist and proliferate, the understanding of Showa history will remain distorted.

The above was just a case that I have encountered in my own field of specialization, but my co-authors of the present book, all of whom are reputable and reliable scholars in their own right, also testify that they, too, have encountered so many similar publications in their respective fields that taking the time to critique them is impossible. Experts wish to devote time and energy to their own academic explorations rather than wasting their resources on correcting such errors and misperceptions. Thus this deplorable situation is left unattended.

My view, however, is that the proliferation of these irresponsible books on Showa history is extremely dangerous. As one advances in his study of Showa, it becomes clear to him that its history is a highly complicated canvas composed of layers and layers of paradoxes. Against this background, over-simplified and irresponsible books on Showa history only hamper this important realization. An abundance of these books does not nurture wise readers and, instead, helps develop persons who are easily manipulated in a certain direction. Erroneous perceptions lead to erroneous conduct. The over-simplification of history only results in a "simplified history" that is moved only by simple-minded people.

What we can and should do first to put an end to this situation would be, in my view, to present readers with an accurate Showa history based only on reliable historical documents. After all, the dearth of such an accurate history is the cause of the current proliferation of inaccurate histories.

Given the above academic environment, it has become extremely difficult for a historian to single-handedly write a history of Showa. Nevertheless, it is still possible to write an accurate Showa history by compiling the works of specialists. And this is how the present book is constructed.

In compiling this volume, I requested each contributor to accurately disclose their most up-to-date research and to incorporate the findings of recent studies as much as possible in the most easy-to-understand manner. It appears that we have succeeded in achieving this goal beautifully. From all the chapters, I can detect the authors' joy in sharing with readers the most recent fruits of their work, and I am convinced that the end result will satisfy readers to the full.

One topic addressed herein that should attract most readers' attention is the US-Japan negotiations on the eve of the Pacific War. The United States responded to Japan's compromise proposal with the extremely strong-worded Hull note demanding that Japan withdraw its troops from China and French Indochina. While it is well known that the Hull note is what made Japan decide to start the war, this volume shall provide the outcome of the most recent exploration of the causes behind the Hull note.

At first, US Secretary of State Cordell Hull was considering presenting the Japanese side with a provisional agreement offering to lift the asset freeze on the condition that Japanese troops be withdrawn from southern French Indochina. Had this provisional agreement been presented to the Japanese side, it is highly probable that the eruption of war could have been avoided. Presentation of the hardliner Hull note instead has been chiefly attributed to China's and Britain's opposition to the provisional agreement proposal.

Given that China's opposition did not matter much to the United States and Britain's opposition to Hull's original idea was so muddied that Britain was later surprised to hear of the US decision to abandon it, it is hard to think that opposition by these two countries was the main factor behind the adoption of the Hull note. Instead, what can be said for certain from the most recent studies is that the United States had given up the option of averting war with negotiations and chosen the option that would force Japan's hand to start war.

The conspiracy theory purporting that the United States had known of Japan's plan to launch a surprise attack on Pearl Harbor beforehand has been repeatedly mentioned from earlier days, and not a small number of people believe this theory. Readers are urged to read the text that follows this foreword to learn more about the most recent findings on this issue.

In addition to descriptions of new research results, each lecture is supplemented with a list of selected reference books with brief annotations. It is my hope that this information provides useful guidance to those readers who wish to study more about the subject.

I wish for this compilation to be widely read, not only by general readers at large but also by students studying Showa history in colleges and universities. It is hoped that this book will help fill the aforementioned gap between the demand and supply of history books and make an accurate Showa history a shared intellectual heritage of the Japanese people. This in turn, I hope, will facilitate the writing of future Japanese history texts by a next generation of Japanese equipped to think based on a well-balanced, multifaceted foundation.

Tsutsui Kiyotada

Fifteen Lectures on Showa Japan:
Road to the Pacific War in
Recent Historiography

Lecture 1

The Washington Treaty System and Shidehara Diplomacy

Watanabe Kota

"New Diplomacy" and the Washington Treaty System

When the power balance—the traditional system of international relations in Europe—collapsed because of the impact of World War I, a new philosophy of the international order called "New Diplomacy" emerged. This New Diplomacy headed by US President Woodrow Wilson rejected the conventional, "the Old Diplomacy" based on traditional secret diplomacy, bilateral military alliances/entente, and competition in quest of overseas colonies. Convinced that these old habits were the main culprits of wars, Wilson appealed to the world that the Fourteen Points he had proposed in January 1918 would truly bring peace to the world.

As far as US-Japan relations were concerned, Wilson's idealistic internationalism worked negatively. During the Paris Peace Conference in 1919, Wilson delivered his criticism on Japan's conduct, including its dispatch of troops to Siberia, making the subsequent bilateral negotiations on the Shandong peninsula issue even more confrontational. At the time of the establishment of the New or Second China Consortium in 1920, Wilson attempted to restrict Japan's China policy, which he judged to be exclusive in nature. Militarily speaking, too, the naval arms race between Japan and the United States became fiercer. By the 1920–21 period, mutual distrust between the two countries had grown so much that some even talked about a war between the two.

It was under these circumstances that the Washington Conference was convened in 1921–22, during the Warren Harding Republican administration in the United States. The conference played the role of mitigating the confrontation across the Pacific between Japan and the United States. The period of international relations in East Asia during the decade sandwiched by the Washington Conference and the Manchurian Incident in 1931 is generally referred to as the "Washington Treaty system." The treaties were an attempt at launching a multilateral cooperative system around Japan, Britain, and the United States, and it has been interpreted as an embodiment of a new international order based on the philosophy of the New Diplomacy (Hosoya Chihiro, *Ryotaisen-kan no Nippon gaiko* [Japan's Diplomacy between Two World Wars], Iwanami Shoten, 1988).

Whether a new system emerged on the basis of several treaties signed at the Washington Conference or not, however, remains quite debatable. While the main agenda of the conference included the China issue, interests in the Pacific Ocean, and the naval arms limitation issue, all of which were causes of conflict among the world powers in those days, it cannot be said that consensus on these issues was reached among participants on the basis of lengthy deliberations. As Ian Nish has pointed out, an abundance of compromises and conformism was witnessed during the Washington Conference, as was the case in many other international talks, and there could not have been a scheme among participants to construct something that could be called a system (Ian Nish, *Japanese Foreign Policy, 1869–1942: Kasumigaseki to Miyakezaka*, Routledge & K. Paul, 1977). As discussed in detail later, there hardly was room for the Wilsonian idealism to intervene in the

Nine-Party Treaty, which, therefore, continued to be strongly affected by the old diplomacy based on the balance of power among the world powers.

In light of the fact that even relatively recent studies still question the wisdom of discussing international relations in those days around the concept of the "Washington Treaty system," it may be high time to reconsider the use of the concept in future studies of the history of international relations (Koike Seiichi, *Manshu jihen to tai Chugoku seisaku* [The Manchurian Incident and Japan's China Policy], Yoshikawa Kobunkan, 2003). And it should be an important future agenda for experts to propose an alternative analytical framework that supersedes the concept of the Washington Treaty system. (Readers should be advised that each author of the following chapters in this volume adopts a different definition of "Washington Treaty system" and no attempt is made to unify the definition.)

Foreign Minister Shidehara Enters

In Japan, it was Shidehara Kijuro—who twice served as foreign minister (1924–27 and 1929–31)—who highly valued the framework of the Washington Treaty system and made the greatest contribution to the construction of the interwar international order in East Asia on the basis of good relations with Britain and the United States.

Shidehara was born in 1872 (5th Year of Meiji) in Kadoma-mura (presently Kadoma City), Osaka, as the second son of wealthy farmer Shidehara Shinjiro. Upon graduation from the Faculty of Law of Tokyo Imperial University, Shidehara passed the 4th Foreign Service Examination in 1896 and entered the Ministry of Foreign Affairs. In the ministry hierarchy, Shidehara served as a consular official in Incheon, consul in London and other locations, director of telegraphic communications, counselor of the Japanese embassy in Washington, D.C., and the Japanese minister to the Netherlands. In these various posts, Shidehara was engaged in the practical side of the revision of unequal treaties and is-

5

sues over immigrants with the United States. From 1915 (4th Year of Taisho), he served as deputy foreign minister for four years under five consecutive foreign ministers (Ishii Kikujiro, Terauchi Masatake, Motono Ichiro, Goto Shinpei, and Uchida Yasuya). He was appointed ambassador to the United States in 1919. In this capacity, he served as plenipotentiary at the Washington Conference, playing a major role, in particular, in the signing of the Nine-Power Treaty affirming the sovereignty and territorial integrity of China as per the Open Door Policy. Although Shidehara had never been stationed in China, repeated negotiations with the Chinese delegation, particularly those members labeled "young China," taught him that a new era of the construction of a modern nation was emerging in China. That was why, after being appointed to foreign minister, Shidehara was determined to construct stable relations with China based on international treaties and agreements.

In June 1924, Shidehara was appointed foreign minister in Kato Takaaki's *Goken-Sanpa* cabinet (cabinet based on the three pro-constitution factions), making him the first foreign minister who had passed the Foreign Service Examination. Both Kato and Shidehara were married to daughters of Iwasaki Yataro, founder of Mitsubishi, making them brothers-in-law. But the appointment of Shidehara was motivated more by Kato's wish to realize his own diplomacy, which he had envisioned since his opposition party days. What this means is that Kato wished to pursue, through Shidehara, a foreign policy called the "Kasumigaseki orthodox diplomacy" based on good relations with Britain and the United States. For Kato, himself an elite bureaucrat, Shidehara, who had accumulated brilliant accomplishments as a career diplomat, was an ideal partner. Also, because Shidehara did not have strong connections with any of the political parties, he was viewed as a neutral figure, inviting hardly any opposition to his appointment. In particular, the high regard that Shidehara's diplomacy had earned from Prince Saionji Kinmochi, one of the Meiji elderly statesmen, made it possible for Kato's Kenseikai party to be one of the two parties, together with the Minseito, to take the helm of the government during the interwar period. By constructing stable relations with the Kenseikai (and also the Minseito), Shidehara prepared an environment to pursue his foreign policy.

Challenge Posed by China's Nationalism

When he assumed the foreign ministership, Shidehara publicly announced his China policy, including compliance with noninterference in domestic affairs and the deepening of economic relations with China based on equal opportunities in China among foreign powers. Through this China policy Shidehara intended to contribute to the construction of an international order in the spirit of the Nine-Power Treaty.

The greatest bottleneck to Shidehara's diplomacy was fierce civil wars in China. The first of those internal disturbances was the Second Zhili–Fengtian War in September 1924 (13th Year of Taisho) between the Fengtian clique based in Manchuria led by Zhang Zuolin and the Zhili clique under the leadership of Wu Peifu.

When the confrontation between those two parties became conspicuous, Foreign Minister Shidehara, in a memorandum issued through Debuchi Katsuji, Director-General of the Asian Affairs Bureau, immediately announced that Japan would refrain from interfering in the confrontation. When battle actually erupted, voices rose within Japan demanding the dispatch of Imperial Japanese Army troops to assist Zhang Zuolin. These voices were so loud that Prime Minister Kato and Agriculture and Commerce Minister Takahashi Korekiyo pressured Shidehara to reconsider and offer assistance to Zhang's army to cater to public opinion. Insisting that dispatching troops to assist Zhang would be tantamount to interference in China's internal affairs, which would inflate anti-Japanese nationalism among the Chinese people, Shidehara adamantly rejected the pressure.

Although at first the Fengtian clique had been losing in battle, the tables turned when opposing troops under Wu Peifu suffered a debacle: one of Wu's chief allies, Feng Yuxiang, deserted the front at a key moment. (It is a known fact that conspiracies engineered by the local out-

7

post of the Imperial Japanese Army were behind the desertion.) In the end, thanks to Shidehara's upholding of the principle of noninterference in internal affairs despite pressures toward the other direction from all corners around him, Japan did not invite international criticism of its conduct and succeeded in retaining its rights and interests in the Chinese continent unthreatened.

Shidehara's handling of the matter was widely praised by his colleagues, including Agriculture and Commerce Minister Takahashi, and his diplomatic skill became highly appreciated. His compliance with the principle of noninterference ended up protecting Japan's rights and interests in civil war-stricken China. Moreover, Japan's conduct at this time was also highly effective as an appeal for Japan's policy to collaborate with the western powers.

Shidehara did interfere, however, albeit in an indirect way, with affairs in Manchuria, where Japan had long been said to have special interests. Nevertheless, even that was done via peaceful measures such as negotiations with Zhang Zuolin instead of conventional militaristic measures that relied on armed forces.

When, all of a sudden, Guo Songling of the Fengtian clique mutinied against Zhang Zuolin in November 1925, Shidehara also took the position of noninterference, refusing to dispatch Imperial Japanese Army troops. When Zhang was endangered by Guo's advance, however, the Japanese government acted upon the recommendation of War Minister Ugaki Kazushige to dispatch troops from Japan as well as Korea to reinforce the defense capabilities of the Kwantung Army on the pretext of protecting Japanese residents in Manchuria. This action had the indirect effect of blocking the advances of Guo's troops, thus contributing to Zhang's victory. Although Zhang's political standing was protected, the occurrence of upheavals one after another destroyed the credibility of the Mukden currency (one of the Manchurian currencies), leading to the worsening of Manchuria's economic conditions and political stability.

In light of this development, Shidehara decided to promote stability in the political situation by encouraging Zhang to consolidate the finances of Manchuria's Three Northeast Provinces. This decision not only followed the conventional policy of Japan to protect Japan's rights and interests in Manchuria by providing assistance to Zhang but also contained the new element of Japan actively giving guidance to Zhang to promote stability in Manchuria. Although Shidehara's goal to attain stability in Manchuria was crippled by the subsequent Northern Expedition by the Kuomintang (1926–28), one can still detect Shidehara's long-term wish to pursue stabilization for Manchuria beyond merely promoting Japan's economic interests there (Nishida 2005).

Shidehara's noninterference principle faced new challenges as nationalism-led movements started in full swing on the Chinese mainland. Plainly speaking, the noninterference principle increasingly became an obstacle to coping with anti-foreign movements in central and southern China, where the western powers, particularly Britain, had maintained enormous rights and interests.

The turning point was a strike in early February 1925 launched by workers of a spinning plant in Shanghai owned by Japanese capital. The strike subsequently evolved into a large-scale demonstration on May 30; participants in the movement had mushroomed to the 10,000 level. During the demonstration, people chanted "Down with Japanese and British imperialism" and demanded the return of foreign concessions in China. Police guarding the British concession fired at demonstrators, inciting fierce clashes between the two sides that led to numerous casualties. This May Thirtieth movement, as it was later labeled, further inflated anti-imperialism sentiment among the Chinese people. Eventually such sentiment developed into a countrywide anti-foreign movement. Of the foreign powers in China, Britain became a particular target of Chinese animosity.

If truth be told, agitation by the Communist Party of China, which had become increasingly active since the First United Front in 1924, was behind the rise of the anti-foreign movement. Knowing this, the British government felt threatened by the expansion of the anti-foreign (particularly anti-Britain) movement, driven mainly by Chinese laborers, which swallowed up Guangzhou. Britain's national power was by this time already not strong enough to exercise the immense influence in East Asia as it did in pre–World War I days. Thus, as a new means to protect its rights and interests in China, Britain chose to strengthen its alliance with Japan, its former ally that had become a major power in East Asia. Britain viewed the alliance as a countermeasure against communist ideas and the anti-Britain movement.

For Japan, particularly Japanese economic organizations in Shanghai, too, closer cooperation with Britain was a desirable choice because rampant demonstrations and boycotts in China had become a serious threat. Shidehara in Tokyo, however, remained negative toward taking concrete action in cooperation with Britain against riots in China. From his viewpoint, the suppression of the anti-foreign movement in China with force in collaboration with the western powers would be tantamount to interfering in internal affairs and a violation of the Nine-Power Treaty.

Britain became quite displeased with Shidehara's noninterference philosophy. As the anti-foreign movement became even fiercer, Britain gradually began to take independent actions that distanced it from the framework of the Nine-Party Treaty supporting cooperation among western powers and noninterference with domestic affairs. For this reason, Britain's conduct became increasingly detached from the China policy that Shidehara had pursued, creating a discrepancy between two of the central signees of the Nine-Power Treaty. Although Shidehara diplomacy has been conventionally regarded as based on good relations with Britain and the United States, the above episode reveals that this evaluation was not always appropriate as far as relations with Britain were concerned (Goto 2006). The episode also shows the limitations of the Nine-Power Treaty.

Special Conference on the Chinese Customs Tariff (October 26, 1925–July 3, 1926)

The rise of nationalism in China accelerated its pursuit for correction of unequal treaties with the western powers. Thus, the Special Conference on the Chinese Customs Tariff convened in October 1925 in Beijing became a venue reflecting the contrast of perceptions between an increasingly nationalistic China and the western powers. While the conference failed to accomplish anything outstanding, it nevertheless was a significant occasion in the sense that the difference of perceptions on China among Japan, Britain, and the United States surfaced at the conference.

The purpose of the conference was to raise the tariff rate on imports to China, in return for China's abolition of Li-chin (a toll imposed in China in those days) as stipulated by the Nine-Power Treaty, and to discuss the timing and method of imposing a surtax. The Republic of China government under the provisional leadership of Duan Qirui was demanding a raise in the tariff rate in order to cope with the financial crunch caused by internal disturbances and to settle foreign loans. From the viewpoint of the western powers, China's tariff issue could facilitate unification of a divided China, with the assistance of the western powers, and expand trade with China.

For this conference, Shidehara appointed Hioki Eki, Minister to China, as Japan's plenipotentiary and Saburi Sadao, Director-General of the Foreign Ministry's Trade Bureau and Shidehara's right-hand man, as the chief attendant and secretary-general of the Japanese delegation. While Shidehara and his colleagues were sympathetic with China's wish to restore its tariff autonomy, they had their own idea on the method for imposing a surtax as an interim step toward tariff autonomy. The Japanese side agreed in principle with the Chinese demand for restoration of tariff autonomy, on the condition that it would be implemented in steps and that a gradation tax rate of 12.5 percent on average would be introduced for every increase in the tariff. In preconference negotiations, Saburi succeeded in obtaining informal consent on this scheme from one of China's chief delegates, Huang Fu.

When the conference was convened, Hioki made a speech at the outset to announce Japan's approval in principle of the restoration of China's tariff autonomy. This came as a surprise to the other participating countries. Nevertheless, because the majority of the participating countries were actually inclined toward the approval of China's tariff autonomy, the November 19 session adopted the resolution approving restoration of China's tariff autonomy in principle, effective January 1, 1929.

After this resolution, the conference moved on to discuss interim measures to be taken until the actual restoration of tariff autonomy. At this juncture, conference participants became embroiled in a heated argument on the issue of the conventional tariff and the use of the increased tax revenue. Representing the Japanese government, Saburi in February 1926 proposed adoption of a seven-gradation tax rate scheme for seven types of commodities. Because this system would not only increase China's tax revenue but also comply with the wish of Britain and the United States, the Japanese side almost succeeded in securing agreements from China, Britain, and the United States.

Almost concurrently, however, the Chinese delegation submitted a proposal requesting an immediate implementation of the 2.5 percent surtax that had been stipulated by the Washington Tariff Treaty. While Britain and the United States were accommodative to the Chinese proposal, Shidehara rejected it because it could hamper the seven-gradation tax rate scheme that Japan had proposed (Miyata 2014).

Because a coup that took place in China around that time brought down the Duan Qirui government, leaving Beijing in an anarchic situation, the conference ended without accomplishing any concrete outcomes. While the direct cause of the failure of this conference was, undoubtedly, the civil wars in China, some argue that Shidehara was also to blame for the failure to get an agreement among Japan, Britain, and the United States due to his single-minded adherence to Japan's economic interests. An opportunity for flexible cooperation among the world powers was lost (Hattori 2006). At the same time, however, it was an indisputable fact that China complicated things at the conference by presenting various demands beyond the stipulation of the Washington Tariff Treaty one after another. And countries including Britain also contributed to the failure to accomplish the original goal of China's fiscal reconstruction because they were too eager to accommodate China's demands.

Responses to the Northern Expeditions

After Sun Yat-sen passed away in March 1925, the Kuomintang established the Nationalist Government of the Republic of China in Guangzhou. To accomplish the unification of China, the Nationalist Government appointed Chiang Kai-shek as commandant of the National Revolutionary Army and launched the First Northern Expedition in July 1926. In the face of the successful campaign of the Northern Expeditions army, the western powers were urged to take measures to protect their rights and interests in China.

In order to cope with the situation within the framework of the Nine-Power Treaty, US Minister to China John MacMurray proposed coordination among the western powers on a reconciliatory policy toward the National Government. Convinced that easy compromise with the Nationalist Government would further worsen the confusion in China, Shidehara tried to persuade the British and US governments to maintain cautious attitudes toward the situation.

Going ahead of Shidehara, however, British Foreign Minister Austin Chamberlain announced in December Britain's adoption of a new China policy and immediate and unconditional approval of the imposition of a surtax. This announcement, which was later to be called a "Christmas message," emphasized the shift in Britain's China policy toward a more conciliatory stance and, at the same time, signified Britain's de facto breakaway from the Nine-Power Treaty.

It may be said that Britain's arbitrary conduct reflected the decline of Britain's presence in East Asia. Realizing that it could no longer carry out its own high-handed China policy backed up by immense military might, Britain attempted to persuade Japan to dispatch troops together with itself when the Nationalist Government started launching its revolutionary diplomacy that included the forceful re-taking of the foreign concessions in China. However, Shidehara held fast to his noninterference principle, instantly crippling Britain's proposal for a Japan-UK joint troop dispatch. Although Shidehara's priority in this episode was to settle the matter without resorting to interventions with military power, British Ambassador to Japan John Tilley and his colleagues regarded Shidehara's stance as a manifestation of Shidehara's unfriendly attitude toward Britain (Goto 2006).

It was on the occasion of the Nanking Incident in March 1927 that Shidehara's noninterference principle ran into difficulty. Entering Nanking triumphantly, the Northern Expedition army of the Kuomintang assaulted foreign legations and residents in the city, which triggered a strong protest from the western powers. When the British government proposed a joint dispatch of troops with Japan, Shidehara again rejected the idea, citing the following reasons: (1) military interference would worsen the resentment among the Chinese people; (2) provision of support to moderate elements within the Nationalist Government would subject them to criticism as traitors; and (3) even if China became a communist country, treaty port trade would become possible within a few years, as it had in the Soviet Union.

But Shidehara's noninterference principle also came under heavy attack from inside Japan. Particularly, civilian Japanese residents in China repeatedly requested the government to dispatch troops immediately. In the end, the first Shidehara diplomacy came to an end with the resignation of the Wakatsuki Reijiro cabinet, which had to step down when it failed to obtain consent from the Privy Council on the proposed measures to cope with the Showa Financial Crisis. Actually, the Wakatsuki cabinet, in which Shidehara served as foreign minister, had long been

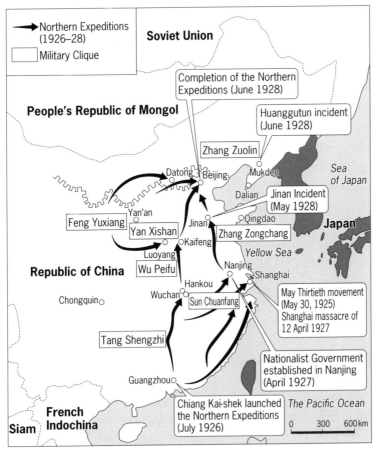

China in the latter half of 1920s

suffering from corruption scandals, suspected attempts at high treason, and public opinion demanding a hardliner foreign policy. The Privy Council's rejection of the proposed measures to deal with the Showa Financial Crisis was the final blow to the cabinet.

Second Shidehara Diplomacy and Its End

Unlike the Wakatsuki cabinet, the succeeding Tanaka Giichi cabinet, formed with the support of the Seiyukai party, sent three waves of Imperial Japanese Army troops to Shandong Province (the First, Second, and Third Shandong Expeditions). The First Shandong Expedition was favorably received by the British government. During the Second Shandong Expedition, the Jinan Incident erupted, which had the effect of shifting the main target of the Chinese anti-foreign movement from Britain to Japan. The Tanaka diplomacy, which aspired to slough off the Shidehara diplomacy, was unable to remedy the situation, giving further momentum to the demise of the Nine-Power Treaty.

Hamaguchi Osachi (of the Minseito), who formed the cabinet to succeed the Tanaka government, announced a platform of ten major policies, including mutual friendship with China, international arms reduction, and tight fiscal policy. Hamaguchi aspired for a more moderate domestic politics and foreign policy. In this spirit, Hamaguchi appointed Shidehara as his foreign minister, giving Shidehara an opportunity to pursue the second Shidehara diplomacy.

The second Shidehara diplomacy, however, was plagued by a grave problem from the outset—that is, important changes to the situation in Manchuria that could nullify the Nine-Power Treaty. This situation had not existed at the time of the first Shidehara diplomacy.

Zhang Xueliang, who had led the Fengtian clique after the death of his father, Zhang Zuolin, chose to have a closer association with the Nationalist Government and actively participated in the anti-foreign movement in Manchuria. Zhang Xueliang's new policy aggravated China's confrontation with Japan and Soviet Union, leading to the Sino-Soviet conflict in 1929. While Shidehara tried to make Japan play the role of mediator in this conflict, at the same time he did not desire the involvement of Britain, the United States, and other western powers in the mediation attempt. Shidehara was aiming for a settlement at the hands of the warring parties themselves. It is obvious from this episode that the Nine-Power Treaty, which was based on cooperation among Japan, Britain, and the United States, had already lost its validity. This behavior of Shidehara to exclude Britain and the United States from mediation of an international conflict could be attributed to Shidehara's loss of confidence in the possibility of cooperation among world powers (Nishida 2005).

Foreign Minister Shidehara on the cover of the *Time* magazine, October 12, 1931 issue

When the Manchurian Incident erupted in September 1931, Shidehara still took the position of blocking interference by Britain and the United States, insisting that the matter was for Japan and China to settle through bilateral negotiations. When the Kwantung Army escalated its military actions in Manchuria, with the majority of public opinion in Japan supporting it, Shidehara, however, was already deprived of an effective means to settle the conflict. Shidehara diplomacy was not equipped with an effective theory to put forth as a counterargument to the self-sufficiency sphere scheme or the Pan-Asianism that had gained power within Japan since the Great Depression (Kurosawa 2013).

One of the causes of the almost complete demise of Shidehara diplomacy from the Manchurian Incident through the end of the Pacific War must be Shidehara's essentially bureaucratic disposition. Scarcely sharing a sense of community with his foreign ministry colleagues, Shidehara was not particularly enthusiastic about establishing his own faction or building special personal networks. As such, he was also uninterested in nurturing disciples who could succeed his policies. While he retained the portfolio, he was able to pursue his policies by handpicking competent ministry officials. Even though this group of competent bureaucrats was later referred to as "the Shidehara faction," they nevertheless remained a loose unit and failed to develop solidarity or group dynamism comparable to the group of young bureaucrats called the Foreign Ministry Young Turks. The reason for this must be Shidehara's disposition.

From the viewpoint of the outcome, it was tragic for Japan to lose Shidehara diplomacy to the complicated tangles of the Nine-Power Treaty, which had been made powerless by changes in the international environment, the rise of "progressive" elements in Japan, and Shidehara's personality that did not conform to the traditional Japanese bureaucrat model. The second comeback of Shidehara diplomacy to the forefront in Japan had to await the end of the Pacific War.

*   *   *

Recommended Readings for Deeper Understanding

Goto Harumi. *Shanhai o meguru Nichiei kankei: 1925–1932-nen—Nichiei domei-go no kyocho to taiko* [Anglo-Japanese Relations over Shanghai: 1925–32—Collaboration and Rivalry after the Signing of the Anglo-Japan Alliance]. Tokyo: University of Tokyo Press, 2006.

The most recent empirical work on Anglo-Japanese relations during the time of the Shidehara-Tanaka diplomacy. It contains a persuasive argument that Shidehara was not always accommodative as far as Japan's relations with Britain were concerned.

Hattori Ryuji. *Shidehara Kijuro to 20 seiki no Nippon—Gaiko to minshushugi* [Shidehara Diplomacy and Japan in the 20th Century—Diplomacy and Democracy]. Tokyo: Yuhikaku Publishing, 2006.

The most recent biographical study based on a wide collection of both domestic and overseas historical documents. For the topics that the current chapter covers, see also *Higashi Ajia kokusai kankyo no hendo to Nippon gaiko—1918–1938* [Changes in the International Environment in East Asia and Japan's Diplomacy—1918–1938] by the same author (Tokyo: Yuhikaku Publishing, 2001).

Kurosawa Fumitaka. *Taisenkan-ki no kyuchu to seijika* [Imperial Palace and Politicians in the Interwar Period]. Tokyo: Misuzu Shobo, 2013.

Comparing the impact of World War I to the second opening of Japan, this book discusses how Shidehara helped Japan cope with this new era using his diplomatic skills.

Miyata Masaaki. *Eibei sekai chitsujo to Higashi Ajia ni okeru Nippon—Chugoku o meguru kyocho to sokoku: 1906–1936* [Anglo-American World Order and Japan in East Asia—Collaboration and Rivalry over China: 1906–1936]. Tokyo: Kinseisha, 2014.

An extremely detailed empirical study on the history of international relations in East Asia from the late nineteenth century through the eve of the Second Sino-Japanese War, including domestic situations in countries concerned. While it is essentially based on strict criticism reliant on historical documents, it includes portions that appear to be overreactions.

Nishida Toshihiro. "Daiichiji Shidehara gaiko ni okeru Manmo seisaku no tenkai—1926–1927-nen o chushin toshite" [Evolution of Manchuria-Mongolia Policy in the First Shidehara Diplomacy—With Special Emphasis on 1926–1927] in *Nihonshi Kenkyu*, No. 514 (June 2005).

An attempt to reevaluate Shidehara diplomacy, whose aspect as an economic diplomacy has been emphasized, from the angle of international perceptions over the long term. It includes other important analyses by the author.

Seki Shizuo. *Taisho gaiko—Jinbutsu ni miru gaiko senryaku-ron* [Taisho Diplomacy—Diplomatic Strategies Embodied by Individuals]. Kyoto: Minerva Shobo, 2001.

Chapter 8 of this book discusses the relations between Shidehara's argument against interference with China and the argument on Japan's special interests in Manchuria and Mongolia from the viewpoint of the decision-making process during the first tenure of Foreign Minister Shidehara.

Shidehara Kijuro. *Gaiko 50-nen* [Fifty Years of Diplomacy]. Tokyo: Chuokoron Shinsha, 2015.

Shidehara's memoir and a rare record of Shidehara's own testimonies. Tsutsui Kiyotada's commentary at the end of the book is also useful in learning about Shidehara's accomplishments.

Shidehara Heiwa Zaidan, ed. *Shidehara Kijuro*. Tokyo: Shidehara Heiwa Zaidan, 1955.

A robust biography of Shidehara published immediately after his death. Compiled essentially to honor Shidehara's accomplishments, this is nonetheless a valuable publication because it also contains precious documents and references.

Taneine Shuji. *Kindai Nippon gaiko to shikatsuteki rieki—Dainiji Shidehara gaiko to Taiheiyo senso e no jokyoku* [Modern Japanese Diplomacy and "Survival Interests"—The Second Shidehara Diplomacy and Prelude to the Pacific War]. Tokyo: Fuyo Shobo Shuppan, 2014.

A robust study on the second Shidehara diplomacy, which has received comparatively less exploration. It analyzes Shidehara's responses to the Sino-Soviet Conflict and the Manchurian Incident, using the concept of "survival interests."

Tsutsui Kiyotada. *Manshu jihen wa naze okita no ka* [Why did the Manchurian Incident happen?]. Tokyo: Chuokoron Shinsha, 2015.

A history of Japan's shifting foreign policy between China and Western powers from after the Russo-Japanese War to the Manchurian Incident. This book is based on the latest findings of the research and author's profound original remarks.

Usui Katsumi. *Nippon to Chugoku—Taisho jidai* [Japan and China—Taisho Era]. Tokyo: Hara Shobo, 1972.

A pioneer study on the history of Sino-Japanese relations in the Taisho era, including a detailed account on Shidehara diplomacy.

Enactment of the General Election Law and the Beginning of Democratic Politics

Koyama Toshiki

Party Politics and the Beginning of Democratic Politics

In 1924 (13th Year of Taisho), Kato Takaaki formed his three-party coalition cabinet based on the principle of constitution protection (the first Kato Takaaki cabinet). This cabinet materialized for its members won the general election by riding the political movement known as the Second Movement to Protect the Constitution. And they responded to popular hopes by enacting the General Election Law which extended suffrage to all males aged 25 and over. The subsequent eight years were the era of party politics in Japan.

What, then, was this Second Movement to Protect the Constitution, which was the genesis of party politics in Japan? The Kiyoura Keigo cabinet, which later became the target of criticism by the Second Movement to Protect the Constitution, had been formed to succeed the second Yamamoto Gonbei cabinet, which had stepped down en masse to take responsibility for the attempted assassination of Prince Regent Hirohito on December 27, 1923 (the Toranomon Incident). Kiyoura had been chairman of the Privy Council before he was appointed prime minister. When Kiyoura formed his cabinet, he requested the cooperation of the Kenkyukai (Study Group, the largest faction within the House of Peers with which Kiyoura had long associated) and proposed partnership with the Seiyukai, which was the largest party in the House of Representatives.

The Seiyukai had once formed a partnership with the House of Peers when Hara Takashi was its president. Nevertheless, it rejected Kiyoura's suggestion. Having been distanced from the position of power for quite some time, the Seiyukai had determined to confront any non-party cabinet even before the fall of the Yamamoto cabinet. In that spirit, it had deepened its partnership with the Kenseikai (formerly the Rikken-Doshikai) headed by President Kato Takaaki. Takahashi Korekiyo, president of the Seiyukai and former prime minister of Japan, criticized the Kiyoura cabinet as a cabinet of the privileged composed only of aristocrats and elite bureaucrats and announced his intention to give up his seat in the House of Peers and run for the House of Representatives. Some senior members of the Seiyukai, including Tokonami Takejiro and Yamamoto Tatsuo, opposed Takahashi's decision, citing the party's traditional partnership with the House of Peers since the Hara Takashi days. These senior members seceded from the Seiyukai to form their own Seiyu Honto.

Thus, the House of Representatives was split between the Seiyu Honto in support of the Kiyoura cabinet, on the one hand, and three parties—the Seiyukai, the Kenseikai, and the Kakushin Kurabu—that wished to topple the government, on the other hand. Those three parties aiming to establish party politics demanded reform of the House of Peers and adoption of universal suffrage. Their slogan was "Dispel the clique group! Defend constitutional government!" They earned the nickname Goken Sanpa, meaning "three groups supporting the constitution." The Goken Sanpa modeled itself after the Campaign for Defending Constitutionalism (the First Constitution Protection Movement) that had

Talk among heads of three pro-constitution parties (1924).
From left to right: Kato Takaaki, Inukai Tsuyoshi, and Takahashi Korekiyo (Photo courtesy of the Mainichi Newspapers)

succeeded in toppling the third Katsura Taro cabinet in the early Taisho
period (1912–13). It was the Goken Sanpa that evolved into what came
to be known as the Second Constitution Protection Movement.

Kiyoura dissolved the House of Representative on the eve of the termination of its tenure and campaigned against the three parties in the
subsequent general election. The election ended in a landslide victory
for the three-party block. The Kenseikai, in particular, was the greatest
winner, claiming 154 seats. The Seiyukai and the Kakushin Kurabu (under the leadership of Inukai Tsuyoshi) did not perform as well, winning
only 101 seats and 29 seats, respectively, upset by the Seiyu Honto which
won 114 seats. In June, Kato Takaaki, president of the victorious Kenseikai, received an imperial mandate to form a new cabinet. In pre–
World War II Japan, this was the only case of a prime minister being
appointed based on the outcome of an election. Kato invited Takahashi
Korekiyo of the Seiyukai and Inukai Tsuyoshi of the Kakushin Kurabu to
join his cabinet, making it a coalition government among the three
pro-constitution parties.

Although this Second Constitution Protection Movement succeeded
in forming a pro-constitution coalition government, it never mustered
the same level of energy as the First Movement in early Taisho. In the

Second Movement, politicians' wishes to control the government were more conspicuous than people's demands for political participation. In terms of coalition policy goals, despite the fact that the realization of party politics was upheld as a common objective, the Seiyukai showed a passive attitude toward universal suffrage and the Kenseikai was passive about reform for the House of Peers. Among historians, these pre–World War II political parties have been regarded as lacking the ability to respond to the wide range of social movements and political demands of their time. Historians in those days generally gave these political parties a low rating.

Recent studies have revealed, however, that the Second Constitution Protection Movement was, in actuality, widely supported, particularly among urban common people and rural youths. In other words, young people in local areas responded favorably to the appeal for the overthrow of the privileged classes; in fact, they underpinned the movement. As it becomes clear that the movement attracted at least some support from common people and contributed to the arrival of the era of party politics by facilitating universal suffrage, the movement is being reevaluated as studies on this period advance.

Enactment of the General Election Law of 1925

A general election gives a citizen the right to vote and the right to be elected regardless of his or her social status, property, or income (universal suffrage). It should be recalled, however, that few countries recognized women's suffrage in pre–World War II days, and thus it is customary to call a system that allows only male citizens to vote a general election. Since the introduction in Japan of elections for the House of Representatives, the minimum amount of direct taxes (land tax and income tax) required to obtain suffrage had been abated in a phased manner. In 1925 (14th Year of Taisho), the Kato coalition government took a step toward universal suffrage by launching a revision of the election law to abolish the tax condition on suffrage.

Because revision of the election law had attracted a lot of attention, the drafting of the law did not go smoothly. First, when the cabinet's draft was presented, the Privy Council raised the minimum age of eligibility for election from 25 years old to 30 years old. The Privy Council also added a clause depriving people receiving public or private aid of the right to vote. Prime Minister Kato and his associates tried to mediate between the two sides by limiting the criteria for disqualification to people receiving public or private charity, rather than those receiving public or private aid. This spurred the House of Peers, which was predominantly opposed to universal suffrage, to pass an amendment that once again disqualified people who received public or private aid. Because the House of Representatives rejected the House of Peers' amendment, the 1925 general election bill was submitted for deliberation at a joint committee of both houses. Those deliberations finally settled on "the receipt of public or private aid for relief of poverty" as the condition for disqualification. With this, the bill was finally enacted.

In addition to above modification of the wording of the bill, the Privy Council also demanded the government take measures to provide proper guidance regarding people's education and thought and to restrict radical words and deeds. The backdrop to this demand was the normalization of diplomatic relations between Japan and the Soviet Union, which was worried to invigorate communist movements in Japan. The suppression of communism had already been started in Europe by that time. As a result, the Public Security Preservation Law of 1925 was enacted along with the Law to keep surveillance over "anyone forming an association aimed at altering the *kokutai* [national polity] or *seitai* [system of government], or the system of private property, and anyone who has joined such an association." This law was the product of a compromise between the Seiyukai, which had been eager to enact a peace preservation act, and the Kenseikai, which had not wanted such a law. In later years, broad interpretation of this law allowed it to be used as a tool for thought censorship in Japan.

In any event, the adoption of universal suffrage had been a long-standing political question for Japan. As people's expectation for democracy rose after World War I (during which the Russian Revolution had started and, in Japan, the Rice Riots of 1918 erupted), a variety of social movements made a sudden rise in the late Taisho Era. These social movements included rampant labor disputes and peasant farmer disputes, the resurgence of socialism, the rise of women's movements, and the *buraku* liberation movement. For most of these movements, the adoption of universal suffrage (and implementation of general elections) was at the core of their political demands.

Thus, when the government responded to people's demands, albeit after many twists and turns, it was perceived in those days that the way was paved for a democracy in which the general "masses" would participate in parliamentary politics. The percentage of those eligible to vote rose to about 20 percent of the entire population, while a number of proletarian political parties were also established. With the enactment of the General Election Law, popular democracy in Japan entered a new phase.

Kensei no Jodo (The Way of Constitutional Politics) and Party Politics

After the enactment of the General Election Law, Takahashi Korekiyo resigned as president of the Seiyukai. Takahashi's successor, former Minister of Army Tanaka Giichi, did not join the Kato Takaaki cabinet in place of Takahashi. Hoping to be the next ruling party, the Seiyukai under Tanaka's leadership merged with the Kakushin Kurabu and formed a partnership with the Seiyu Honto in an attempt to win over a majority of votes. Subsequently, the Seiyukai became antagonistic to the Kenseikai over the tax reform issue, forcing the three-party coalition cabinet to step down en masse because of disagreement within the cabinet.

By that time, Saionji Kinmochi was the last of the Meiji elder statesmen holding the role of recommending the next prime minister to the Emperor. The Seiyukai and the Seiyu Honto were hopeful that Saionji, former president of Seiyukai, who was known for his aversion to Kato Takaaki, would not recommend Kato. However, Saionji recommended Kato as the next prime minister without any hesitation. Kato's successful handling of enactment of the General Election Law and his pursuit of steady diplomacy made Saionji revise his opinion of Kato. Saionji now had high hopes for Kato's leadership. In the second Kato cabinet, the Kenseikai was the sole government party, while the Seiyukai and the Seiyu Honto went out of government. Prime Minister Kato, as it happened, passed away suddenly during the Diet session; the Kato cabinet's Home Minister, Wakatsuki Reijiro, who succeeded Kato as president of the Kenseikai, was recommended as the next prime minister.

Now that the structure of conflicts between the government party and the opposition parties was clear, interparty rivalry grew fiercer, leading to reciprocal disclosures of scandal. Among the numerous cases that became the talk of the town in those days were the Matsushima Brothels scandal in which Prime Minister Wakatsuki was accused of perjury; the scandal involving the Imperial Japanese Army's secret fund, which Tanaka Giichi was suspected to have presented to the Seiyukai when he joined the party; and the Park Yeol–Fumiko Incident in which the Seiyukai accused the government of noncompliance with oversight responsibility. In the last case in particular, a scandalous photo of the couple suspected of high treason for plotting to bomb the wedding of Crown Prince Hirohito was widely circulated through the media to catch people's attention. What one should detect from this episode is, first, the influence of the media on politics, which had been expanding rapidly in those days, and, second, the growing prominence of the Emperor's presence as a political symbol. This second point was echoed in such later incidents as the violation of the supreme command at the time of the London Naval Conference (see Lecture 4).

When the Seiyukai and the Seiyu Honto jointly submitted a no-confidence motion against the cabinet, Prime Minister Wakatsuki refused to dissolve the House of Representatives, citing the demise of Emperor Taisho as the reason. Hinting at his resignation in a meeting with Presi-

27

dent Tanaka of the Seiyukai, Wakatsuki persuaded the opposition parties to withdraw the motion. When the secret scheme of the governing Kenseikai to form a partnership with the Seiyu Honto was disclosed, however, the Seiyukai was displeased and started attacking the cabinet in the Diet sessions. When Finance Minister Kataoka Naoharu was grilled by the Seiyukai at a Diet session on the Earthquake Loss Compensation Bond Bill, he erroneously declared the bankruptcy of the Tokyo-Watanabe Bank. The Showa financial crisis triggered by Kataoka's verbal blunder was, thus, very much a product of political strife.

The Wakatsuki cabinet also attempted to rescue the Bank of Taiwan with an emergency imperial ordinance. When its plea for the imperial ordinance was turned down by the Privy Council, the Wakatsuki cabinet was forced to step down. Lord Keeper of the Privy Seal Makino Nobuaki consulted with Saionji Kinmochi about who should be the next prime minister. When Makino told Saionji that, in compliance with *Kensei no Jodo* (the way of constitutional politics), he had decided to recommend Tanaka Giichi as the succeeding prime minister, Saionji concurred.

Kensei no Jodo was the procedure during the era of party politics for the succession of the prime ministership. The procedure stipulated that the succeeding president of the ruling party would become prime minister when a cabinet resigned due to its prime minister's contingency. The procedure also stipulated that the president of the leading opposition party would form the succeeding cabinet when a cabinet resigned due to a policy impasse. The conventional view has been that, even though Saionji was willing to comply with *Kensei no Jodo*, he was, at the same time, ready to allow a non-party cabinet to be formed any time if necessary. Recent studies have revealed, however, that Saionji clearly intended for the alternation of government among political parties to fully come into effect. In other words, after the Kato Takaaki cabinet, Saionji actively approved the continuation of party politics and aimed to promote the future embedding of the system in Japan.

Thus, an environment conducive to party politics appeared to be in place. Mitani Taichiro, an expert on Japanese political history, enumerates the following five "realistic conditions" for the party cabinet system's survival in pre–World War II Japan: (1) confirmation of the supremacy of the House of Representatives over the House of Peers; (2) common acceptance of constitutional theory that legitimizes party politics; (3) neutralization of the Privy Council; (4) a political appointee system for senior bureaucrats; and (5) relaxation of international tensions and a decline in the political weight of the military. During the early Showa period when the party politics system was in full bloom, the theory of the Emperor as an organ of government, which legitimized the party politics system, was firmly established. At that time, not even the House of Peers or the Privy Council was powerful enough to launch a frontal attack on political parties. Government bureaus including the Home Ministry and the Ministry of Foreign Affairs as well as the Imperial Japanese Army and Navy were urged to cope with the increasing presence of the party cabinet. Political parties in those days continued to monopolize the government, despite criticisms of the trend, and they began to exercise influences on other political forces.

Domestic Policies of the Two Major Political Parties

What kind of domestic policies did two pre–World War II major political parties have?

The domestic policies of the Kenseikai and the Minseito were characterized by fiscal austerity measures. These measures featured fiscal and administrative rationalization (including arms reductions for the Imperial Japanese Army and Navy) so as to reduce the issuance of public bonds by cutting the budget as well as personnel. Taking advantage of the improvement of government finances and gold reserves, the Hamaguchi Osachi cabinet pushed through the lifting of the gold embargo a long-standing issue for the Japanese business circle in an attempt to stabilize the exchange rate. Furthermore, the cabinet took measures to improve the competitiveness of Japanese companies by promoting cost reduction as well as mergers and cartelization (industrial rationalization) of companies through enactment of the Strategic Industries Control Act. It is well known, however, that the lifting of the gold embargo in the wake of the Great Depression was poorly timed; it triggered the Showa Depression in Japan.

In the realm of politics, the Hamaguchi cabinet tried a number of reforms, including exploration of the possibility of women's suffrage and the proportional representation system under the banner of electoral reforms as well as enactment of a labor union law. None of these initiatives was realized. Although some question the ruling parties' enthusiasm regarding these social policies, it should be recalled that the Labor Dispute Arbitration Law was enacted during the tenure of the Kenseikai government. The Kenseikai repeatedly stressed its determination to sincerely address policy issues that had been included in its campaign platform. It can be said that the policies of the Kenseikai and the Minseito emphasized financial austerity, social policy, and expansion of political rights.

The figurehead domestic policy of the Seiyukai, in contrast, was tax reform and the decentralization of government power. Although the Tanaka Giichi cabinet established an Administrative Reform Council to deliberate the delegation of land tax to local authorities as their source of revenue, the popular election of prefectural governors, and the adoption of the Doshusei (a proposal to organize Japan into one circuit of Hokkaido (*do*) and several new states (*shu*) that are each a combination of several prefectures), none of these initiatives materialized. Furthermore, when Inukai Tsuyoshi became the party president, the Seiyukai advocated industrialism and rural development and criticized the Minseito's financial austerity and the lifting of the gold embargo. After the Inukai cabinet was formed, its finance minister Takahashi Korekiyo restored the ban on gold exports and implemented the departure from the gold standard as well as the policy of letting the yen fall in value on foreign exchange markets.

In the political realm, the Tanaka cabinet strengthened surveillance of the communist party and launched a group arrest of party members and sympathizers after the general election on February 20, 1928. In what came to be known as the March 15 Incident, more than 1,500 individuals were apprehended. Furthermore, the Tanaka cabinet relied on an emergency imperial ordinance to push through an amendment to the Public Security Preservation Law that raised the maximum penalty from ten years to death. In recent years, the addition of a clause to illegalize any activity that contributes to attainment of the communist party's goals has come to be regarded as an important step in allowing future extension of the application of this law. We can summarize, then, that the Seiyukai's policy put priority on expansionary fiscal policy, the promotion of industrial development, and the strengthening of legislation to preserve the public order. As stated above, the two major political parties in those days tried to appeal to voters with their own characteristic policy packages.

In the past, it has been found problematic that domestic policies during the party cabinet days suffered from inconsistency, swinging widely between the platforms of the two major parties. Others point out that the policies of the two major parties were mutually complementary in coping with international economic competition and bringing about improvements in people's livelihood. Seeing as the era of party politics itself turned out to be short-lived, there were few cases of their policies being realized. Nevertheless, the party cabinet era produced a few important policies that were succeeded by subsequent eras, including the Strategic Industries Control Act and the Public Security Preservation Law. In light of this two-sidedness, studies on policies during the party cabinet era have been pursued mainly in terms their relations with the years immediately preceding and following the era, including their connection with policy debates in Japan in the 1910s–20s and their influences on the wartime regime in the 1930s–40s.

Intraparty Factions of the Two Major Political Parties

A prototype of intraparty factions that used to exist within the postwar

Liberal Democratic Party (LDP) had already been seen in the Seiyukai and the Minseito. Leaders of factions raised political funds, taking advantage of the human networks they had cultivated that would allow them to expand their clout and exercise strong influence on their respective party's decisions regarding its executive members (e.g., the general council chairman and secretary-general) as well as party policies. The Seiyukai had a number of members with strong ties with the Mitsui zaibatsu, while some Minseito members had good connections with the Mitsubishi zaibatsu. The source of political funding was not limited to these zaibatsu, however.

Inter-faction feuds in the Seiyukai were fierce in the early Showa period. Senior members who had long been with the party were joined by former senior members of the Seiyu Honto and the Kakushin Kurabu as well as such newly emerging leaders as Suzuki Kisaburo and Kuhara Fusanosuke, all of whom competed for a bigger voice in the Seiyukai. Unlike the days of Hara Takashi, Seiyukai presidents such as Takahashi Korekiyo, Tanaka Giichi, and Inukai Tsuyoshi could not afford to ignore the wishes of those influential members within the party.

Of all the factions, the faction led by Suzuki Kisaburo successfully expanded its influence by forming partnerships with such party seniors as Hatoyama Ichiro and Mori Tsutomu until the Suzuki faction became the most powerful faction within the party at the time of President Inukai. But the Suzuki faction, of course, had to face strong resistance from other factions, too. When Suzuki successfully mobilized the power of his faction to be elected as Seiyukai president after Inukai Tsuyoshi was killed during the May 15 Incident, anti-mainstream factions opposing Suzuki intensified their support for the formation of a non-party cabinet. Because of this intraparty feud, the Seiyukai after Inukai's death lost control over its members and gradually became removed from the center of the contest for the government.

Compared to the Seiyukai, the authority of the president was greater in the Kenseikai-Minseito. Under the long reign of President Kato Takaaki, such ex-bureaucrats as Wakatsuki Reijiro stood at the center of the party. Opposing those ex-bureaucrat politicians were those with a long history as parliamentarians known as party politicians. The party politicians were headed by Adachi Kenzo, who was the Home Minister of the Hamaguchi cabinet. The ex-bureaucrats overwhelmed the party politicians, monopolizing executive posts, and exercised strong influence on policy decisions of the party.

Even though Hamaguchi Osachi, who became the Kenseikai-Minseito president, was an ex-bureaucrat, he had been a member of the House of Representatives and was well respected by both factions. When Hamaguchi was attacked by a right-wing fanatic and died, however, this party, too, could not remain immune to intra-party feud. When President Wakatsuki turned his back to the scheme for a national unity government that Adachi had contemplated since the Manchurian Incident, Adachi defected from the party. The resignation of the Second Wakatsuki cabinet was partly attributable to the sense of crisis on the part of some party politician members over the austere fiscal policy pursued by Finance Minister Inoue Jun'nosuke and their discontent over the Wakatsuki government's decision-making and budget formulation. Clearly, the two major parties being unable to function as a unifying force in the 1930s was partially attributable to factional feuds within these parties.

The inner workings of the prewar political parties were highly complicated. Only a few personal documents of individual politicians are available to us today. This means there is still a lot to be explored. In recent years, the advancement of studies in this area has shown a promising trend with the publication of personal historical documents, such as the *Hamaguchi Osachi nikki* (Diary of Hamaguchi Osachi) and the *Saito Takao nikki* (Diary of Saito Takao), as well as the histories of several local autonomies containing substantial references to the party cabinet days. The exploration into the thinking and behavior of individual politicians and the structure of factions has been pursued to clarify relations between the policies and political situations and obtain new insights on those days.

Implementation of Japanese General Election, 1928

In February 1928 (3rd Year of Showa), general election was held in Japan, the first one after the introduction of universal male suffrage. What, then, was the real state of what appeared to be a democratic political regime based on political participation of the masses?

In this first general election in Japan, in order to cope with the sudden increase in voters, the election campaign itself became a spectacular affair. Political parties resorted to the aggressive use of such campaign tools as posters, audio records, and advertisements in newspapers. There also were cases of outright campaign interferences. In prewar elections, illegitimate vote buying was rampant, and police were kept busy clamping down on violations of the rules. The General Election Law was not just about expanding the ranks of voters. It also included attempts at improving election operations—such as prohibiting door-to-door canvassing—that could become a hotbed of vote buying, and at imposing restrictions on campaign workers and expenses.

As party politics got into full swing, the bureaucrats of the Home Ministry (including prefectural governors and police) began to be increasingly affected by the intentions of the government party. As a matter of fact, the Tanaka Giichi–Seiyukai cabinet resorted to explicitly pro-bureaucrat appointments, including appointing former justice ministry official Suzuki Kisaburo to Home Minister. Those prefectural governors and police heads who were under the patronage of the governing party maintained strict but lopsided control of the opposition parties. According to a police statement on the election day, there were 164 offenders to the General Election Law on the Seiyukai side compared to 1,701 on the Minseito side. From this one can detect the actual state of the election interference that took place.

In spite of these and other election interferences, the ruling Seiyukai was forced to engage in a hard-fought campaign, partly due to the unpopularity of the Tanaka cabinet. Home Minister Suzuki was in charge of the election campaign on the ruling party side. His attack on the opposition on the eve of the election—in which he said that British/American-style "parliamentarism" (a term that was featured in the Minseito's platform) was not compatible with Japan's national polity—backfired and, contrary to expectations, drew harsh criticism of

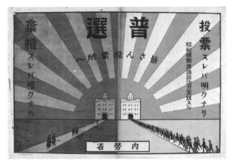

Poster for Japanese General Election, 1928 produced by the Ministry of Home Affairs. The left half of the poster is in a darker color with the caption saying, "It gets darker when you don't vote"

Suzuki instead of the opposition. In this election, the Seiyukai won 217 seats while the Minseito won 216; in terms of votes cast, however, the Minseito defeated the Seiyukai. Voter turnout exceeded 80 percent, and eight proletariat party candidates were elected. In the Diet session convened after the election, there was near parity between the government and opposition parties. In this Diet session, Home Minister Suzuki was forced to resign to take responsibility for the campaign interferences. The ruling Seiyukai, which had suffered a de facto defeat in the election, managed to stay in power by forcing through a partnership with other parties. These actions of the Seiyukai cast a dark shadow on the general election and the start of party politics.

Subsequently, two House of Representatives elections were held by the same universal male suffrage implemented during the remaining days of party politics. Although each time votes received by the two major parties fluctuated widely, the government party achieved a landslide victory in both elections—meaning, therefore, there was no instance of the ruling party stepping down, defeated in an election. The government party held the advantage because it could interfere with the election and it could raise campaign funds easier than the opposition parties.

This "national swing" of votes received by parties was partly attributable to fluctuations in voting trends in urban areas. Although politicians had begun to organize their own personal associations of supporters by that time, their numbers were limited. In urban areas, where the number of eligible voters mushroomed due to the General Election Law, a large number of unaffiliated voters emerged. This contributed to the conspicuous fluctuations of votes.

Each political party actively engaged in vote-gathering activities. Partly due to the political appointee system of senior bureaucrats, there were numerous cases of public officials and representatives of associational organizations and other groups being arrested for graft and vote buying. More and more cases were seen of vote buying being skillfully camouflaged by, for instance, voters being recruited to politicians' personal associations of supporters. Although conspicuous cases of vote buying and interference were often severely criticized, inviting voters' antipathy in many cases, the expected eradication of wrongdoing in the elections failed to be accomplished.

Proletarian parties failed to win seats while the two major parties won overwhelming support in terms of votes, and strong criticisms were heard on this discrepancy. Accusations flew about the difference in financial capacity among the parties as well as about wrongful acts. People's suspicion about elections and their sense of injustice became deeply intertwined with their suspicion about the legitimacy of parliamentary government.

To be sure, the enactment of the General Election Law did expand people's political participation and further advance democracy. The repeated change of government between parties through elections helped party politics become a norm. At the same time, however, it also helped people squarely face the evils of party politics. Thus, people's expectation of and disillusionment with political parties gradually became one of the factors that prepared the rise of the military as economic depression and social unrest deepened.

* * *

Recommended Readings for Deeper Understanding

Awaya Kentaro. *Showa no seito* [Showa's Political Parties]. Tokyo: Iwanami Shoten, 1983 and 2007.

A study on political parties in the prewar Showa Era focusing on the Seiyukai and the Minseito, the two major parties, including such viewpoints as the actual state of elections, the structure of local politics, and public opinion reactions. An overview of the history of political parties starting from the party politics period to the dissolution of political parties during World War II and the start of postwar party politics.

Ito Takashi and Nakamura Takahide, eds. *Kindai Nippon kenkyu nyumon, zohoban* [Introduction to Study on Modern Japan, augmented edition]. Tokyo: University of Tokyo Press, 2011. First edition published in 1983.

An introduction to modern Japan's political history compiled by leading experts in the field. It contains 12 treatises, i.e., six discussions by period including Mitani Taichiro's "Seito naikaku-ki no joken [Conditions for an Era of Party Cabinet]," and six thematic discussions on diplomacy, the judiciary, business, education, labor & industry, and fiscal and monetary affairs. It also contains a discussion on historical documents.

Koyama Toshiki. *Kensei jodo to seito seiji—Kindai Nippon nidai seito-sei no koso to zasetsu* [*Kensei no Jodo* and Party Politics—Plans and Setbacks Surrounding the Two Party System in Modern Japan). Kyoto: Shibun-kaku Shuppan, 2012.

An exploration of the birth and fail of the two major political parties using Kensei no Jodo, a key word in prewar party politics, as the key concept. The book analyzes how the Kensei no Jodo rule promoted political strife without resorting to a change of government through election or the government party–opposition party coalition. It also analyzes the logic followed by Saionji, who attempted to embed Kensei no Jodo, in recommending the next prime minister.

Masumi Jun'nosuke. *Nippon seiji-shi 3—Seito no choraku, soryokusen taisei* [Political History of Japan 3—Decline of Political Parties and the Total War Regime]. Tokyo: University of Tokyo Press, 1988.

A popular edition of the monumental seven-volume *Nippon seito-shi ron* [History of Japan's Political Party] in four volumes. The original edition provided the foundation for the study of the history of prewar political parties. While this work quotes an abundance of historical documents, its unique narratives make it easy to read. It contains chapters on the development of party politics in the 1920s and the structure of the two-party system.

Murai Ryota. *Seito naikaku-sei no seiritsu: 1918–27 nen* [Establishment of the Party Cabinet System: 1918–27]. Tokyo: Yuhikaku Publishing, 2005.

An analysis of the origin of party politics, with special attention paid to Saionji Kinmochi's political guidance. It describes how Saionji, who had grudgingly appointed Kato Takaaki as prime minister, came to approve of the two-party system and nurture it against the backdrop of the public opinion in favor of party politics. The book also describes the growing soundness of the Kenseikai's diplomatic policy and the changes in the method for appointing a prime minister.

Nakazawa Shunsuke. *Chian Ijiho—Naze seito seiji wa akuho o unda ka* [Public Security Preservation Law—Why Did Party Politics Give Birth to a Bad Law?]. Tokyo: Chuokoron Shinsha, 2012.

A study on the enactment and transformation of the Public Security Preservation Law, which was enacted concurrently with the General Election Law. The study pays special attention to the role played by political parties. By focusing on the intentions of the two major parties (the Seiyukai and the Minseito) and the regulating authorities (the Home Ministry and the Ministry of Justice), the study reveals the causes behind the extended application of the law under party politics.

Naraoka Sochi. *Kato Takaaki to seito seiji—Nidai seito-sei e no michi* [Kato Takaaki and Party Politics—Road to the Two-Party System]. Tokyo: Yamakawa Shuppansha, 2006.

The first full-fledged biographical study of Kato Takaaki, who led the Kenseikai and formed the foundation of the two-party system. An attempt to portray the real person—the Kato who took to Britain, who grew Rikken Doshikai-Kenseikai into the government party, and who contributed to the establishment of party politics—by making full use of a variety of historical documents.

Oku Kentaro. *Showa senzen-ki Rikken Seiyukai no kenkyu—Tonai habatsu no bunseki o chushin ni* [A Study on the Rikken-Seiyukai in the Prewar early Showa Era—With Special Emphasis on Analysis of Intra-Party Factions]. Tokyo: Keio University Press, 2004.

A detailed study on the Seiyukai in the early Showa Era relying not only on such primary sources as politicians' diaries but also on reporting by various media, including newspapers and magazines. Included are analyses on the intra-party factions around Hatoyama Ichiro, who had been a member of the Suzuki Kisaburo faction, the trends toward the New Socio-Political Structure, and the center-periphery relations via elections.

Suetake Yoshiya and Takeda Tomoki, eds. *Nippon seito-shi* [History of Japan's Political Parties]. Tokyo: Yoshikawa Kobunkan, 2011.

A concise history of Japan's modern and contemporary history through the lens of the political party. The study ranges from the perception of political parties at the time of the Meiji Restoration to the establishment of political parties and their development after the launching of parliament, the dissolution of parties during the war and then their postwar revival, the 1955 System, and to contemporary days. The list of important references on political party studies organized by period is also a useful guide to contemporary political party studies.

Tsutsui Kiyotada. *Showa senzenki no seito seiji—Nidai seito-sei wa naze zasetsu shita no ka* [Party Politics in the Prewar Showa Era—Why Did the Two Party System Suffer a Setback?]. Tokyo: Chikumashobo, 2012.

An exploration of problems faced by prewar political parties during the party cabinet era, using primary sources and media reports. Its analysis that "theater politics" born under "mass democracy," which was promoted by adoption of universal male suffrage and the development of the mass media, prompted disillusionment with party politics among the Japanese people, thus allowing the military to rise, is thought-provoking in the context of contemporary politics.

Lecture 3

From the Northern Expeditions to the Assassination of Zhang Zuolin

Iechika Ryoko

What Was the Northern Expedition?

The Xinhai Revolution erupted on October 10, 1911, ending the Qing Dynasty's rule over China that had lasted for more than 260 years. Although it is generally said that it was the Tongmenghui, also known as the Chinese United League, that led the revolution, the reality was much more complicated. The Tongmenghui was formed by the August 1905 merger of Sun Yetsen's Xingzhonghui (Revive China Society, located in Guangdon), the Huaxinghui (China Revival Society, located in Hunan) founded by Huang Xing and Song Jiaoren, and the Guangfuhui (Revive the Light Society, in Zhejiang and Shanghai) led by Cai Yuanpei and Zhang Binglin. While its platform was "to expel the Tatar barbarians, to revive Zhonghua, to establish a Republic, and to distribute land equally among the people," there were various differences among the three groups in terms of policies. Aside from the Tongmenghui, there were other groups that were engaged in efforts to overthrow Qing and build a state based on the Han ethnic nation, including the Progressive Association in the Yangtze River basin and the Literary Society in Wuchang. One important point here is that most of these groups were based in the south of the Yangtze River.

The revolutionary movements traveled from south to north. Local leaders in southern China, who had long been placed in the political periphery by the Manchurian conquerors, shifted their manpower and economic energy, which previously had been directed overseas, to their homeland with hopes for the construction of their own country. At the Wuchang Uprising, which was the catalyst for the Xinhai Revolution, members of the Progressive Association and the Literary Society played the central role. Hearing the news of the uprising, Sun Yatsen immediately departed for China from Denver, Colorado, where he had been in exile; but it was already December 25, 1911, when he finally reached Shanghai. Elected as "Provisional President," Sun declared the founding of the Republic of China on January 1, 1912, in Nanjing. Qing Emperor Puyi had not abdicated yet, and the Republic of China had to ask for help from Yuan Shikai, leader of the Beiyang Clique, to realize the abdication of Puyi. This was an origin of the Northern Expedition.

The provisional government of the Republic of China sent a telegram to Yuan Shikai announcing that it intended to (1) make the Qing emperor abdicate and (2) make Nanjing the provisional capital of the republic. While Yuan agreed with the first proposition, he refuted that it would be de facto impossible for the provisional government to control northern China and declared that he intended to establish the northern region's own provisional government. Hearing this, Sun dispatched Cai Yuanpei and Song Jiaoren to Beijing to persuade Yuan to visit Nanjing. In response to this request from Sun, the Third District of the Beiyang Army fabricated a coup d'état. Yuan telegraphed Sun, insisting that the provisional government should be established in Beijing. Yuan continued to refuse to visit Nanjing and, on March 10, 1912, he was sworn in as provisional president of the Republic of China in Beijing to replace Sun.

Sun, however, continued to persist with the capital city issue. When he spoke at the welcoming reception of the House of Councilors in Beijing on August 31, 1912, he stated that he opposed making Beijing capital of the republic, because (1) Beijing housed too many foreign settlements, special districts (e.g. foreign concessions), and foreign military forces; and (2) Beijing was problematic from the viewpoint of national defense, etc. Sun warned that Russia and Japan, which had controlled traffic in south Manchuria and Korea by that time, both had territorial ambitions toward China. Should either of them decide to invade China, access to Beijing was an easy, five-day journey. For these reasons, Sun insisted that either Wuchang or Nanjing should be the permanent capital city of the Republic of China (*Min Li Pao*, September 6, 1912).

Subsequently, Yuan continued to suppress revolutionary parties in the south and, in the end, he restored the imperial system, making himself emperor. These actions put him in sharp confrontation with the revolutionary forces in the south, splitting China into the provisional government in Beijing, on the one hand, and the revolutionary government in the south, on the other. This standoff between the two sides persisted even after Yuan's death in June 1916. In August 1921, the Nanjing provisional government decided to launch the Northern Expedition as an attempt at north-south unification by Sun's own hand. Opposed by Chen Jiongming, commander-in-chief of the Guangdong Army, in October, the expedition did not materialize at that time. To augment his inadequate military power, Sun went into partnership with the Soviets, formed the First United Front with the Communist Party of China in January 1924, and founded the Republic of China Military Academy in Whampoa. After the death of Sun Yatsen in March 1925, completing the national revolution by means of the Northern Expedition and founding the state based on the Three Principles of the People with its capital in Nanjing became the greatest political goals for the Kuomintang.

The Northern Expedition and Japan

After Sun Yatsen passed away, the Kuomintang became divided between the left and the right in terms of relations with the communist party. Chiang Kai-shek, commandant of the Whampoa Military Academy, was regarded as a middle-of-the-roader in those days. His position on the Northern Expedition did not contradict too much with Wang Jingwei, a representative left-winger. In his closing remarks at the Second National Congress on January 20, 1926, Wang stressed that "to accomplish early national unification is to live up to the late Sun Yatsen's teaching" and that "it is imperative to put at least areas south of the Yellow River basin under our party's guidance by the Third National Congress of Kuomintang." With these remarks Wang prompted the early launching of the Northern Expedition. On June 5, 1926, the Kuomintang elected Chiang Kai-shek as the Generalissimo of the Nationalist Revolutionary Army (NRA). The army set off on the Northern Expedition from Guangzhou on July 1 (see map on page 45). Its initial target was to defeat Wu Peifu, who had maintained a power base in Hubei and Henan in central China, and Sun Chuanfang, who had controlled Fujian, Chekiang, and the Yangtze River basin.

On July 14, 1926, the Manifesto of the Northern Expedition was issued which said, "The sole cause of the Chinese people's sufferings is the invasion of the imperialists and the tyranny of traitor military cliques, the 'imperialists' running dogs.' The sole demand of the Chinese people is to construct a unified government with their own hands." As can be seen from from this manifesto, the Nationalist Revolution was heavily influenced by the communist party. And, thus, it might be said that the Northern Expedition had been launched in the framework of anti-imperialism. It was true that local military leaders called military cliques had divided China into several regions; they ruled their own regions with military power, and they were connected with the western powers that had rights and interests in the regions they controlled (see map).

At first, Japan obtained rights and interests in Manchuria-Mongolia and the Shandong province in response to the Twenty-One Demands of 1915. With the signing of the Nine-Power Treaty at the Washington Naval Conference convened in November 1921, which made the Open-Door Policy advocated by the United States an international rule and stipulated equality of opportuni-

China divided by military cliques on the eve of the Northern Expedition (July 1926) (Source: *Sho Kaiseki hiroku 7* [Series Notes of Chiang Kai-shek 7], Sankei Shimbunsha, 1976)

ties among the signees, as well as the Shandong Treaty signed by Japan and Qing on February 4, 1922, through the mediation of Britain and the United States, Japan's vested interests in Shandong became mostly invalid, forcing the Imperial Japanese Army stationed in the peninsula to withdraw. Still, because Japan succeeded in retaining the loan to the Jiaoji Railway and control of the mines along the railway as a Japan-Qing joint venture, the number of Japanese residents in Shandong rose to the level of 18,000.

In Japan this Nationalist Revolution in China coincided with the accession of the Crown Prince the throne as Emperor Showa. Recent studies have come to disclose much of the true person of Emperor Showa. According to Furukawa Takahisa, Emperor Showa "idealized the realization of a popular constitutional monarchy combining Confucius rule of virtue and party politics of the West, particularly that of Britain, as well as cooperative diplomacy" (Furukawa 2011). In other words, cooperative diplomacy had been the basic principle for Emperor Showa from the beginning.

Chiang Kai-shek's First Northern Expedition was characterized by the rampant destruction of foreign facilities and assaults on foreign set-

tlers by mobs mobilized by the communist party. This made confrontation with foreign countries fiercer as the Northern Expedition advanced.
Chiang Kai-shek became increasingly confrontational with the Wuhan
government that tolerated these misconducts, while the communist party began to openly launch an anti-Chiang campaign. It was against this
backdrop that the Hankou Incident and the Nanjing Incident (1927)
erupted one after another.

On January 5, 1927, a mob in protest of violence by British soldiers
burst into the foreign settlement in Hankou. In response, the British government decided to return to China jurisdiction over incidents within
the Hankou foreign settlement in which Chinese citizens were accused.
Jurisdiction over administrative and police authorities in Hankou was
also returned to China (Miyata 2014). Encouraged by what appeared to
be a substantial compromise on the part of Britain, the Chinese mob
movement became even more energized. On March 23, units of the Nationalist Revolutionary Army under the direct command of Chiang Kai-
shek occupied the city of Nanjing. Catching the momentum, mobs and
NRA soldiers started large-scale rioting against foreign interests, burn-
ing houses and churches, attacking the British, American and Japanese
consulates, and killing or harming several foreign residents. In response,
British and American soldiers fired on the mob, citing the protection of
foreign residents as justification. A large number of Nanjing citizens
died. The Imperial Japanese Army did not take part in the shoot-out.
According to the investigation by the Kuomintang reported by a local
newspaper, an American, two Britons, and a Japanese were killed, while
two Americans, two Britons, and two Japanese were injured. In contrast, as many as 2,000 Chinese people were killed by the exchange of
fire between the two sides (*Chen Bao*, April 3, 1927). This was what the
Nanjing Incident was about.

In the aftermath of the Nanjing Incident, Foreign Minister Shidehara
Kijuro of the Wakatsuki cabinet on March 30 demanded (1) strict punishment of the NRA soldiers responsible for the violence, (2) reparation
for damages, and (3) indemnity for victims. The Imperial Japanese Army

and Navy, however, were not satisfied with this demand and insisted that all the countries whose nationals were residing in the region should jointly dispatch troops to maintain public order. The Japanese government instructed the consul-general in Shanghai to request Chiang Kai-shek to "suppress the communist elements as much as possible" and "return from Nanjing to Shanghai to maintain public order there" (*Chen Bao*, April 1, 1927). Also, Chinese businessmen based in Shanghai (e.g., the Soong family and Yu Ya-ching) requested a crackdown on the communist party's mass movements.

On April 12, Chiang Kai-shek launched an anti-communist coup d'etat in Shanghai and established the Nationalist government in Nanjing, separate from the Wuhan government. In response, on April 19 Wang Jingwei declared his intention to continue the Wuhan government's own northern expedition. Because the Whampoa Military Academy had sworn allegiance to Chiang and Wang did not have his own military capabilities, Wang attempted to carry out the northern expedition by incorporating local military cliques' troops into the Nationalist Revolutionary Army. Appointing Yan Xishan, Feng Yuxiang, Tang Sheng-zhi, Li Zongren, and Zhang Fakui to the Generalissimo or supreme commander, Wang organized the Wuhan Northern Expedition Army. As these military leaders played the role of temporarily filling the military vacuum of the Wuhan government, their political clout increased, allowing them to exercise influence on the Nationalist government (Iechika 2002).

On April 20, two days after the founding of the Nationalist government in Nanjing, Tanaka Giichi formed his cabinet in Japan. Holding up his public pledge for aggressive policies toward the Chinese continent, Tanaka abandoned the Shidehara diplomacy of non-interference in internal affairs, which had been criticized as weak-kneed diplomacy. On May 28, Prime Minister Tanaka resolutely carried out the First Shandong Expedition on the pretext of protecting local Japanese residents (the expedition was withdrawn in September). Chiang Kai-shek later described this change of policy as a shift "from moderate diplomacy to invasive diplomacy" (*Sho Kaiseki hiroku 7*). At the same time, Tanaka instructed Yoshida Shigeru, who was consul-general at Mukden, to scout around Zhang Zuolin in Beijing. He had judged that the movements of the Northern Expedition forces would greatly affect Japan's rights and interests in China.

A Chiang Kai-shek–Tanaka Giichi Meeting

In an attempt to unify the Nanjing government and the Wuhan government, Feng Yuxiang met Chiang Kai-shek and Hu Hanmin in Xuzhou on June 20, 1927, and Wuhan government representatives on the next day in Wuhan to request the dismissal and extradition to Moscow of Mikhail Borodin (Comintern's advisor), expulsion of the communist party, and joint continuation of the Northern Expedition. In response, Wang Jingwei convened a conference on the segregation of communists in Wuhan on July 15. Participants at this conference decided on the termination of the First United Front with the communists. The Wuhan side made Chiang Kai-shek's resignation from his official post a condition of their agreement. Chiang was forced to resign as the Generalissimo of the Nationalist Revolutionary Army on August 13.

At 7:00 a.m. on September 28, 1927, Chiang departed from the port of Shanghai, accompanied by nine confidents of his including Zhang Qun, to arrive in Nagasaki at 12:45 p.m. on September 29. After visiting scenic spots in Nagasaki, Obama, Unzen, Kobe, Arima, Nara, Osaka, Tokyo, Hakone, Nikko, Shiobara, etc. Chiang and his party returned home from Nagasaki on November 8. Chiang's activities during this trip are disclosed in the *Chiang Kai-shek Diaries*, which since 2006 have been available to the public at the Hoover Institution of Stanford University.

Generally, it has been believed that Chiang's purpose for this visit was to ask permission from Soong Mei-ling's mother, who had been staying in Arima Onsen, Hyogo prefecture, to marry her daughter and to have a talk with Prime Minister cum Foreign Minister Tanaka Giichi. The meeting with Tanaka was not initially confirmed in Chiang's itinerary. Whether this meeting materialized or not had a very important meaning for Chiang. Even though Zhang Qun had arrived in Tokyo ahead of Chiang on October 4 to confirm the meeting with Tanaka, he had difficulty confirming the appointment. In an interview that took place in Tokyo on October 24, Chiang answered that, "My visit to Tokyo this time had no political purpose. . . . Because Prime Minister Tanaka is on trip, I do not think I can see him this time" (*Tokyo Asahi Shimbun*, October 24, 1927). From the *Chiang Kai-shek Diaries*, it can be detected that Chiang was strongly displeased by Japan's reception of him as if he were a refugee.

Chiang Kai-shek in Kobe (Source: *Kobe Shimbun*, October 3, 1927)

It was on November 5 that Chiang was finally able to meet with Tanaka. On that day, after paying a visit to President Hamaguchi Osachi of the Minseito in the morning, Chiang met Prime Minister Tanaka in the afternoon. In both meetings, Chiang discussed the future of Sino-Japanese relations. The meeting with Tanaka was held at Tanaka's private residence in Aoyama, not at the prime minister's official residence; as such, it was an informal meeting. November 5 was a Saturday, but the weekend itinerary of the prime minister released by newspapers made no reference to this meeting with Chiang. Because Tanaka had been scheduled to depart for his villa in Kamakura on board the 3:42 p.m. train from Tokyo Station (*Tokyo Asahi Shimbun*, November 5, 1927), it can be conjectured that his meeting with Chiang was the outcome of last minute arrangements.

The meeting was attended by Zhang Qun and Major General Sato Yasunosuke, Tanaka's confidant. Sato kept a verbatim account of the meeting that is now available in "Tanaka shusho Sho Kaiseki kaidanroku" [Record of the Dialogue between Prime Minister Tanaka and Chiang Kai-shek] (*Teikoku no taishi-gaiko seisaku kankei ikken*: *Matsumoto kiroku*, Diplomatic Archives of Ministry of Foreign Affairs, and *Sho Chusei soto bunbutu*, Generalissiomo Chiang Kai-shek Archives at Academia Historica Archives, Taiwan). The dialogue between the two can be summarized as follows:

> **Tanaka Giichi:** From a broader perspective, it is a matter of urgency at this point to get the south of the Yangtze River under control. For this reason, we beg for Your Excellency's prudence.
>
> Of all the world powers, it is Japan that has the greatest stake in your country. While Japan would not interfere with your civil war, we nevertheless find it hard to remain indifferent to the rampancy of the communist party. In this sense, we are pleased that Your Excellency, who is a known anti-communist, intends to consolidate southern China. As long as Japan's rights and interests are not damaged, we would not hesitate to render substantial cooperation to your endeavors.
>
> . . . and this is Japan's attitude toward Zhang Zuolin. Although some claim that Japan intends to assist Zhang, nothing is farther from the truth. Japan absolutely will not assist Zhang either by providing materials or advice or any other form of assistance. You can rest assured that all Japan hopes for is maintenance of security in Manchuria.
>
> **Chiang Kai-shek:** I wholeheartedly agree with Your Excellency's view that it is impossible to immediately launch the Northern Expedition. I also concur with your assertion that the rear attack should be launched only after the south is consolidated.
>
> It is my conviction that I should take action when the communist party becomes rampant.
>
> **Tanaka:** I am now convinced that your view on the communists is exactly the same as mine.
>
> **Chiang:** The anti-Japan movements are attributable to the misperception that Japan is assisting Zhang Zuolin. . . . The Chinese people have the misunderstanding that military cliques in China have relied on Japan for assistance. Therefore, it is imperative that Japan helps our comrades to accomplish the revolution posthaste.

Doing so should eliminate all the misunderstandings regarding Japan among the Chinese people. If that is accomplished, it should become easy for Japan to solve the Manchurian-Mongolian problem, and all the anti-Japan movements in China will perish.

This meeting, which became possible by delaying Tanaka's train for Koshigoe near Kamakura by 25 minutes, lasted for more than two hours. When leaving the meeting, Tanaka told Chiang that he wished to see Chiang again if his stay in Japan could be extended, to which Chiang responded that he would have Zhang Qun stay behind. It appears that Chiang thought that he had succeeded in reaching some understanding with Tanaka through this meeting (Iechika 2013). In actuality, however, there emerged a great misperception between the two, and it can be said that this misperception "spawned the Second and Third Shandong Expeditions" (Huang Tzuchin 2011).

Jinan Incident

Returning to Shanghai, Chiang Kai-shek was reinstated as the Generalissimo of the Nationalist Revolutionary Army in Nanjing on January 4, 1928. He restarted the Second Northern Expedition in April with the purpose of advancing to the north of the Yangtze River and unifying the nation. Meanwhile, in the Beijing government, Zhang Zuolin of the Fengtian clique assumed the post of grand marshal of the army and navy of the Republic of China in June 1927. Since the days of the Terauchi Masatake cabinet, Japan had supported Zhang and, in return for a massive loan to Zhang, Japan had monopolized soy and other crops in Northeast China and advanced its economic and military interference with Manchuria.

The Nationalist Revolutionary Army (or *Nangun*, Southern Army, as it was called in Japan) was organized into four armies—the First Group Army (Chiang Kai-shek, the Generalissimo, 290,000 troops organized into 18 divisions), the Second Group Army (Feng Yuxiang, the Generalissimo, 310,000 troops organized into 25 divisions), the Third Group Army (Yan Xishan, the Generalissimo, 150,000 troops organized into 11 divisions), and the Fourth Group Army (16 divisions and 9 independent divisions). Each group army separately advanced toward Beijing. To meet these forces, the Fengtian Clique Army (or *Hokugun*, Northern Army, as it was called in Japan) boasted seven area armies and one million troops. On April 8, Chiang issued the order for an all-out attack, upon which the First Group Army conquered Taierzhuang, Shandong, by April 10 and moved on to Jinan. It was Japan, instead of Zhang Zuolin, that responded to this move promptly.

On March 6, the eve of the relaunching of the Northern Expedition, Chiang invited the Japanese press corps to dinner and made a speech in which he said, "We believe that Japan, of all our friendly nations, understands the significance of the nationalist revolution best and that you would never try anything to obstruct us. . . . I wish you, gentlemen of the press corps, could bring this message back to your people and the government in Japan" (*Sho Kaiseki hiroku 7*). Chiang's wish was in vain because Prime Minister Tanaka decided at the cabinet meeting on April 19 to launch the Second Shandong Expedition for the reason of protecting Japanese residents. The Sixth Division of the Imperial Japanese Army thus dispatched reached Jinan via Tsingtao on April 26.

Hearing of Japan's dispatch of troops to Shandong, Chiang wrote as follows in his April 20 diary: "Should the Northern Expedition be hampered, our republic has no future. The only thing we can do now is to bear shame, shoulder heavy burdens, and fight with firm determination." From this entry, it can be detected that Chiang accepted it as inevitable that to successfully complete the Northern Expedition a compromise with Japan would be necessary.

The First Group Army under Chiang's command arrived in Jinan on May 1. About this Chiang wrote in his diary as follows:

> Tight security was in place with barbed wires and bayonetted soldiers of the Imperial Japanese Army deployed along the road be-

hind the wires. Neither our troops nor people were allowed to pass the security line. Such an oppressive country is bound to fall. All we can do is to endure. I must also persuade my troops and people, who are enraged by the Japanese army's high-handedness, to do the same.

In service of his higher objective, which was to conquer Beijing, Chiang instructed all the divisions under his command to avoid a clash with the Japanese troops. In spite of this precaution, armed clashes occurred inside Jinan on May 3 when the Imperial Japanese Army bombarded the city. Hearing of this incident, Chiang wrote in his diary that he did not know how the clashes came about. After this incident, Chiang retreated to Taian in order to prevent further clashes with Japanese troops. On May 7, Lieutenant General Fukuda Hikosuke, division commander of the 6th Division of the Imperial Japanese Army, placed five demands on Chiang. Three of the demands were the execution of senior military officers who were involved in the incident, the disarmament of the Nationalist Revolutionary Army troops that had antagonized the Japanese troops, and the strict prohibition of anti-Japan propaganda (see photo). The demands were written at noon on May 7 but not handed to Chiang until 4 o'clock in the afternoon. Chiang was given only twelve hours to respond.

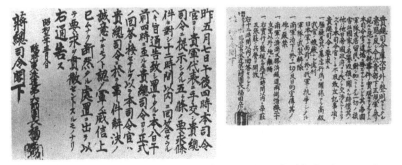

Five Demands (Source: Kindai Chugoku Shuppansha ed., *Kin hyakunen rai no Chunichi kankei zuroku* [Pictorial Record of Sino-Japanese Relations in the Past 100 Years], 1985)

From May 8, the Japanese Army launched an all-out attack, including air raids. On May 11, it conquered Jinan completely. Chiang chose to move north, bypassing Jinan and preventing an all-out battle between the two sides. Still, this incident in Jinan had a tremendous impact on Chiang. In his May 9 diary, he wrote, "Those who are determined to avenge humiliation but unable to put up with it even for a while only have brute courage. They can never accomplish the task that wipes away a disgrace. I must bear with the humanly unbearable." The next day, he scribbled his inner distress, saying, "I have made a resolution . . . to get up at 6 o'clock without fail every day to spend time commemorating the national humiliation. I will continue this habit without a break until the national humiliation is completely avenged." From May 9, Chiang made it a rule to start his daily diary entry with two Chinese characters that meant "to avenge humiliation."

Huanggutun Incident: Assassination of Zhang Zuolin

The Japanese government policy toward Zhang Zuolin had been basically determined as of 1927. Thus, Miyata writes as follows:

> In Japan's Ministry of Foreign Affairs in the wake of World War I, there emerged an atmosphere urging a review of the traditional China policy that had made much of relations with specific military cliques such as Zhang Zuolin. With the advent of Shidehara diplomacy, the momentum to abandon Zhang was further accelerated significantly. (Miyata 2014)

It had been the foreign ministry's perception that "it is a widely known fact that [Prime Minister Tanaka and Zhang] have been on friendly terms for a long time." Although, in order to settle various outstanding issues involving Zhang, it would be "a wise policy" to request "Prime Minister Tanaka to reprimand Zhang Zuolin on his high-handed attitudes toward Japan." Should Zhang not listen, the foreign ministry was of the view that, "we have no other recourse than to correct his wrongdoings by force, and the best timing for doing so is when the Fengtian Clique's situation worsens and Zhang finds it necessary to withdraw to north of the Great Wall" (Ministry of Foreign Affairs, *Toho kaigi oyobi Cho Sakurin bakusatsu jiken kankei bunsho* [Documents related to the Far Eastern Conference and the Assassination of Zhang Zuolin], Military Archives at the National Institute for Defense Studies).

Zhang Zuoling, "Mussolini in Beijing," in an $8,000 newly acquired military uniform (Source: *Kyoto Hinode Shimbun*, May 28, 1928)

As the Northern Expedition armies closed in on Beijing from multiple directions, Zhang Zuolin sent a telegram on May 11 requesting Sun Chuanfang, Yang Yuting, Zhang Xueliang, and Zhang Zuoxiang to visit Beijing. On May 15 a supreme military conference was convened among them at the grand marshal's office. The conference discussed whether the assembled should all resign en masse or fight until the end. Zhang Zuolin alone insisted on fighting until the end; the other participants recommended withdrawing to Mukden. Because Zhang continued to fight in Baoding and its vicinities and suffered a devastating defeat, an emergency conference was convened at the grand marshal's office on May 30. There the resignation of Zhang Zuolin and withdrawal of the Fengtian Army to the north of the Great Wall was decided (*Kyoto Hinode Shimbun*, May 12 and 16, 1928; June 1, 1928).

After giving a last audience as grand marshal on June 2, Zhang left Beijing for Mukden on June 3 on board an 18-coach special train that left Beijing station at 1:10 a.m. The train ran on the Beijing–Mukden Railway, bypassing Tianjin, Shanhaiguan, and Jinzhou. At half past five in the morning on June 4, as Zhang's train approached the Laodaokou junction with the South Manchuria Railway, the train exploded (*Kyoto Hinode*

Exploded train car (Source: China Foundation for International and Strategic Studies, ed., *Tainichi senso shiroku—Shashin/kiroku shu* [Historical Record of the War against Japan—Photo & Record Edition], 1995)

Shimbun, June 3–5, 1928). At this junction, the Beijing–Mukden Railway ran underneath the South Manchuria Railway overpass. Japanese newspapers mostly immediately reported that the explosion had been caused by "bombs buried by plain-clothed *Nangun* soldiers." And the first report had it that Zhang was only slightly wounded.

China's *Central Daily News* reported that General Wu Junsheng, who was seated next to Zhang Zuolin, was killed, while the survival or death of Zhang himself was unknown. The *Central Daily News* also attributed the explosion to "bombs set beforehand by plain-clothed soldiers of *Nangun.*" This Chinese newspaper subsequently reported that Zhang Xueliang and Sun Chuanfang had departed Beijing for Mukden on board the train belonging to the 3rd and 4th Area Armies' command at 10:15 p.m. on June 4. As for the condition of Zhang Zuolin, the newspaper commented that "the view that he has already died seems to be most plausible" (*Central Daily News,* June 5–6, 1928). From this article, it can be conjectured that Zhang Xueliang had departed for Mukden on the very day of the explosion.

The Truth of the Incident

The truth of the Huanggutun Incident has been mostly disclosed by past studies. The theory that Kawamoto Daisaku was the mastermind has been firmly entrenched beyond any doubt, by his own memoir ("Watashi ga Cho Sakurin o koroshita: Kawamoto shuki" [Kawamoto Notes: I Killed Zhang Zuolin], *Bungeishunju*, December 1954 issue) and the memoir of Kawagoe Moriji, staff officer of the Kwantung Army and Kawamoto's assistant during the incident. According to Kawagoe,

It was decided at the Far Eastern Conference (*Toho Kaigi*) that, in light of the war minister's lopsided reliance on Zhang Zuolin, the incompetence of the foreign ministry, and the passive attitude of the executives of the South Manchuria Railway, Zhang's assassination was the only way to settle the outstanding issues in Manchuria-Mongolia, to promote the Japanese people's prosperity and the Chinese people's happiness, and to make Manchuria and Mongolia a paradise. It was also decided that the only

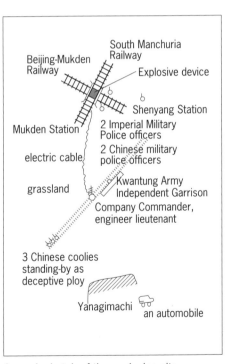

A rough sketch of the explosion site (constructed on the basis of Moriji Kawagoe's illustration)

recourse was to eliminate Zhang in accordance with proper planning by the Kwantung Army and that the army commander, Kawamoto Daisaku, and myself should be responsible for execution of the army's plan. I determined to do so as soon as I assumed my current post in the Kwantung Army [author's note: August 1927]. (Kawagoe's memoir)

It was Kawamoto that set the bomb on the railroad bridge the night of June 2, after which he returned to Port Arthur (Lushun). Kawagoe's company pushed the button to detonate the bomb.

As written in the *Chiang Kai-shek Diaries*, the bomb was first believed to have been buried along the rails like a landmine. Close scrutiny of the photograph of the scene, however, reveals that the rails of the Beijing-Mukden Railway remained intact, while upper parts of the train as well as the railroad bridge of the South Manchuria Railway were blown off. Although Prime Minister Tanaka had known of the truth of what was in Japan called "A Certain Important Incident in Manchuria" from an early stage, his attempt to make the truth public was resisted by others. On December 24, 1928, Prime Minister Tanaka reported to Emperor Showa an outline of the incident; War Minister Shirakawa Yoshinori also made a report on the incident to the emperor on March 27, 1929. In this meeting with the emperor, Shirakawa explained the incident as something premeditated by Kawamoto Daisaku singlehandedly and presented the government's view that the truth of the incident should not be revealed lest it would do harm to the country (Furukawa 2011).

Rapprochement between Zhang Xueliang and Chiang Kai-shek

We have reason to believe that Zhang Xueliang had known of his father's death almost immediately because, as stated earlier, he had departed for Mukden on the very day of the incident. However, in an interview in

Taipei in January 1992, Zhang Xueliang said he had learned of his father's death twelve or thirteen days after the incident (Tominaga 2014).

According to a Ministry of Foreign Affairs' document, Zhang Xueliang returned to Mukden on the night of June 5. After confirming the death of his father, Zhang Xueliang invited local media people who were stationed in Mukden to announce that anybody who reported on the death of his father would be executed (*Toho kaigi oyobi Cho Sakurin bakusatsu jiken kankei bunsho*). This announcement was the cause of subsequent confusion over whether Zhang Zuolin had lived or died and the reason that newspaper reporting on this issue changed again and again. After this announcement, Zhang Xueliang headed for Hebei Province; he later returned to Mukden.

Telegraph informing Chu Pei-teh of Zhang Zuolin's death by explosion (Source: *Sho Chusei soto bunbutsu: Kakumei bunken 1—Hokubatsu shiryo* [Generalissimo Chiang Kai-shek Archives 1: Revolutionary Documents—Historical Documents on the Northern Expeditions] at Academia Historica, Taiwan)

Chiang Kai-shek, who knew of the assassination of Zhang Zuolin on the day of the incident, wrote in his June 4 diary that Zhang had been injured by explosions at the Mukden station and had died due to his injury. But on June 5, he found out that "Zhang Zuolin was injured by the explosion of the landmine that the Kanto Army had set at the Mukden station and died of this injury." Thus, Chiang not only detected the engineering of the Kanto Army behind the incident from the beginning but also confirmed the death of Zhang Zuolin at an extremely early stage. On June 6, Chiang sent a telegram to Chu Pei-teh to inform him of Zhang's death and Ho Heng-chun's appointment as Commissioner of Police of Beijing (*Sho Chusei soto bunbutsu* [Generalissimo Chiang Kai-shek Archives]). Ho Heng-chun was personally close to Zhang Xueliang and a useful presence when negotiating with the younger Zhang. Thus, it is possible to conjecture that Zhang Xueliang announced his father's death on June 19 after he succeeded in peace negotiations with Chiang.

On June 7, the Northern Expedition army made a triumphant entry to Beijing, where Zhang Zuolin was no longer to put up resistance, and declared the completion of the Northern Expedition. Subsequently, on December 29, Zhang Xueliang announced compliance with the Three Principles of the People and allegiance to the Nationalist government. That same day, he conducted the Northeast Flag Replacement (replacing all banners of the Beiyang Government in Manchuria with the Blue Sky, White Sun, and Wholly Red Earth flag of the Nationalist Government). This made Chiang Kai-shek's unification of all of China complete. Had Zhang Xueliang and Chiang Kai-shek successfully concluded peace negotiations immediately following the Huanggutun Incident, however, Chiang's unification of China would have been completed on June 7.

It was only natural that possible formation of a nation-state in China with Zhang Xueliang's joining the Kuomintang posed a threat to the Japanese dream of controlling Manchuria and Mongolia by separating these regions from China proper.

＊　＊　＊

Recommended Readings for Deeper Understanding

Basic Historical Documents
Chen Bao [Morning News] and *Zhongyang Ribào* [Central Daily News, Shanghai edition].
　　Official newspaper of the Kuomintang.

Chiang Kai-shek Diaries in the collection of the Hoover Institution, Stanford University.
　　The Hoover Institution is entrusted with these documents by the bereaved family of Chiang Kai-shek. From March 2006, the Institution gradually began making these documents public, and the entire "diary" (from 1917 to July 21, 1972) became open to public in July 2009. Entries prior to 1917 are compiled as "memories."

Kawagoe Moriji. "Cho Sakurin bakushi jiken" [Zhang Zuolin's Death from Explosion], Military Archives at the National Institute for Defense Studies.

Memories written in 1962 of Kawagoe Moriji, a staff officer of the Kwantung Army who assisted Kawamoto in the assassination of Zhang Zuolin.

Kawamoto Daisaku. "Watashi ga Cho Sakurin o koroshita: Kawamoto shuki" [Kawamoto Notes: I Killed Zhang Zuolin], *Bungeishunju*, December 1954.

Although the article was published under Kawamoto's name, it was actually dictated by Hirano Reiji, Kawamoto's brother-in-law.

Kyoto Hinode Shimbun.

In my limited knowledge, this is the newspaper that provided the most detailed account of the Zhang Zuolin assassination among the dailies published in Japan in those days. Dispatching special correspondents to Beijing and Mukden, this newspaper provided reports from the site without relying on foreign wire services.

Ministry of Foreign Affairs (Japan). *Toho kaigi oyobi Cho Sakurin bakusatsu jiken kankei bunsho* [Documents related to the Far Eastern Conference and the Assassination of Zhang Zuolin], Military Archives at the National Institute for Defense Studies.

A compilation of documents on diplomatic history related to the Far Eastern Conference and the Assassination of Zhang Zuolin.

Sho Chusei soto bunbutsu [Generalissimo Chiang Kai-shek Archives], Academia Historica, Taiwan.

Official historical documents in Taiwan are mainly preserved at Academia Historica and the Institute of Modern History, Academia Sinica, where documents have been digitized and made open to public. Academia Historica houses the Presidents' and Vice-Presidents' Archives as well as general official historical documents. Included in the former are documents on Chiang Kai-shek, Chiang Ching-kuo, Yen Chia-kan, Lee Teng-hui, Chen Cheng, and Hsieh Min. The latter includes archives of the Nationalist Government, the Committee on Natural Resources, the Taiwan Provincial Government Office of Land Administration, the Ministry of Foreign Affairs, and the Yan Xishan Archives and the Wang Jingwei archives.

Sho Kaiseki hiroku 7 & 8 [Secret Notes of Chiang Kai-shek, Vols. 7 & 8]. Tokyo: Sankei Shimbunsha, 1976.

A 15-volume record of Chiang Kai-shek's memories complied before his death. A basic document for the study of modern to contemporary history of China, which frequently quotes the *Chiang Kai-shek Diaries*.

Books and Treatises

Furukawa Takahisa. *Showa Tenno—"Risei no kunshu" no kodoku* [Emperor Showa—Solitude of the "Monarch of Reason"]. Tokyo: Chuokoron Shinsha, 2011.

An attempt to analyze Emperor Showa's thinking relying on primary sources including diaries and memos of the emperor's aides that have been made public lately.

Hata Ikuhiko. "Cho Sakurin Bakusatsu jiken no saikosatsu" [Assassination of Zhao Zuolin Revisited], *Seikei Kenkyu*, Vol. 44, No. 1. Tokyo: Nippon Daigaku Hogakkai, 2007.

A rebuttal of the theory of the KGB's involvement in the incident. Summarizing the history of studies on this incident, it provides empirical reconfirmation and reconstruction of the theory of Kawamoto Daisaku as the mastermind.

Huang Tzuchin. *Sho Kaiseki to Nippon—Tomo to teki no hazama de* [Chiang Kai-shek and Japan—On the Threshold between Friend and Foe]. Tokyo: Takeda Random House Japan, 2011.

An analysis of Chiang's perception of Japan throughout his life, relying on the Chiang Kai-shek Diaries and historical documents of Academia Historica.

Iechika Ryoko. "Sho Kaiseki no 1927-nen aki no Nippon homon—*Sho Kaiseki nikki* to Nippon no shimbun hodo ni yoru bunseki" [Chiang Kai-shek's Autumn 1927 Visit to Japan—Analysis Using the *Chiang Kai-shek Diaries* and Japan's Newspaper Reporting] in *Sho Kaiseki kenkyu—Seiji, senso, Nippon* [Study of Chiang Kai-shek—Politics, War, and Japan], edited by Yamada Tatsuo and Matsushige Mitsuhiro. Tokyo: Toho Shoten, 2013.

An attempt at reconstruction of Chiang Kai-shek's Japan visit based on the *Chiang Kai-shek Diaries* and reports of Japan's local newspapers (*Tokyo Asahi Shimbun, Nagasaki Shimbun, Kobe Shimbun, Kobe Yushin*

Nippo, Osaka Asahi Shimbun, and Shimotsuke Shimbun), which covered the trip closely.

Iechika Ryoko. *Sho Kaiseki to Nankin kokumin seifu* [Chiang Kai-shek and the Nanjing Government]. Tokyo: Keio University Press, 2002.
An analysis of the process from the founding of the Nanjing government (from the Sun Yatsen Revolution to completion of the Northern Expeditions) to the civil war in China, using the process and structure of Chiang's seizure of power as a key element.

Kitaoka Shin'ichi. *Nippon no kindai 5: Seito kara gunbu e* [Japan in Modern Days 5: From Political Party to the Military]. Tokyo: Chuokoron Shinsha, 1999.
It reveals the Japanese government's policy toward the Chinese continent in the 1920s.

Kitaoka Shin'ichi and Bu Ping, eds. *Nitchu rekishi kyodo kenkyu hokokusho dainikan—Kin-gendai-shi hen* [Final Report of the Japan-China Joint History Research Committee, Vol. 2—Modern to Contemporary History]. Tokyo: Bensei Publishing, 2014.
Final report of the Japan-China Joint History Research Committee that was organized in December 2006. It clarifies the contending issues in history between Japan and China.

Miyata Masaaki. *Eibei sekai chitsujo to Higashi Ajia ni okeru Nippon* [Anglo-American World Order and Japan in East Asia]. Tokyo: Kinseisha, 2014.
A monumental work that analyzes Japan's East Asia strategy in modern times from an international perspective.

Nishimura Shigeo. *Cho Gakuryo* [Zhang Xueliang]. Tokyo: Iwanami Shoten, 1996.
A biography of Zhang Xueliang, including analyses of the relations among Manchuria, Japan, and the Kuomintang. It reveals how Zhang Xueliang, who was deprived of his father and his homeland by Japan, viewed Japan.

Tominaga Takako. *Kuni to seiki o kaeta ai* [Love that Changed the Country and the Century]. Tokyo: KADOKAWA, 2014.

A portrayal of Zhang Xueliang based on the author's interview of Zhang. This work discloses the relations between Zhang Xueliang and Soong Mei-ling.

Lecture 4

London Naval Conference, Imperial Court, Political Parties, and the Imperial Japanese Navy

Hatano Isamu

On Historical Evaluation of the London Naval Treaty Issue

In January 1930 (5th Year of Showa), the London Naval Conference was convened to restrict the tonnage of auxiliary vessels possessed by world naval powers. It appears that the political process around Japan's responses to this conference has already been almost thoroughly explored. For instance, in the realm of political history, Ito Takashi's *Showa shoki seiji-shi kenkyu* [Political History of Early Showa Period] published in 1969 is regarded as a pioneer work that analyzes in detail the partnerships and confrontations among various political groups over responses to this issue. In the field of diplomatic history, *Nippon gaiko bunsho* [Documents on Japan's Foreign Policy] about the London Naval Conference days has been published by the Ministry of Foreign Affairs. Subsequently, exploration has been continued through new historical documents, including the diary of Hamaguchi Osachi, prime minister of Japan around that time.

Advances in academic studies based on these publications and other historical documents have also been seen in a variety of other areas including naval history and the history of international treaties, trends of the emperor, the imperial court and the Privy Council. Seki Shizuo's *Rondon kaigun joyaku seiritsu-shi* [History behind the Conclusion of the London Naval Treaty] published in 2009 is an attempt at a chronological description of what took place, incorporating these advances in academic inquiries. As an overview of history in the target years, it is representative of the findings available today.

How, then, do these recent studies evaluate Japan's responses to the London Naval Treaty from a historical perspective? While at first the issue of the London Naval Treaty had been limited to criticism of the government from anti-treaty advocates in Japan, it soon encompassed more versatile issues. Linked with such wide-ranging questions as cooperative diplomacy based on good relations with Britain and the United States, the arms reduction regime, and the issue of supreme command authority, the London Naval Treaty evolved beyond and above a single policy issue. In other words, it is customary to view the London Naval Treaty as a genesis for or a remote cause of the collapse of the Washington Treaty regime and party politics in Japan. It cannot be said, however, that details of this process have been clarified to general readers. Thus, allow me first to confirm the overall flow of events and reactions to them that have so far been disclosed by past studies.

From Dispatch of Japan's Plenipotentiary to the London Naval Conference to Ratification of the Treaty

The Hamaguchi Osachi cabinet, which was formed in July 1929 (4th Year of Showa), decided Japan would participate in the London Naval Conference and dispatched the delegation headed by former Prime Minister Wakatsuki Reijiro as chief plenipotentiary and Navy Minister Takarabe Takeshi as plenipotentiary to London. In Takarabe's absence the administrative tasks of the navy minister were assumed by Prime Minister Hamaguchi. As preparation for the conference, the Imperial Japanese Navy had determined "Three Principles" in regard to its goals for the conference. The Three Principles were (1) to set the overall ratio of auxiliary vessel tonnage to 70 percent of US tonnage; (2) to set the number of heavy cruisers (less than a displacement of 10,000 metric tons loaded with guns up to 8 inches caliber) to 70 percent of that of the United States; and (3) to maintain the status quo in terms of the number of submarines (78,000 metric tons).

On March 15, 1930, Wakatsuki in London sent home a request for instructions on the signing of the treaty along a US-Japan compromise proposal known as the Reed-Matsudaira compromise. This agreement would entitle Japan to possess 69.75 percent of the United States' gross tonnage for auxiliary vessels, 60.23 percent for heavy cruisers, 70 percent for light cruisers and destroyers, and a parity for submarines at the status quo of 52,700 metric tons. Because these proportions were only slightly below the Three Principles, Vice Navy Minister Yamanashi Katsunoshin and Hori Teikichi, director-general of the Navy Ministry's Military Affairs Bureau, were of a view that agreement along this line was unavoidable "from a broader perspective of the state." In contrast, Kato Hiroharu (Kanji), chief of Naval General Staff, and Deputy Chief Suetsugu Nobumasa took the position that Japan should not give in even an inch from the Three Principles.

On March 27, Prime Minister Hamaguchi had an audience with the emperor, who instructed Hamaguchi to "make the utmost effort to promptly settle the issue for the sake of world peace." After also consulting with the grand chamberlain at the Imperial Court, Prime Minister Hamaguchi firmly resolved to sign the agreement.

Naval Chief of Staff Kato decided to report to the emperor on March 31 to convey his opposition to the agreement. Apprehensive of the risk of the emperor being forced to take sides when the prime minister and the chief of Naval General Staff report different things, Grand Chamberlain Suzuki Kantaro (Admiral, retired) advised Kato to forgo the imperial audience. Kato concurred at first.

On April 1, Prime Minister Hamaguchi invited top navy leaders including Admiral Okada Keisuke, military councilor on the Supreme War Council, Naval Chief of Staff Kato, and Vice Navy Minister Yamanashi to the prime minister's office before the cabinet meeting and requested the Imperial Japanese Navy's support for the signing of the treaty. In response, Okada, representing the Imperial Japanese Navy, approved submitting to the cabinet meeting the draft government response to Wakatsuki's request for instructions. At this meeting with Hamaguchi, Kato only said, "From the viewpoint of tactics and operations, the American proposal is unacceptable . . . from the viewpoint of tactics and operations. . . ." At the subsequent cabinet meeting, aside from the decision on the government's response to Wakatsuki's request, the Imperial Japanese Navy's request for replenishment of its shortage in manpower was granted. On April 2, after repeated petitions, Naval Chief of Staff Kato was granted an imperial audience. During the audience Kato stated, "Because the US proposal contains terrifying elements that could cause grave defects in the operations of the Imperial Japanese Navy, it should be deliberated with caution." On March 26, prior to this meeting, when the "Imperial Japanese Navy's Future Directions" was decided by the Imperial Japanese Navy General Staff, both Kato and Suetsugu had concurred that the numerical strength of the Imperial Japanese Navy would be decided by the government. Moreover, even Admiral of the Fleet Togo Heihachiro and Admiral Prince Fushimi Hiroyasu, two of the top elders in the Imperial Japanese Navy in those days, had announced that, "When the government makes the decision, this decision must be followed." In any event, it was the problem of "inadequate defense capabilities" that the Imperial Japanese Navy General Staff and other anti-treaty advocates stressed immediately before and after the decision on the government's response to Wakatsuki's request was made on April 1. There was absolutely no movement to take issue with the problem of supreme command authority.

From the Emergence of the Problem of the Infringement on the Independence of the Supreme Command to Ratification of the London Naval Treaty

On April 20, 1930, the Japanese government sent back its response to Wakatsuki's request. The London Naval Treaty was signed on April 22, marking the conclusion of a treaty on naval arms reduction among Japan, Britain, and the United States based on the aforementioned US-Japan compromise proposal. The treaty would remain valid until the end of 1936, like the Washington Naval Treaty that had been signed in February 1922. A ten-year pause, or "holiday," in the construction of capital ships (battleships and battle cruisers) stipulated by the Washington Treaty was also extended to 1936. When the 58th extraordinary session of the Imperial Diet was convened on April 22, however, the opposition party Seiyukai, in an attempt to topple the cabinet, launched an attack on the government by accusing it of infringing on the independence of the supreme command. This soon evolved into a major political strife.

To begin with, "supreme command authority" referred to an authority over military operations and tactics/strategy; Article 11 of the Constitution of the Empire of Japan declared that such authority belonged to the emperor. Supreme command authority was exercised only by the emperor with assistance from the naval/army high com-

Prime Minister Hamaguchi announcing the conclusion of the London Naval Treaty on radio in respective countries. Heads of governments of Britain, Japan, and the United States spoke for eight minutes on radio on October 28, 1930, to the attention of the entire world. (Source: *Zusetsu Nippon kaigun* [Illustrated Imperial Japanese Navy], Kawade Shobo Shinsha, 1997)

mand—that is, the Imperial Japanese Army General Staff Office and the Imperial Japanese Navy General Staff—and the army and navy did not have to obey the cabinet or the Imperial Diet. However, as stipulated by Article 12, the decision on the numerical strength of the military force was a part of the emperor's prerogative to organize the army and navy with the assistance of the cabinet (ministers of state). Those who opposed the London Naval Treaty stretched their interpretation of supreme command authority to insist that the decision on the numerical strength of the military force was also deeply related to the supreme command authority. They attacked the government, saying, "The government's decision on the reply to Wakatsuki's request in disregard of the chief of the Naval General Staff or without his consent was tantamount to an infringement on the independence of the supreme command." Encouraged by this development, Naval Chief of Staff Kato suddenly changed his attitude and started arguing that the government's decision this time did constitute infringement on the independence of the supreme command, saying, "The numerical strength of the military force is only a peripheral issue. The real issue is the independence of the supreme command." Even Togo and Prince Fushimi hardened their attitudes and started demanding denunciation of the treaty.

The conduct of the Seiyukai, which was an opposition party at that time, later became criticized as the first step toward the demise of party politics in prewar Japan. Leaders of the Seiyukai at that time must have thought that, in order to topple the Minseito cabinet, it would be necessary to team up with the military, the Privy Council, or any other extra-cabinet organization or group that could harm the government or to cash in on any confrontation between the government and such organizations/groups. Harada Kumao, who was a de facto secretary to the elder Meiji statesman Saionji Kinmochi at that time, wrote in his diary, "Behind Naval Chief of Staff Kato's unbending words and deeds is Deputy Chief Suetsugu, behind whom is Hiranuma Kiichiro of the Privy Council." Moreover, because Hiranuma kept close relations with Suzuki Kisaburo, leader of the largest faction within the Seiyukai, as well as secretary-general of the party, Mori Tsutomu, it can be said that the campaign to topple the Hamaguchi cabinet initiated by the Seiyukai was actually a conglomerate effort by a wide range of actors.

Although the Hamaguchi cabinet managed to survive the Imperial Diet session where the Minseito occupied the majority of the House of Representatives, it was feared at one point that ratification of the treaty may not pass the deliberation of the Privy Council. However, because Naval Chief of Staff Kato tendered his resignation directly to the emperor on June 10 to become a member of the Supreme War Council and the conference of naval members of the Supreme War Council conveyed its agreement with the London Treaty to the emperor on June 23, the Hamaguchi cabinet was able to make the Privy Council approve the ratification of the treaty on October 1. Inside the Imperial Japanese Navy, Naval Chief of Staff Kato as well as Navy Minister Takarabe were replaced. Out of fairness to both sides, Deputy Chief Suetsugu and Vice Minister Yamanashi were also relegated to lower positions.

Thus, the London Naval Treaty was finally ratified on October 2, 1930.

Roles the Emperor and the Imperial Court Played in Ratification of the Treaty

In November 1930, the month after the ratification of the London Naval Treaty, Prime Minister Hamaguchi was assaulted by a right-wing youth who was "indignant at the government's infringement on the independence of the supreme command." Foreign Minister Shidehara Kijuro became acting prime minister in place of the injured Hamaguchi, but the cabinet resigned in April 1931 and Hamaguchi died from his wounds in May. Nevertheless, the cabinet's conclusion of the treaty in the face of resistance from hardliners within the military and the Privy Council was an epoch-making accomplishment in the history of prewar party politics in Japan.

What, then, were the forces that contributed to the conclusion of the

treaty in line with the Hamaguchi cabinet's intention during deliberations at the conference of the Naval Supreme War Council as well as the
Privy Council? First of all, as Ito Takashi points out, we must recognize
the role that those around the emperor, including the elder statesman
Saionji and the emperor's confidants in the Imperial Court (Lord Keeper
of the Privy Seal, Minister of the Imperial Household, and Grand Chamberlain, etc.), played in helping the emperor make up his mind. Particularly noteworthy were the contributions of Saionji, who had expressed
his full support to the government in order to uphold the Washington
Treaty regime and placed under his direct influence the Lord Keeper of
the Privy Seal, the Minister of the Imperial Household, and the Grand
Chamberlain, to whom he had attached great importance. Saionji devoted his effort to enable the conclusion of the treaty via Suzuki Kantaro,
Grand Chamberlain of the time and former chief of Naval General Staff,
as well as such heavy weights within the military as Okada Keisuke and
Ugaki Kazushige (minister of war at that time). It can be said that stren-
uous efforts to have the treaty be concluded— regardless of whether the
Three Principles were accomplished—by Suzuki and Okada on behalf of
Saionji contributed greatly to the settlement of the issue. It should be
pointed out, however, that unlike Yamagata Aritomo, who had coordinated the interests of all the political forces under his auspices in the
olden days, Saionji's influence was contained within a circle made of the
Imperial Court, the House of Peers, and elders of the Imperial Japanese
Army and Navy (such as Okada, Ugaki, and Saito Makoto, former navy
minister in the Saionji cabinet).

In recent studies on prewar Showa history, more attention has been
paid to the views Emperor Showa expressed as formidable political incidents erupted and to how those views profoundly affected the subsequent development of the incidents. In the case of the London Naval
Treaty, the emperor had been pro-treaty from an early stage; he had repeatedly expressed his position to his aides, the prime minister (see
above the emperor's remarks on March 27 when Prime Minister Hamaguchi reported to him), and others who came to report to him. As intro-

duced earlier, after due deliberation, the Naval Supreme War Council reported to the emperor that it had decided to support the conclusion of the treaty. Behind this decision was, first, the conversion of Prince Fushimi, who had expressed his strong displeasure with the treaty, to a pro-treaty advocate by the emperor's expression of his pro-treaty stance. Togo, another staunch opponent of the treaty, was also converted by the emperor, who said words to the effect of, "As admiral of the fleet, you must take a farsighted view all the time. You should not put restraints on the 1935 conference [London Naval Conference]." From Hamaguchi's standpoint, he was supported by the emperor, Prince Saionji, and the entire Imperial Court. With such support, he could contend with any resistance from the military or the Privy Council.

Although the Hamaguchi cabinet had anticipated strong opposition from the Imperial Japanese Navy General Staff and many other directions, it was resolute about the prompt conclusion of the London Naval Treaty. This was because, first of all, a breakdown of this conference was thought likely to worsen Japan's relations with Britain and the United States. Moreover, a breakdown could have been interpreted as a result of Japan's frontal challenge to the Washington Treaty regime, which had been the foundation of the international order in East Asia. Also, it so happened that the London conference coincided with the timing of refinancing the foreign bonds that Japan had obtained to wage the Russo-Japanese War. British and American banks requested conclusion of the naval arms reduction treaty as a condition for the refinancing. For this reason, two of the central pillars of the Hamaguchi-Minseito cabinet—the fiscal policy of Finance Minister Inoue Jun'nosuke and the closely related foreign policy of Foreign Minister Shidehara Kijuro—both required collaboration with Britain and the United States. Thus, commitment to the London Naval Treaty was an important element of the Washington Treaty regime and party politics in Japan in the hands of the Minseito government.

Problems in the Government's Responses and Its Basic Stance

What evaluation, then, should we give the policies that the Hamaguchi government took for the maintenance and strengthening of the international cooperative regime and party politics? In retrospect, it is undeniable that there were a few grave problems with the policies. First, the Hamaguchi cabinet had initially adopted the Three Principles proposed by the Imperial Japanese Navy without any modification and instructed the delegates in London to negotiate on the basis of these principles. As Ito Takashi pointed out, however, that does not seem to have been a thoroughly thought-out decision. As Hori Teikichi, director-general of the Bureau of Military Affairs of the Imperial Japanese Navy at that time, reminisces, the Three Principles were not at all precise and rigorous guidelines drawn from the long tradition of the Imperial Navy (see Hori Teikichi, *Rondon kaigi to tosuiken mondai* [London Naval Conference and the Problem of Supreme Command Authority]). Nevertheless, the Imperial Navy, which had been made keenly aware of the need to muster the support of public opinion in Japan from the bitter experiences at the Washington Naval Conference, used the Three Principles frequently as a propaganda tool on the eve of the London Naval Conference. Consequently, it became difficult, ironically, for the Imperial Navy to make compromises at the arms reduction negotiations, while the sense of discontent over the outcome of the arms reduction negotiations grew sharply within the navy (Sato 1969).

While at the beginning of the London conference the Hamaguchi government had adopted the requests from the navy almost without any modification for use in the negotiations, it seems highly implausible that the government had had a clear vision about carrying through these principles or had anticipated that major political turmoil would erupt should those principles not be carried through. Foreign Minister Shidehara, for instance, reminisced as follows:

. . . the last request for instruction came [from the Japanese delegation in London], asking for advice on what to do now that the negotiations with Britain and the United States have almost come to a dead end. At this point, we have no other choice than to boldly finalize the deal. You can never accomplish anything if you have to listen to briefings from the Imperial Navy (Shidehara Kijuro, *Gaiko 50-nen* [50 Years of Diplomacy], Chuokoron Shinsha, 2015).

Because Vice Minister Yamanashi and Director-General of Military Affairs Hori were capable of departing from a purely militaristic viewpoint and assess situations from a much wider perspective, it is easy to agree with such an assertion as "Even the Imperial Japanese Navy General Staff would not have caused such trouble had Foreign Minister Shidehara repeated frank consultations with top leaders of the Ministry of Navy, mitigating the sense of discontent in the Bureau of Military Affairs" (from commentary attached to *Gendaishi shiryo 7: Manshu jihen*). Prime Minister Hamaguchi was concurrently acting minister of the navy at that time. When Vice Minister Yamanashi requested Hamaguchi to visit Togo to persuade the admiral of the fleet, Hamaguchi instead demanded that Togo come to see him. As exemplified by this episode, Hamaguchi maintained an unbending attitude toward anti-treaty elements within the Navy Ministry; this appears to have invited a lot of animosity.

Harada Kumao left references in his diary to the Hamaguchi government's basic policy after the eruption of the dispute over the infringement on the independence of the supreme command. According to Harada:

[The government] reached a general conclusion that "it is obvious that no infringement on the independence of the supreme command has been committed." Consequently, the government set up three principles for its reply in the Imperial Diet on this issue: (1)

The government took into fullest account the advice of the Imperial Japanese Navy General Staff; (2) The government would be fully responsible for national defense vis-à-vis the Imperial Diet; and (3) The government is not obliged to answer questions on internal procedures when it replied to requests from the Japanese delegation in London or to any question related to the constitutional argument.

Despite such an uncompromising attitude on the part of the Hamaguchi cabinet toward the military and the Privy Council, it was able to accomplish the conclusion of the treaty thanks to the support from the emperor and the Imperial Court, as introduced earlier. But that was not the end of the aftermath of this incident. There followed an upsurge of counteraction to what was perceived as the party cabinet's "monopoly of the monarch's sympathy." The movement of anti-treaty advocates was in no time transformed into an ideological argument concerning what was seen as a change of the constitutional monarch in the form of denunciation of the party cabinet and the emperor's confidants (Masuda 1999).

To borrow the expression of Ito Takashi and Sato Seizaburo to describe this transformation in detail, the anti-treaty advocates viewed the conclusion of the London Naval Treaty from an ideological perspective and succeeded in unifying forces that shared the same vector. Discontent and a sense of crisis within the Imperial Japanese Navy, for instance, easily resonated with the sense of crisis within the Imperial Japanese Army over the worsening of the Manchuria-Mongolia issue. Inside the navy, a group was formed that later became the core force of the May 15 Incident (1932). The Sakurakai (Cherry Blossom Society, an ultranationalist secret society established by young officers) was organized among officers of the army and later became engaged in the planning of coup d'états and overseas military advances. Also, the mainstream of the Seiyukai formed a partnership with the military and the Privy Council over the dispute over the infringement on the independence of the supreme command. The radicalization of right-wing groups also became conspicuous. Thus, while the Hamaguchi cabinet succeeded in concluding the London Naval Treaty, it also gave birth to a formidable anti-arms reduction united front that aimed at hardliner foreign policy and the overthrow of party politics (reorganization of the state). In contrast, the government side lacked the determination to consolidate a group of likeminded forces based on the active image that it had projected at the time of the formation of the cabinet and to establish the conclusion of the treaty as a victory of the "progressive" faction. (Author's note: Here "progressive" refers to "progress" on the path toward a civilized society including constitutional government). Politically, the government side obviously lost the competition.

As Tsutsui Kiyotada has convincingly argued recently, the Hamaguchi cabinet was reliant not only on the emperor and the Imperial Court but also public opinion led by the newspapers (especially pro-treaty arguments after the government's response to Wakabayashi's request for instructions was issued) (Tsutsui 2012). But these forces were not something political parties could continue to rely on after the incident. The weakening of the Imperial Court's attitude toward the military in later years (particularly after the February 26 Incident) and the drastic change in the newspaper commentaries after the eruption of the Manchurian Incident well testified to this.

The Greatest Beneficiary of the Positive Evaluation of the Naval Treaty

Finally, let us confirm if the content of the London Naval Treaty was really disadvantageous to the Imperial Japan Navy. And let us see what kind of political forces in Japan perceived the treaty as such. Admiral Kobayashi Seizo, chief of the Imperial Japanese Navy Technical Department at that time who later became governor-general of Taiwan, observes as follows in his memoir *Rondon gunshuku kaigi ron* [Review of the London Naval Conference]: Until the expiration of the London Treaty in 1936, the tonnage of auxiliary vessels that Japan possessed was only 0.25 percent short of the 70 percent of the tonnage of the United States that Japan had wanted. The tonnage of heavy cruisers was actually maintained at 70 percent the level of the US tonnage until the end of 1935 due to the delay in shipbuilding on the US side. It turned out that the actual tonnages of vessels possessed by the United States and Britain were kept lower than initially expected. Moreover, the Imperial Navy benefitted from the budget for its Naval Armaments Supplement Program in return for agreement with the government's instructions to Wakatsuki.

What one can detect from the above observation is that the London Naval Treaty was not necessarily disadvantageous to Japan. It was indeed far from being the imposition of "anxiety about national defense" that the anti-treaty faction claimed. Indeed, it was the challengers to the Washington Treaty regime, instead of its advocates, who recognized the reality of the equilibrium of naval power between Japan and the United States and fully utilized it. Itagaki Seishiro, one of the masterminds behind the Manchurian Incident in September 1931, made the following in-house lecture in May on the eve of the Incident:

> In order to rank with the world powers in terms of national defense capabilities and industrial resources, Japan must make Manchuria and Mongolia our territory. . . . Although the United States is likely to interfere strongly when Japan carries out this policy, our Imperial Navy is capable of defeating the US Navy. As the gap in naval power between Japan and the United States is expected to widen as a result of the London Treaty as time goes on, we might as well start a war promptly if we have to fight anyway.

Ishihara Kanji, another mastermind behind the Manchurian Incident, in later years told Kaya Okinori (later day finance minister), "Because close examination revealed that American naval power in those days fell far short of powerful military or diplomatic interference with Japan (particularly in terms of the number of cruisers possessed), we launched the Manchurian Incident believing that the United States would not interfere." (Kaya Okinori, *Senzen sengo 80-nen* [80 Years before and after the War], Keizai Oraisha, 1976). While the military action in Manchuria was totally unexpected by anyone except for those directly involved, those military officers who took action had known of the objective conditions that would make their actions viable.

The dispute over the London Naval Treaty has often been judged to be a starting point of the rise of the military (or the forces that opposed the Washington Treaty regime and party politics) in Japan. For instance, explanations such as the following are often heard: "The argument over the infringement on the independence of the supreme command triggered by the conclusion of the London Naval Treaty, coupled with the deadlock over the Manchuria-Mongolia problem under Shidehara diplomacy, gave the military an acute sense of crisis. Ideologies denouncing cooperation with Britain and the United States and party politics became rampant."

While, perhaps, this comment itself might be accurate, the following supplementary explanation may be in order now that the political process associated with the conclusion of the treaty has been more or less clarified: The Hamaguchi-Minseito cabinet was successful in the sense that it was able to conclude the treaty. In the process toward the conclusion, however, it made the military and other anti-treaty advocates feel an acute sense of defeat and failure. The effect was that these forces unified. They saw an excuse to initiate military action in Manchuria, allowing them to take advantage of the power equilibrium between the Japanese and American navies under the Washington Treaty regime. Therefore, we cannot say that the Hamaguchi cabinet's measures did not contribute to the subsequent difficulty to maintain cooperative diplomacy and party politics in Japan.

From now on, studies on the London Naval Treaty should not be confined to the search for and denunciation of those who were responsible for the destruction of the international as well as domestic order. In the future study of this issue, it still remains significant to keep in mind that miscalculation, halfway measures, minor errors, and lack of communication among prominent actors of the party politics system could, if allowed to accumulate, lead to the malfunctioning of the system and allow the emergence of elements that could cash in that malfunctioning to destroy the system. This is true even today.

*　*　*

Recommended Readings for Deeper Understanding

While there exist numerous historical documents related to the matters introduced in this lecture, the following documents offer an abundance of information and viewpoints to readers:

Ikei Masaru, Hatano Masaru, and Kurosawa Fumitaka, eds. *Hamaguchi Osachi nikki: Zuikanroku* [Hamaguchi Osachi Diary: Compilation of Random Thoughts]. Tokyo: Misuzu Shobo, 1991.

A first-class historical document left to us by the prime minister of Japan at that time.

Ito Takashi. *Showa shoki seiji-shi kenkyu—Rondon kaigun gunshuku mondai o meguru sho seiji shudan no taiko to teikei* [Study of Politics in Early Showa Era—Confrontation and Partnership among Various Political Groups over the London Naval Treaty Issue]. Tokyo: University of Tokyo Press, 1969.

A compilation of historical documents, memoirs of those who were directly involved, a wide range of newspaper and magazine articles of the time, and records of interviews on survivors of the incidents. A highly valuable, pioneering, and comprehensive study in areas of political history.

Japan Association of International Relations, ed. *Taiheiyo senso e no michi* [Road to the Pacific War]. Tokyo: Asahi Shimbunsha, 1963.

An eight-volume compilation, the first volume of which addresses the Washington-London Naval Treaties with clear-cut explanations on trends within the government and the navy. Its annex volume contains the primary sources that were used to write this chapter, making the entire compilation more valuable.

Kobayashi Tatsuo and Shimada Toshihiko, eds. *Gendaishi shiryo 7: Manshu jihen* [Reference Materials on Contemporary History 7: Manchurian Incident]. Tokyo: Misuzu Shobo, 1964.

A collection of precious primary historical documents by the hand of those directly involved in historical events, including Okada Keisuke, with meticulous explanations.

Ministry of Foreign Affairs (Japan), ed. *Nippon gaiko bunsho: 1930-nen Rondon kaigun kaigi* [Documents on Japan's Foreign Policy: 1930 London Naval Conference], published in 1983–84.

Although this document is not quoted in the text, it is the basic document on the negotiations between the Japanese and foreign delegations during the London Naval Conference.

Sato Seizaburo. "Kyocho to jiritsu no aida" [Between Cooperation and Self-Reliance] (1969) in his *"Shi no choyaku" o koete—Seiyo no shogeki to Nippon* [Beyond *Salto Mortale*—Impact of the West and Japan]. Tokyo: Toshi Shuppan, 1994.

A treatise Sato wrote for the journal of the Japanese Political Science Association. A pioneering work in the field of international relations history.

Seki Shizuo. *Rondon kaigun joyaku seiritsu-shi—Showa doran no jokyoku* [History of Conclusion of the London Naval Treaty—Prelude to Turmoil in the Showa Era]. Kyoto: Minerva Shobo, 2007.

The most handy and yet comprehensive descriptions of the subject that is available today. It incorporates contents of documents that have only recently been made public.

Tsutsui Kiyotada. *Showa senzenki no seito seiji—Nidai seito-sei wa naze zasetsu shita no ka* [Party Politics in Prewar Showa Era—Why Did the Two-Party System Experience a Setback?]. Tokyo: Chikumashobo, 2012.

History of the prewar party politics from its beginning to its end, viewing it as the historical precedence for contemporary "performance politics" and the confusion in the two-party system, with attention paid to such extra-party actors as the emperor, the imperial court, and the media.

The following two books attempt to clarify the historical position of the constitutional monarchy from the viewpoint of the management of a constitutional monarchy state.

Ito Yukio. *Showa Tenno to rikken kunshusei no hokai—Mutsuhito, Yoshi-hito kara Hirohito e* [Emperor Showa and the Fall of Constitutional Monarchy—From Mutsuhito and Yoshihito to Hirohito]. Nagoya: University of Nagoya Press, 2005.

Masuda Tomoko. *Tenno-sei to kokka—Kindai Nippon no rikken kun-shu-sei* [The Emperor System and State—Constitutional Monarchy in Modern Japan]. Tokyo: Aoki Shoten, 1999.

Lecture 5

From the Manchurian Incident to Japan's Withdrawal from the League of Nations

Tohmatsu Haruo

Japan's Involvement in Manchuria and the Manchuria/ Mongolia Situation in the 1920s

Japan's full-scale involvement in Manchuria began at the time of the Russo-Japanese War. As a result of the Russo-Japanese War, Lushun on the Liaodong Peninsula and Dalian became Japanese concessions through the Treaty of Portsmouth in 1905. These concessions were re-named the Kwantung Leased Territory and placed under the Kwantung Government-General (Reorganized to Kwantung Bureau after 1919). Although Qing China still exercised nominal sovereignty over this territory, Japan obtained such economic concessions as railway management, use of ports, and mining development. The territory's core organ was the parastatal South Manchuria Railway (Mantetsu) established in 1906 (see Kato Kiyofumi, *Mantetsu zenshi—"Kokusaku gaisha" no zenbo* [Entire History of Mantetsu: The Full Scope of a Statutory Company], Kodan-sha, 2006). The Kwantung Garrison was established to protect these concessions; it was reorganized into the Kwantung Army (Kanto Army)

83

in 1919. Thus emerged the colonial army that later became the ringleader of the Manchurian Incident (see Nakayama Takashi, *Kanto Gun* [Kwantung Army], Kodansha, 2000). Japan's rights and interests in these regions were confirmed in 1905 through 1907 by treaties and agreements Japan concluded with Russia, France, Britain, United States, and Qing China, making southern Manchuria a part of Japan's "informal empire."

Subsequently, in 1915 during World War I, the Okuma Shigenobu cabinet placed the Twenty-One Demands on the Republic of China government (the Beijing government led by Yuan Shikai), with the aim of expanding Japan's rights and interests in China south of the Great Wall while retaining its vested interests in southern Manchuria (Naraoka Sochi, *Taika 21-kajo yokyu to wa nandatta noka—Daiichiji sekai taisen to Nitchu tairitsu no genten* [What Were the Twenty-One Demands All About?—World War I and Origin of the Sino-Japanese Confrontation], University of Nagoya Press, 2015). While the Twenty-One Demands were met by resistance from the Chinese nationalists, the Japanese government managed to make the Beijing government accept the major portion of them by threatening the Chinese with an ultimatum. However, Japan was forced to give up most of the concessions after the US-led Washington Naval Conference in 1921–22. The Nine-Power Treaty concluded during this conference confirmed the principle that major world powers with vested interests in China would maintain an "open door" to allow all nations equal rights and equal access to China market and that Chinese territorial and administrative integrity should be maintained. Not only the United States, Britain, France, Japan and other world powers with vested interests in China but also the Republic of China itself became a signee of the treaty, making it legal grounds on which to restrain Japan's conduct after the Manchurian Incident (Usui Katsumi, *Chugoku o meguru kindai Nippon no gaiko* [Modern Japan's China-Related Diplomacy], Chikumashobo, 1983).

When, in the mid-1920s, Chinese nationalists, in the form of Chiang Kai-shek's Northern Expeditions, closed in on southern Manchuria, Japan was filled with a sense of crisis about the possible loss of its vested interests in China. After the warlord Zhang Xueliang, who had de facto control over Manchuria (the Fengtian clique), conducted the Northeast Flag Replacement in December 1928, Manchuria went under the control of the Republic of China. As Manchuria's position went through such a fundamental change, Japan's rights and interests in southern Manchuria became the target of anti-Japan movements, not only of the Fengtian clique but also of the nationalism throughout China (Nishimura Shigeo, *Cho Gakuryo—Nitchu no haken to "Manshu"* [Zhang Xueliang—Japan's and China's Hegemony and Manchuria], Iwanami Shoten, 1996).

Manchuria's situation from the late 1920s through the early 1930s can be overviewed as follows: Japan tried to maintain and expand its vested interests held since the Russo-Japanese War. The Republic of China aspired to retrieve the rights and interests of which it had been deprived by the world powers, with Japan as its primary target. The Soviet Union, on its part, attempted to retain its rights and interests in northern Manchuria including, most notably, the Chinese Eastern Railway, which it had obtained before the Russian Revolution. Surrounded by Japan, China, and the Soviet Union, the Mongolian people were striving to obtain autonomy or independence. And the western powers were very much interested in Manchuria's development as a potential market, as well as a part of the international order, namely the Nine-Power Treaty (or the Washington Treaty).

Sino-Soviet Conflict

Prior to the Manchurian Incident, a large-scale conflict known as the Sino–Soviet Conflict of 1929 erupted in this region. After the fall of the Qing Dynasty with the 1911 Xinhai Revolution, and the Republic of China established in 1912, confusion ensued, as the central government reigned only nominally. The entire Chinese continent was in constant turmoil from assorted confrontations among military cliques. During such times, the Mongolian people, who had been under the control of the Qing Dynasty, began a movement to obtain their autonomy and inde-

pendence. One of those Mongolian independence movements succeeded in establishing the Mongolian People's Republic in 1924 in Outer
Mongolia with help of the Soviet Union. Meanwhile, the Imperial Japanese Army also exercised their angle on the Mongolians in Inner Mongolia in order to strengthen its defense structure against the Soviet Union
(Mori Hisao, *Nippon rikugun to naimo kosaku—Kanto Gun wa naze
dokuso shita ka* [Imperial Japanese Army and Its Inner Mongolia Operations—Why Was the Kwantung Army Allowed Arbitrary Conduct?], Kodansha, 2009).

But from the viewpoint of Chiang Kai-shek, an anti-communist who
wished to inherit the entire former territory of the Qing Dynasty and
who was, essentially, a believer in a tributary regime tradition, the separation and independence of the Mongols, which would allow the Soviet
Union and Japan to establish puppet governments, was totally unacceptable (Iechika Ryoko, *Sho Kaiseki no gaiko senryaku to Nitchu senso*
[Chiang Kai-shek's Diplomatic Strategy and the Second Sino-Japanese
War], Iwanami Shoten, 2012). For the Fengtian clique government as
well, the emergence of a Soviet puppet government in neighboring Outer Mongolia was a great threat.

Under these circumstances, Zhang Xueliang attempted to take over
the Chinese Eastern Railway in northern Manchuria, which had been
under the joint management of the Soviet Union and the Fengtian clique
government, with the support of Chiang Kai-shek in the year after of his
Northeast Flag Replacement. This attempt resulted in a large-scale military confrontation with the Soviet Union in November 1929. Chiang Kai-
shek's army however did not move to assist Zhang. A landslide victory
resulted for the Soviet army, which had far superior military equipment
and well-trained troops. Thus Zhang Xueliang failed in his attempt to
seize the rights and interests in northern Manchuria (Asada Masafumi,
Manmo—Nichi-Ro-Chu no "saizensen" [Manchuria-Mongolia—The
Frontline among Japan, Russia, and China], Kodansha, 2014).

The Imperial Japanese Army, particularly the Kwantung Army, which
had been charged with the task of protecting Japan's rights and interests

in southern Manchuria, showed strong interest in this development. It is beyond doubt that the outcome of the Sino–Soviet Conflict made the Kwantung Army realize not only the threat of the quickly modernizing Soviet Army in the Far East but also the possibility as well as the necessity of protecting Japan's vested interests in southern Manchuria against the rising Chinese nationalism (Taneine Shuji, *Kindai Nippon gaiko to "shikatsuteki rieki"—Dainiji Shidehara gaiko to Taiheiyo senso e no jokyoku* [Modern Japan's Diplomacy and "Critical Interests"—The Second Shidehara Diplomacy and Prelude to the Pacific War], Fuyo Shobo Shuppan, 2014).

Road to the Manchurian Incident

The Great Depression was triggered by the stock market collapse on Wall Street in October 1929, and Japan, too, had to endure a serious recession. The Manchurian Incident is inseparable from the economic crisis in Japan.

Japan's China policy on the eve of the Manchurian Incident had been a cooperative one based on good relations with Britain and the United States led by Minister for Foreign Affairs Shidehara Kijuro of the Wakatsuki Reijiro cabinet (Shidehara diplomacy). Nonetheless, Shidehara diplomacy did not advocate abandoning the rights and interests that Japan had legally obtained in China since the Russo-Japanese War. On the contrary, it aimed to maintain Japan's vested interests through negotiations with the Republic of China government in cooperation with the western powers. Since the successful completion of the Northern Expeditions, however, the Republic of China government wanted to hasten the prompt retrieval of concessions from the Western powers and Japan. Japan's negotiations with China were thus deadlocked. In the face of intensified boycotts of Japanese goods and anti-Japanese movements, even Foreign Minister Shidehara had been forced to wait as Sino-Japanese negotiations became "firmly cornered." (Shigemitsu Mamoru, *Gaiko kaiso-roku* [Memoir on Diplomacy], Chuokoron Shinsha, 2011).

Particularly, the planned construction of a parallel railway to the South Manchuria Railway by the Fengtian clique government made the Japanese gravely uneasy (Usui Katsumi, *Manshu jihen* [Manchurian Incident], Chuokoron-sha, 1974).

Such a deadlock stiffened public opinion in Japan, where people had suffered from serious economic recession. Party politics, which appeared to finally have become embedded in Japan, fell into the bad habit of catering to public opinion rather than leading it in the right direction (Tsutsui Kiyotada, *Showa senzenki no seito seiji—Nidai seito-sei wa naze zasetsu shita no ka* [Party Politics in the Prewar Showa Period—Why Did the Two-Party System not succeed?], Chikumashobo, 2011). On January 23, 1931, during the 59th Session of the Imperial Diet, Matsuoka Yosuke, a Seiyukai member of the House of Representatives, pressed Foreign Minister Shidehara hard with questions. Matsuoka, an ex-diplomat who had served as vice-president of the South Manchuria Railway before entering politics, had been critical of Shidehara's accommodative diplomacy toward China. The phrase "Manchuria and Mongolia are Japan's lifeline" that Matsuoka used in his Diet speech became the rage of the time. As if to make the trend more irreversible, frictions between China and Japan that followed one after another, including the Nakamura Incident[1] and the Wanpaoshan Incident[2], made the slogan "Manchuria and Mongolia are Japan's lifeline" even more convincing.

The sense of crisis over the Republic of China's revolutionary diplomacy and the hardline policy of the Fengtian clique government toward Japan was particularly strong among Japanese residents in Manchuria, and personnel of the South Manchuria Railway and the Kwantung Army.

---

1 Extrajudicial killing of Imperial Japanese Army Captain Nakamura Shintaro and three others on a survey mission in Daxing-Anling region, on June 27, 1931, by Fengtian clique soldiers in Manchuria.
2 A minor dispute between Chinese and Korean farmers that occurred on July 1, 1931, over Korean settlers entering the Wanpaoshan region.

It was in the face of the rise of public opinion in Japan demanding more hardliner policies toward China that the Kwantung Army started planning the use of force on its own.

And it was Lieutenant Colonel Ishihara Kanji, a staff officer of the Kwantung Army, who masterminded this plan. Well-versed in western military theories, Ishihara was also an avid member of the Kokuchukai, a religious organization advocating Nichiren-shugi founded by the philosopher Tanaka Chigaku[3]. Having thoroughly studied the history of war from the Napoleonic Wars through World War I, Ishihara had developed his own unique view on war. His view was that because Japan, representing Oriental civilization, and the United States, as the representative of western civilization, were destined to fight out the world's final war by the 2,500th anniversary of Buddha's death (in 2014 or 2038), Japan had to nurture its national power in preparation for the final showdown. The seizure of Manchuria was, therefore, the first step that Japan should take in order to secure a supply of natural resources (Ishihara Kanji, *Saishu senso-ron* [Theory of the Final War], Chuokoron Shinsha, 2001).

Around 1931, the strength of the Kwantung Army, which was allowed to be stationed in the Kwantung Leased Territory and the territory adjacent to the South Manchuria Railway in accordance with the Portsmouth Treaty, was about 10,000-men strong. Zhang Xueliang's army boasted some 450,000 soldiers including the police forces. Although this army had nominally been an army of the Republic of China since Zhang's Northeast Flag Replacement, it was, in actuality, Zhang's private army. Zhang's army was far inferior to the central army directly attached to the republic, which was mainly staffed with graduates of the Whampoa Military Academy, in terms of equipment, training, and political loyalty. Nevertheless, the fact remained that the Kwantung Army had to deal

---

3 *Nichiren-shugi* (Nichiren-ism) is based on Tanaka's interpretation of the writings of Nichiren (1222–82), Buddhist priest and founder of the Nichiren Sect.

with Zhang's army, which was more than 40 times larger than itself. To cope with this situation, Ishihara developed operational strategies based on relentless preemptive and surprise attacks.

The Manchurian Incident and the Founding of Manchukuo

On the night of September 18, 1931, the Kwantung Army itself blew out the rails of the South Manchuria Railway at Liutiaohu in the suburbs of Mukden, giving it an excuse to mobilize troops on the pretext of restoring public order. In no time the Kwantung Army conquered Beidaying, the headquarters of Zhang Xueliang's army. In the subsequent invasion operations, the Kwantung Army and the Imperial Japanese Army dispatched from Korea as reinforcement conquered not only south Manchuria but the entire Manchurian region by the end of the year. This quick success of the Kwantung Army was attributable to a combination of factors, including the meticulous surprise attack operation planned by Ishihara; the Fengtian clique government being off-guard; Soviet restraint on interference with northern Manchuria due to under-preparedness of its military buildups because the First Five-Year Plan was unfinished; the western powers being too busy to interfere because they were preoccupied with their economic reconstruction in the aftermath of the Great Depression; and the non-resistance policy ("unify the country before eliminating foreign aggression") of Chiang Kai-shek, who prioritized domestic consolidation and suppression of the communist party (Lu Xijun, *Chugoku kokumin seifu no tainichi seisaku 1931–1933* [Republic of China's Japan Policy 1931–33], University of Tokyo Press, 2001). In spite of its far superior numerical strength, Zhang Xueliang's army abstained from full-scale resistance and instead fled to south of the line of the Great Wall in compliance with Chiang's instructions.

The Kwantung Army rallied forces in Manchuria's occupied territory, which had pledged allegiance to Japan, to establish a Northeast Administrative Committee, which later became the foundation of the new

Puyi (left) at his inaugural ceremony as chief executive of Manchukuo on March 9, 1932

state of Manchukuo declared on March 1, 1932. By making Aisin Gioro Puyi, the last emperor of the Qing Dynasty whom Japan's special service agency had helped escape Tianjin, chief executive of Manchukuo (emperor after 1934), Japan made it appear as though the new state was the outcome of an indigenous independence movement in the birthplace of the Qing Dynasty with the assistance of the Kwantung Army. It appeared that even the Kwantung Army, which seemed to be so fearless, could not straightforwardly declare the annexation of Manchuria, probably in consideration of the worldwide climate in the inter-war period advocating no territorial annexation and the principle of ethnic national self-determination.

The following arguments were applied when founding Manchukuo. First, Manchuria is located at the periphery of the former Qing Empire and, as such, it should not be regarded as an integral part of the Republic of China. Manchuria became a part of China only when the Jurchens (the Manchu) in Manchuria conquered the China mainland south of the Great Wall in the early seventeenth century. Second, Manchuria was a critical area for Japan's security, being a buffer zone for Japan with China, the Mongolian People's Republic (a satellite state of the Soviet Union), and the Soviet Union. Therefore, Japan had to acquire Manchuria, which was Japan's "lifeline." Third, the multiethnic composition of Manchuria defied the unilateral territorial claims of the Republic of China. Although the proportion of Han Chinese had risen to 80 percent of Manchurian residents by the early 1930s, this region was the ancient homeland of the ethnic Manchus, and had been inhabited for a long time by the Manchus, the Mongols, the Koreans, the Russians, and the Japanese (Tsukase Susumu, *Manshukoku—"Minzoku kyowa" no jitsuzo* [Manchukuo—The Reality of "the Harmony among the Five Ethnic Groups"], Yoshikawa Kobunkan, 1998). The Japanese side used this situation to justify the slogan of "Arcadia Manchukuo, Five Races under One Union.[4]" In reality, many residents of Manchuria loathed Zhang Xueliang's oppressive rule and were distrustful of the Republic of China government. But they also resented the Kwantung Army's occupation of Manchuria. Whether there was a genuine Manchuria/Mongolia independence movement at that time is a debatable topic (Nakami 2013), though there certainly were various movements seeking more autonomy (Shibuya 2008).

International Repercussions and the Lytton Report

The occupation of Manchuria by the Kwantung Army stirred up a variety of international repercussions. The Western powers including Britain, France, Germany, and Italy, which had been apprehensive about being deprived of their rights and interests in China by the Republic of China's revolutionary diplomacy, initially showed a certain level of understanding regarding Japan's "act of self-defense." Yet as suspicion about the Kwantung Army's conspiracy behind the Liutiaohu Incident became

---

4 The original word of Arcadia is *odo rakudo*, literally meaning 'a utopia ruled by a virtuous king.'

widespread, as Japan continued military actions that were far beyond a mere "act of self-defense," and as the establishment of Manchukuo was declared, attitudes toward Japan hardened (Usui 1995). In particular, the United States' attitude toward Japan became remarkably tougher. In January 1932, US Secretary of State Henry Stimson of the Herbert Hoover administration announced that the United States would not recognize any change to existing states by the accumulation of faits accomplis in violation of the Nine-Power Treaty or the Kellogg–Briand Pact. This Stimson Doctrine became the base of subsequent US policy toward Japan (Takamitsu Yoshie, "1930-nendai ni okeru Amerika no Chugoku ninshiki to tainichi seisaku" [China Perception and Japan Policy of the United States in the 1930s] in Sugita Yoneyuki, ed., *Amerika gaiko no bunseki—Rekishiteki tenkai to genjo bunseki* [Analysis of American Diplomacy—Historical Development and Analysis of Current Status], Daigaku Kyoiku Shuppan, 2008). In the League of Nations, smaller member countries apprehensive about the domineering conduct of the world powers, including Belgium, the Netherlands, Czechoslovakia, and Spain, were critical of Japan's conduct (Shinohara 2010; Thorne 1972).

Under these circumstances, the Republic of China government filed a complaint with the League of Nations about Japan's actions that were in violation of the Covenant of the League of Nations. The League dispatched a fact-finding mission to Manchuria. This mission was headed by V. A. G. R. Bulwer-Lytton, the second Earl of Lytton of the United Kingdom and former governor of Bengal. The mission included one member each from the other League member countries, Germany, Italy, and France. A representative of the United States, a non-member country, participated as an observer. All of the members of the mission were experts on colonial issues. The activities of the mission (known as the Lytton Commission) were meticulously recorded by Heinrich Schnee, the German member of the mission (Heinrich Schnee, *Völker und Mächte im Fernen Osten. Eindrücke von einer Reise mit der Mandschurei-Kommission* (Peoples and Powers in the Far East. Impressions from a Voyage with the Manchuria Commission), translated by Kana-

93

The Lytton Commission members visiting Prime Minister Inukai Tsuyoshi on February 29, 1932. Far left in the front row is Bulwer-Lytton, chairman of the Commission; Schnee is on the left in the middle row. (Photo courtesy of Kyodo News)

mori Shigenari, Kodansha, 2002). The Lytton Commission visited China, Japan, and Manchuria for three months starting in the spring of 1932 and published its report in early October that same year.

The final report of the Commission, *Report of the Commission of Enquiry into the Sino-Japanese Dispute* (Lytton Report henceforth), can be summarized as follows: (1) While China's conduct violated Japan's legal rights and interests, (2) Japan's conduct went far beyond the range of an act of self-defense. Therefore, (3) the founding of Manchukuo was both legally and politically problematic. Thus, (4) Japan, China, and the Soviet Union should conclude an agreement of mutual nonaggression and withdraw their troops from Manchuria and (5) place Manchuria tentatively under international custody under the League of Nations' auspices (Kokusai Renmei Kyokai, ed., *Kanzen fukkoku Ritton hokokusho* [Unabridged Reprint of the Lytton Report], Kadokawa Gakugei Shuppan, 2006).

The scheme proposed by the Lytton Report incorporated the mandate system stipulated by Article 22 of the Covenant of the League of Nations as well as the League's experience in administering the international custodies of Saarland and Danzig in Europe. The Chinese side was prepared to accept this proposal on the condition of an additional safety measure (holding a local referendum in the relatively near future) to

prevent the international custody of Manchuria from stretching on for-
ever (Tohmatsu, *Kokusai Ho-Gaiko Zasshi*, 2001). A blueprint of what
appeared to resemble today's UN Peacekeeping Force was also prepared for the maintenance of security in Manchuria (Tohmatsu Haruo,
"1932-nen mihatsu no 'Manshu PKF'—Ritton hokokusho ni mirareru
tokubetsu kenpeitai koso" [Unimplemented 'Manchurian PKF' of 1932—
A Special Military Police Force Scheme Found in the Lytton Report], in
Gunji-shi Gakkai, ed., *Saiko Manshu jihen* [Manchurian Incident Revis-
ited], Kinseisha, 2001). While the proposal showed a view to "kill three
birds with one stone," by paying due attention to China's sovereignty, as
well as Japan's rights and interests, and, at the same time, protect the
dignity of the League of Nations, the success of the Lytton Report's proposal was dependent on whether Japan would accept it or not.

The End of the Manchurian Incident

For the half year between the declaration of independence of Manchukuo in March 1932 and publication of the Lytton Report in October 1932,
Japan's Ministry of Foreign Affairs studied relatively recent cases of the
founding of a new state and its international recognition, including Iraq
and Panama. Even the Imperial Japanese Army, the initiator of the Manchurian Incident, had taken a cautious stance toward the establishment
of Manchukuo at first to the extent that it had studied how deteriorated
relations with the League of Nations could have an impact on Japan's
international standing, immediately after the Manchurian Incident
(Tohmatsu, *Kokusai Ho-Gaiko Zasshi*, 2001). As the Fengtian clique
government was successfully removed from Manchuria, the feared Soviet intervention became improbable, and it became clear that the United
States could do nothing more than issue moralistic accusations such as
the Stimson Doctrine; however, the Japanese Army became quickly
inclined to hasten the construction and development of Manchukuo. Japan's earlier diplomacy of caution shifted toward the retention of Manchukuo. During the 63rd session of the Imperial Diet on August 25, 1932,

Foreign Minister Uchida Kosai (Yasuya) of the Saito Makoto cabinet declared that Japan was "solidly determined not to concede a foot even if the country turned into scorched earth," giving his diplomacy the nickname of "Shodo gaiko [burned-down diplomacy]" (Usui 1974).

After these developments, the Japanese government officially recognized Manchukuo on September 15, 1932. The Japan-Manchukuo Protocol was approved on the same day. With the signing of this protocol, the Japanese government succeeded in making the Manchukuo government recognize Japan's vested interests and the permanent stationing of the Kwantung Army to defend the country. The Manchukuo government employed a large number of Japanese bureaucrats and engineers in its governmental institutions. Even though the nominal heads of governmental organizations may have been Han Chinese, Manchu, or Mongolian, the real power of the organizations was in the hands of Japanese bureaucrats. Manchukuo became a de facto protectorate of Japan. From this point on, the Japanese view became widespread that the acceptance of solutions based on the Lytton Report, which denied the existence of Manchukuo, went against Japan's prestige and its national interest.

Subsequently, in order to stabilize the southern and western borders of Manchukuo, the Kwantung Army confronted and defeated Zhang Xueliang's troops in January through March 1933 in Rehe Province (Battle of Rehe). Japanese troops marched into Hebei Province in May, fighting off the Republic of China army, which attempted a counterattack along the Great Wall line (Battle of the Great Wall). On May 31, 1933, the Tanggu Truce was signed between the Chinese and Japanese armies, upon which the Kwantung Army withdrew to north of the line of the Great Wall, establishing the southern border of Manchukuo (Uchida Naotaka, *Kahoku jihen no kenkyu—Tanku teisen kyotei to Kahoku kikika no Nitchu kankei 1932–1935* [A Study on the Hebei Incident—Tanggu Truce and Sino-Japanese Relations under Hebei Crisis1932–35], Kyuko Shoin, 2006).

With the signing of the Tanggu Truce, the Manchurian Incident was virtually terminated. Concluding a general peace treaty with Japan would be tantamount to recognizing the legal existence of Manchukuo. That, therefore, was an utterly unacceptable choice for Chiang Kai-shek in light of rising hardliner public opinion against Japan not only in the Kuomintang but also in the entire country. A ceasefire agreement made between two warring troops on the spot was a mere tentative measure that allowed both sides to shelve the territorial issue for future final settlement (Lu 2001).

Japan's Withdrawal from the League of Nations and the Situation of Manchukuo Thereafter

Around the time of the military confrontation between the Japanese and Chinese armies in Rehe, the League of Nations in Geneva became a theatre of diplomatic battle regarding the existence of Manchukuo. The majority opinion in Japan—from the government to the public—leaned toward Japan's withdrawal from the League of Nations if it did not recognize the existence of Manchukuo (Usui 1995). The League of Nations' Special Session of Assembly on February 24, 1933, deliberated on whether to adopt the Final Report of the League of Nations' Special Session of Assembly on the Sino-Japanese Conflict based on the Lytton Report. This final report renounced the independence of Manchukuo and recommended the guarantee of Japan's vested interests on the basis of the principle of the Nine-Power Treaty, which stipulated the territorial integrity of China. Forty-two member countries agreed with adopting the final report, one member opposed doing so, and one member abstained.

The Japanese plenipotentiary who attended this special session was Matsuoka Yosuke, who formerly had denounced Shidehara diplomacy. Following the instructions from the home government, Matsuoka announced Japan's withdrawal from the League of Nations and walked away from the assembly with the rest of the Japanese delegation. Truth be told, Matsuoka later resented this decision of the Japanese government. As a matter of fact, prior to his departure for Geneva, Matsuoka had promised Prince Saionji Kinmochi, the "last *genro* (or elder states-man)," who had feared that withdrawal from the League of Nations would result in Japan's isolation in the international community, that he would make efforts to prevent Japan's withdrawal from the League. When Matsuoka returned home, however, he found himself fervently welcomed by public opinion (Miwa Kimitada, *Matsuoka Yosuke—Sono ningen to gaiko* [Matsuoka Yosuke—His Person and Diplomacy], Chuo-koronsha, 1971). This perception gap over withdrawal from the League of Nations between Matsuoka and public opinion bared the danger of mass democracy when the norm of party politics still remained imma-ture (Tsutsui 2012).

On March 27, 1933, about a month after the Special Session of Assembly of the League of Nations, the Japanese government sent an official notice of withdrawal to the Council of the League of Nations. Because it was stipulated that a country was obliged to comply with its duties as a member for two years after the official notice of withdrawal, Japan's withdrawal actually became effective on March 27, 1935.

The Soviet Union, whose interference the Kwantung Army feared most, did not officially recognize Manchukuo, but it sold the Chinese Eastern Railway to Manchukuo on March 23, 1935, removing its military forces from North Manchuria, and agreed with the establishment of Manchukuo legations in several locations on Soviet territory (Asada 2012). Public order in Manchukuo was secured in a relatively short peri-od of time, and by 1936, the majority of anti-Japanese movements were successfully suppressed. Economic construction under a four-year plan, modeled after the Soviet five-year plan, was promoted by Japanese bu-reaucrats. By 1943, Manchukuo had become the most industrialized re-gion in East Asia except for Japan proper. If public order and economic development are two important conditions for nation building, it can be said that Manchukuo fulfilled these conditions to a significant degree. Given the reality of Manchukuo, which advocated "harmony among the five ethnic groups" without enacting a nationality law and preserved the Japanese concessions (Asano Toyomi, *Teikoku Nippon no shokumin-*

chi hosei—Hoiki togo to teikoku chitsujo [Legislation in Colonies of the Empire of Japan—Unification of Jurisdiction Area and Imperial Order], University of Nagoya Press, 2008), it is highly debatable whether Manchukuo deserved to be called a genuine state (Yamamuro Shin'ichi, *Manchiria under Japanese Dominion*, translated by Joshua A. Fogel, Philadelphia: University of Pennsylvania Press, 2006). Nonetheless, sixteen countries had recognized Manchukuo by 1941.

Although it was at one time feared that withdrawal from the League of Nations might adversely affect Japan's mandate on the Micronesia islands (South Sea Islands) based on Article 22 of the League Covenant, this turned out to be mostly a false alarm (Tohmatsu Haruo, *Nippon teikoku to inin tochi—Nanyo gunto o meguru kokusai seiji 1914–1947* [Japanese Empire and Mandate System—International Politics around the Micronesia Islands 1914–47], University of Nagoya Press, 2011). Japan's cooperation with the League of Nations continued after its withdrawal in the form of a collaborative opium crackdown and the dispatch of judges to the Permanent Court of International Justice (Kamiyama Akiyoshi, *Nippon no Kokusai Renmei dattai to josetsu Kokusai Shiho Saibansho to no kankei ni tsuite* [Japan's Withdrawal from the League of Nations and Its Relations with the Permanent Court of International Justice] in Ministry of Foreign Affairs, *Gaiko Shiryokan Ho*, No. 6, 1993).

In the League of Nations, which had no coercive power on members unless by unanimous decision, Japan's position as a member of the Council was quite powerful. Despite the unfavorable voting outcome at the Special Session of Assembly in February 1933, China's move for economic sanction against Japan based on Article 16 of the Covenant was rejected (Unno Yoshiro, *Kokusai Renmei to Nippon* [League of Nations and Japan], Hara Shobo, 1972). Tachi Sakutaro, professor of Tokyo Imperial University and a well-known scholar of international law who was also an advisor to the Ministry of Foreign Affairs, claimed that the only thing the League of Nations could do was to issue "recommendations" with no binding power and, judging from the world major powers' abstention from intervening in Sino-Japanese relations over Manchuria, Japan should have remained in the League as if nothing had happened, ignoring the Lytton Report (Tachi Sakutaro, *Kokusai Renmei ki-yaku-ron* [Discussion on the League of Nations Covenant], Kokusai Renmei Kyokai, 1932). As Tachi points out, Japan did have the option of remaining in the League and attempting a certain level of international cooperation while retaining Manchukuo (Inoue Toshikazu, "Kokusai Renmei dattai to kokusai kyocho shugi" [Withdrawal from the League of Nations and the Principle of International Cooperation] in *Hitotsubashi Ronso*, Vol. 94, No. 1, September 1985). Furthermore, the League of Nations and the world powers continued to calmly watch the development of the Manchurian issue even after Japan's withdrawal from the League in the hope that Japan might come back to the League in two years before its withdrawal became effective in March 1935 (Tohmatsu, *Kokusai Ho-Gaiko Zasshi*, 2011).

In the face of the rapidly rising political influence of the Imperial Japanese Army, which had won a brilliant military victory in Manchuria, and the fervent public opinion in Japan, which had praised the founding of Manchukuo as a glorious accomplishment of Japan's diplomacy, however, cool-headed realism had no chance to prevail. By withdrawing from the League of Nations, Japan narrowed its own diplomatic options. The presence of Manchukuo also narrowed to the extreme the margin for subsequent improvement of Japan's relations with China.

*   *   *

Recommended Readings for Deeper Understanding

While, conventionally, the period covered in this lecture has tended to be regarded as the "starting point of Japan's full-scale China invasion that led to the Second Sino-Japanese War," in recent years, multifaceted analyses and studies from the perspective of "politico-economic changes in East Asia after the fall of the Qing Dynasty" have emerged, taking in the viewpoints of not only the major powers including Japan, China, and the Soviet Union but also other actors such as Manchus, Mongolians, Koreans, White Russians, mounted bandits, and the League of Nations.

Asada Masafumi. *Chuto tetsudo keieishi—Roshia to "Manshu" 1896–1935* [History of Management of the Chinese Eastern Railway—Russia and Manchuria 1896–1935]. Nagoya: University of Nagoya Press, 2012.

An analysis of Russian/Soviet involvement in Manchuria with special attention to the railroad concessions that they had established in northern Manchuria in the days of the Russian Empire.

Hironaka Issei. *Nise Chaina—Chugoku kairai seiken* [Fake China—Puppet Governments in China]. Tokyo: Shakai Hyouronsha, 2013.

An attempt at an overview of local regimes collaborative with Japan in various locations in China and Manchukuo's relative position.

Kawada Minoru. *Manshu jihen to seito seiji—Gunbu to seito no gekito* [Manchurian Incident and Party Politics—Fierce Struggle between the Military and Political Parties]. Tokyo: Kodansha, 2010.

A study with focus on trends in domestic politics in Japan, particularly those of political parties.

Matsusaka Yoshihisa Tak. *The Making of Japanese Manchuria, 1904–1932*. Cambridge: Harvard University Asia Center, 2003.

A comprehensive account of Japanese influence and penetration in Manchuria between the Russo-Japanese war and the creation of Manchukuo.

Nakami Tateo. *"Manmo mondai" no rekishiteki kozu* [Historical Structure of the Manchuria-Mongolia Problem]. Tokyo: University of Tokyo Press, 2013.

An overview of trends among the Manchus and Mongolians in the process of dissolution of the Qing Empire.

Nish, Ian. *Japan's Struggle with Internationalism: Japan, China, and the League of Nations 1931–33*. London: Kegan Paul International, 1993.

A detailed study of responses of Japanese intellectuals to the Manchurian Incident.

Ogata Sadako. *Manshu jihen—Seisaku no keisei katei* [The Manchurian

Incident—Process of Policy Formulation]. Tokyo: Iwanami Shoten, 2011.
Usui Katsumi. *Manshukoku to Kokusai Renmei* [Manchukuo and League of Nations]. Tokyo: Yoshikawa Kobunkan, 1995.

These two books are still invaluable classics in the realm of orthodox study on political and diplomatic history related to the Manchurian Incident.

Shibuya Yuri. *"Kankan" to eiyu no Manshu* [Manchuria of Chinese Traitors and Heroes]. Tokyo: Kodansha, 2008.

A study of Manchuria with special focus on various local forces including mounted bandits.

Shinohara Hatsue. *Kokusai Renmei—Sekai heiwa e no yume to zasetsu* [League of Nations—The Dream of World Peace and Its Setback]. Tokyo: Chuokoron Shinsha, 2010.

A useful work when viewing the Manchurian Incident from the perspective of the League of Nations and the international order in the interwar period.

Tamanoi Mariko. ed. (under supervision of Yamamoto Taketoshi). *Manshu– Kosaku suru rekishi* [Manchuria: Crossroads of History]. Tokyo: Fujiwara Shoten, 2008.

A compilation of studies on geographical, ethnical, and cultural diversities and a complicated history of Manchuria by experts, including overseas scholars, in their respective fields.

Thorne, Christopher. *The Limits of Foreign Policy: The West, the League and the Far Eastern Crisis of 1931–1933*. London: Hamilton, 1972.

A meticulous analysis of the Manchurian Incident from the viewpoints of the western powers and the League of Nations.

Tohmatsu Haruo. "Manshu kokusai kanri-ron no keifu—'Ritton hokokusho' no haigo ni aru mono" [Genealogy of the Argument to Put Manchuria under International Custody—What Lied behind the Lytton Report] in *Kokusai Ho-Gaiko Zasshi*, Vol. 99, No. 6, February 2001.

An anatomy of the Manchurian Incident from the viewpoint of international order, through reevaluation of the Lytton Report as a means for the solution.

Wilson, Sandra. *The Manchurian Crisis and Japanese Society, 1931–33.* London: Routledge, 2001.

An overall account of Japanese society' reaction to the Manchurian Incident and the creation of Manchukuo.

Lecture 6

The Emperor-as-Organ Theory Incident

Shibata Shin'ichi

What Is the Emperor-as-Organ Theory?

The Emperor-as-Organ Theory Incident occurred when this theory, which had been controversial since as early as the Taisho Era, was found to be a violation of Japan's national polity by the movement for clarification of the fundamental concepts of national polity (Kokutai Meicho Movement) in 1935 and the chief advocate of the theory, constitutional scholar Minobe Tatsukichi, began to be denounced.

Minobe, when interpreting the Constitution of the Empire of Japan (Meiji Constitution), recognized the principle of imperial sovereignty in the sense that "the supreme source of sovereignty lies in the emperor." Nevertheless, he declared that sovereignty ultimately belonged to the state, a legal entity, and the emperor was the supreme organ of this entity. This was the Emperor-as-Organ Theory.

At this point, let me quote the writings of Ienaga Saburo, a historian particularly renowned for his study of Minobe. He writes:

[The Emperor-as-Organ Theory] had played a political function as an ideology of the bureaucratic cabinet in the Meiji period and, subsequently, of the party cabinet during the period from the Taisho era to the early years of the Showa era. As such, among rulers of the state, it had retained a position of an officially recognized orthodox theory. It is undeniable, though, that this theory had relatively strong liberalistic and democratic connotations. For this reason, Minobe's constitutional theory was attacked in the first year of Taisho by Uesugi Shinkichi, who had taken the position of imperial sovereignty, triggering a dispute involving numerous scholars from both camps. At that time, the dispute remained an argument within the academic circle and did not result in persecution of advocates of the theory. When fanatic Japanism became rampant at the time of the Fifteen Years War [including the Mukden Incident, the Second Sino-Japanese War, and the Pacific War between 1931 and 1945], however, a movement to attack the Emperor-as-Organ Theory as evil and traitorous erupted. During this movement, Minobe lost his position in the 10th Year of Showa (1935), and all books and lectures on the constitution that subscribed to this theory were banned. Until Japan's defeat in the Pacific War in the 20th Year of Showa (1945), this school of thought remained banned by the state. (*Kokushi daijiten* [Great Dictionary of National History], Yoshikawa Kobunkan, 1979–97)

According to Ienaga, the Emperor-as-Organ Theory is a mere nickname and it was more proper to call it the "state authority theory." Because Minobe himself declared that the sovereignty of Japan obviously belonged to the emperor, it was a misperception to set the Emperor-as-Organ Theory against the theory of imperial sovereignty. Ienaga suggested that it was this misperception that caused an academic argument to escalate into a political incident (*Kokushi daijiten*).

What Was the Emperor-as-Organ Theory Incident?

Toriumi Yasushi, one of the pioneers in the study of modern Japan's political history from the historiographical position, characterized the Emperor-as-Organ Theory Incident as a political issue triggered by the
denunciation of Minobe's theory rather than an academic debate.

About the factors behind the denunciation of Minobe, Toriumi writes
as follows:

> Particularly at the time of the conclusion of the London Naval
> Treaty in the 5th Year of Showa (1930), in response to the attack
> on the Hamaguchi Osachi cabinet (of Rikken Minseito) from the
> Imperial Japanese Navy General Staff and various ultra-national-
> ist organizations for its infringement on the independence of the
> supreme command, Minobe refuted the accusations as being com-
> pletely ungrounded and defended the Hamaguchi cabinet's sign-
> ing of the treaty as perfectly legitimate. For this reason, Minobe
> and the Emperor-as-Organ Theory became the target of increas-
> ingly harsh reactions from the military and ultra-nationalists.
> Minoda Muneki and other members of the Genri Nipponsha (Fun-
> damental Japan Society) had already been criticizing Minobe even
> earlier. (*Kokushi daijiten*)

For details of Minoda's criticism, readers are recommended to refer to
Uemura Kazuhide's treatise "Tenno kikansetsu hihan no 'ronri'—'Kanryo' hihansha Minoda Muneki" [Logic of Criticism on the Emperor-as-Organ Theory—Minoda Muneki, Criticizing Bureaucrat] in *Nippon
shugi-teki kyoyo no jidai* [The Age of Japanist Culture], edited by
Takeuchi Hiroshi and Sato Takumi, Kashiwa Shobo, 2006).

Subsequently, from February 1934 through the ensuing year, inter-
pellations harshly criticizing Minobe were repeated in both the House of
Representatives and the House of Peers. Minobe, a member of the House

of Peers, delivered a speech at the Imperial Diet to defend himself in February 1935. Meanwhile, in January 1935, the Kokutai Yogo Rengokai (League for the Protection of National Polity) started a movement to denounce the theories of Minobe and Sue-hiro Izutaro, who was dean of the Faculty of Law at Tokyo Imperial University at that time, as "thoughts that would corrupt the state."

Minobe Tatsukichi delivers a speech to defend the Emperor-as-Organ Theory at the House of Peers. (Photo courtesy of Mainichi Newspapers)

Meanwhile, Prime Minister Okada Keisuke stayed away from the dispute, saying it was more appropriate to leave an academic matter to scholars. After Minobe's speech in the House of Peers, the Kokutai Yogo Rengokai and the Zaigo Gunjinkai (Veterans' Association), which was one of the most powerful ultra-nationalists organizations, radicalized their activities and demanded that the government (1) announce that the Emperor-as-Organ Theory was totally incompatible with the national polity; (2) ban all books and writings subscribing to this theory; and (3) expel all professors and bureaucrats who supported the theory. These two groups also demanded that the prime minister and Ichiki Kitokuro, president of the Privy Council, take responsibility by resigning their posts. For details of the responses of those including the Okada cabinet, see Sugaya Yukihiro, "Okada naikaku-ki ni okeru kikansetsu mondai shori to seigun kankei—Dainiji kokutai meicho seimei o meguru kobo o chushin ni" [Handling of the Emperor-as-Organ Theory Incident during the Okada Cabinet and Relations between the Government and the Military—With Special Reference to Exchanges about the Second *Kokutai Meicho Seimei* (Declaration on Clarification of the National Polity)] in *Gakushuin Daigaku Daigakuin Seijigaku Kenkyuka Seijigaku Ronshu*, No. 18, 2005 and "Tenno kikansetsu jiken tenkai katei no saikento—Okada naikaku-kyuchu no taio o chushin ni" [The Process of Development of the Emperor-as-Organ Theory Incident Revisited—With Special Reference to Responses of the Okada Cabinet and the Imperial Court] in *Nippon Rekishi*, No. 705, Yoshikawa Kobunkan, 2007.

Turning our attention to political parties, while the Rikken Minseito, the government party of the Okada cabinet, remained aloof from the debate, the Rikken Seiyukai took a hardline attitude, partly in hopes of toppling the Okada cabinet. Meanwhile, the military was firmly determined to denounce the controversial theory led by the Imperial Way Faction. Emperor Showa, who had consistently approved the theory, was reported to have expressed strong displeasure at the military officers' denunciation of the theory against his wish (see the diary of Honjo Shigeru, chief aide-de-camp to the emperor). The military, particularly the Imperial Japanese Army, was one source of the power behind the ultra-nationalistic "reformists."

The matter went far beyond a mere academic controversy or a personal attack on Minobe. It developed into a campaign to topple the government by those who were discontented with the moderate Okada cabinet. It further developed into a movement promoted by the ultra-nationalistic "reformists" against status quo elements including the elder statesmen, senior vassals, and political parties. While the matter was at last settled with the Okada cabinet's Dainiji Kokutai Meicho Seimei (The Second Declaration on Clarification of the National Polity, which stated that the government would cut away any theory going against the national polity) in October 1935, Makino Nobuaki, Lord Keeper of the Privy Seal, Ichiki Kitokuro, president of the Privy Council, and Kanamori Tokujiro, director-general of the Legislation Bureau of the cabinet, all of whom were criticized by the "reformists" as advocates of the Emperor-as-Organ Theory and leaders of the status quo forces in the Imperial

Court, were made to resign one after another from late 1935 through early 1936, following the resignation of Minobe from the House of Peers. This is the gist of the Emperor-as-Organ Theory Incident as summarized by Toriumi.

The Kokutai Meicho Movement and the Seiyukai's Ulterior Motive

The Emperor-as-Organ Theory Incident was extremely broad-based in that a variety of factors and individuals were involved for a variety of reasons by a variety of means. While it is hoped that explorations of historical documents and empirical studies on each individual actor will continue to be pursued, it will also be important to verify how this incident relates with the larger background of the times. The impact on the incident of such elements as the "1935–36 crisis" theory that the military as well as the media had bruited since 1933 and the commemorative ceremony for the 2,600th anniversary of the founding of Japan, which provided an impetus to the bid to host the 1940 Olympic Games in Tokyo, for instance, should be studied closely. It will be equally important to find out about the real impact that this incident had on subsequent days.

It also would be essential to analyze the relationship between this incident and the Kokutai Meicho movement as well as the February 26 Incident. The mutual inter-connectedness among various movements that are usually lumped together as "statist movements" and/or the individualities/uniqueness of each movement should also be examined.

One such study that comes to my mind first is Yoshimura Michio's "Showa shoki ni okeru kokugo kosho mondai—Kokutai Meicho Undo to no kanren ni oite" [Name of the Country Issue in the Early Showa Era—In Relations with Kokutai Meicho Movement], *Kokushigaku*, No. 119, Kokugakuin University, 1983, which analyzed the process of externally unifying Japan's country name to the Empire of Japan in April 1936 retroactive all the way to its origin in the late Taisho Era, using records of deliberations in the Imperial Diet and Ministry of Foreign Affairs' documents.

Another good source of information is Gomyo Yuki, "Tenno kikansetsu haigeki undo no ichi danmen—'Kobayashi group' o chushin ni" [An Aspect of the Denunciation Movement against the Emperor-as-Organ Theory—With Special Focus on the Kobayashi Group] in *Nippon Rekishi*, No. 649, Yoshikawa Kobunkan, 2002. Gomyo discovered that what Kobayashi Jun'ichiro and Shiga Naokata, central members of the group, aimed at through the denunciation movement was, among other things, the formation of a Konoe Fumimaro cabinet.

Showa Tokyo monogatari [Tale of Tokyo in the Showa Period] by Yamamoto Shichihei, which is included in the list of useful references at the end of this chapter, introduces interesting trivia that have been often overlooked, such as the reason behind the change of one Chinese character in the name of the movement. One reason, according to Yamamoto, was that the particular character first used for "*cho*" of Kokutai Meicho was the same character that was used in the name of Prince Suminomiya, younger brother of Emperor Showa, who had enrolled in the Imperial Japanese Army Academy, and the army might have found it improper to use this character back-to-back with another character, "*mei*," which was used in the name of Emperor Showa's father and the personal name of the crown prince.

The ninety-page verbatim, an annex to Volume II of Miyazawa Toshiyoshi's *Tenno kikansetsu jiken* [The Emperor-as-Organ Theory Incident], is the record of a colloquium which took place in the mid-1950s among several participants including Hatoyama Ichiro (former member of the House of Representatives from the Seiyukai). It includes not a small number of testimonies on the Meicho Movement and the aims of the Seiyukai that can be substantiated with newly recovered historical documents, however fragmented they might be.

To begin with, why did the Seiyukai attack Minobe so persistently? Although the Seiyukai won a landslide victory over the Minseito in the February 1932 General Election, it lost to the Minseito by a small margin in the subsequent February 1936 General Election. After reading the above Yamamoto, Banno Junji's statement that "voters turned their backs on the Seiyukai, which caused Minobe's fall through the Emperor-as-Organ Theory Incident" seems quite plausible (Banno Junji, *"Kaikyu" no Nippon kindaishi* [Japan's Modern History of "Class"], Kodansha, 2014). Incidentally, studies on the relations between the Emperor-as-Organ Theory Incident and the Seiyukai include Kanda Mitsushi, "Kokutai meicho undo to Seiyukai" [Kokutai Meicho Movement and Seiyukai] in *Nippon Rekishi*, No. 672, Yoshikawa Kobunkan, 2004, Daba Yuji, "Teijin jiken kara tenno kikansetsu jiken e—Minobe Tatsukichi to 'kensatsu fassho'" [From the Teijin Incident to the Emperor-as-Organ Theory Incident—Minobe Tatsukichi and Prosecutor Fascism] in *Seiji Keizai Shigaku*, No. 389, 1999, and Shibata Shin'ichi, "'Jushin burokku haigeki ronja' toshiteno Kuhara Fusanosuke" [Kuhara Fusanosuke as a Denouncer of the Senior Vassal Block] in *Kokugakuin Daigaku Nippon Bunka Kenkyusho Kiyo*, Vol. 83, 1999.

Shinsetsu jurin no Inukai naikaku [The Inukai Cabinet that Treaded on Vassals' Fidelity] (Shunjusha Publishing, February 1932) compiled by the Kokutai Yogo Renmei reveals another reason behind the Seiyukai's attack on Minobe. This forty-six-page booklet was a harsh criticism of Prime Minister Inukai Tsuyoshi by twelve university professors and journalists in the form of personal notes or commentaries on Inukai's decision to withdraw, upon the emperor's persuasion, his resignation to take responsibility for the Sakuradamon Incident (an assassination attempt against Emperor Showa by a Korean independence activist). They argued that because the Yamamoto Gonbei cabinet had stepped down nine years earlier due to the Toranomon Incident (an assassination attempt on Prince Regent Hirohito on December 27, 1923, by communist agitator Nanba Daisuke), so should have the Inukai cabinet. Heading the list of the twelve contributors to this booklet was Minobe Tatsukichi, who had contributed the opening article, followed by Sasaki Soichi, professor of Kyoto Imperial University, who also subscribed to the Emperor-as-Organ Theory.

From the Seiyukai's viewpoint, it had just won the election and returned to the position of power, when it received another relentless attack from Minobe. There might have been resentment or fury within the Seiyukai that held on emotional grounds rather than reason that Minobe simply couldn't be forgiven. It is indeed quite plausible to look at the Emperor-as-Organ Theory Incident as the Seiyukai's revenge against Minobe.

Several Viewpoints

One of the characteristics of Japan's modern history was the rampancy of assassinations. Also characteristic among attackers of the government in those days was a tendency to either bash those authorities backing the government or borrow those authorities as a means to accomplish their objectives. Particularly conspicuous was the denunciation of close aides of the emperor—by, for example, calling them "wily vassals surrounding the emperor"—as exemplified by the 26-Seiki (26th Century) Incident in 1896 (29th Year of Meiji) in which the magazine *26 Seiki* denounced the former Minister of the Imperial Household Hijikata Hisamoto. This led to the resignation of the vice minister and the director-general of the police bureau of the Home Ministry.

Other cases of denunciation of the emperor's close aides included a harsh attack on Katsura Taro's comeback to prime ministership, right after he had just been appointed Lord Keeper of the Privy Seal cum grand chamberlain at the time of the Taisho Political Crisis in 1913; denunciation of the elder statesman Yamagata Aritomo, Imperial Household Minister Hatano Yoshinao, and Prime Minister Hara Takashi at the occasion of the marriage of the crown prince ("The Certain Serious Incident of the Imperial Court") in 1920 (9th Year of Taisho); a scandal of defamatory literature involving the Imperial Household Ministry in 1925 (14th Year of Taisho) in which Makino Nobuchika, Lord Keeper of the Privy Council, was accused by Kita Ikki and Nishida Mitsugi of accepting a bribe over the sale of an imperial woodland; and the killings and assaults of close aides of the emperor during the February 26 Incident (1936) and various assassination attempts before and after the incident. The Emperor-as-Organ Theory Incident was also connected to the genealogy of these incidents.

Occasionally, history was used as a trump card when attacking an opponent's legitimacy. During the first interpellation on the Emperor-as-Organ Theory Incident in the Imperial Diet, the interpellator raised the issue of the Commerce and Industry Minister Nakajima Kumakichi's written praise of Ashikaga Takauji in the fourteenth century prior to mentioning Minobe's theory, as if to rekindle the argument on the legitimacy of either the Northern or the Southern Dynasty in the Imperial Diet toward the end of the Meiji Era. (Nakajima had resigned his post immediately.) In Japan, it often happens that one takes up positions and arguments that are difficult to refute or brings up indicators and goals that are hard to reject in order to push one's assertions and conduct and to bash opponents.

The Impact of the Incident

What kind of impact did this Emperor-as-Organ Theory Incident have on the subsequent fate of Japan, particularly its political development and the conduct of Emperor Showa? In an attempt to answer this question, allow me to introduce three remarks that attract my attention most.

The first of these remarks is the unpublicized private memo of the Taisho-Showa novelist Shiga Naoya. Being a nephew of Shiga Naokata, a close confidant of Konoe Fumimaro, and the brother-in-law of Matsumura Giichi, member of the House of Peers and one time director-general of the Police Bureau of the Ministry of Home Affairs, Shiga appeared to have been equipped with his own information network. Shiga left a private memo on the February 26 Incident that was not published in his lifetime. Agawa Hiroyuki, novelist and a disciple of Shiga, discovered and published this memo (Agawa Hiroyuki, a serial "Shiga Naoya" No. 52 Tennosei <1>" [Shiga Naoya: No. 52, The Emperor System of Japan

<1>], *Tosho*, October 1991, Iwanami Shoten). Thus, Agawa writes:

> The February 26 Incident was an extraordinarily unpleasant oc-
> currence rarely seen in recent years. In fact it was the most un-
> pleasant incident in 50 some years since I was born. The rebels
> murdered the so-called wily vassals surrounding the emperor in
> the name of Kokutai Meicho and attempted to degrade the emper-
> or to their thinking level. This itself is enough evidence that they
> do not recognize the personality of the emperor and, therefore,
> they themselves do not regard the emperor any higher than an
> organ. Once they killed the emperor's close aides, however, they
> found that the emperor did not act in the way they wanted him to.
> In other words, the emperor functioned as more than a mere or-
> gan. This incident contains these kinds of highly nonsensical con-
> tradictions.

And:

> Having heard that the emperor had been righteous in this incident,
> I was deeply impressed and became convinced that there indeed
> is such a thing as traditional righteousness. I love the emperor. I
> believe, among the small number of surviving monarchs in the
> world, that Emperor Showa is the most righteous monarch and
> we are so fortunate to be his subjects.

This kind of personal reflection was undoubtedly one of the conclusions
of the Emperor-as-Organ Theory Incident.

The second remark I wish to introduce here is from *Tenno—Tenno
tochi no shiteki kaimei* [Emperor of Japan—Historical Clarification of
the Rule of the Emperor] (Koubundou Publishers, 1950) by Ishii Ryo-
suke, scholar of legal history. Only five years after the end of the Pacific
War, Ishii refuted the argument or the tendency to claim that the symbolic emperor system of postwar days was severed and removed from the

history of Japan.

First, Ishii pointed out that one of the unique characteristics of the Constitution of the Empire of Japan (Meiji Constitution) was that because its provisions were brief there was considerable room for discretion in their actual application. In fact, in the Meiji Constitution, there was no reference to premier or cabinet or even prime minister. Instead, there was the single definition of a state minister. The late Fujii Sadafumi (professor emeritus of Kokugakuin University and mentor of the present writer) often reminisced that, in Japan under the Meiji Constitution, this unique feature of the constitution allowed politics that fitted the needs of the time, and that was how the Meiji Era had *han*-clique government, the Taisho to early Showa Era had party politics, and generals became prime ministers in subsequent days.

To summarize Ishii's analysis, up until the 6th Year of Showa (1931), efforts had been made to interpret the Meiji Constitution in a way that was consistent with constitutional democracy, adopting state sovereignty theory and "monarch-as-organ" theory in order to make the emperor's supreme authority compatible with constitutional democracy. This was a way of preparing for the social acceptance of the Emperor-as-Organ Theory. After this period, however, the Meiji Constitution was slighted. When Japan experienced the post–World War I economic recession and, then, the Manchurian Incident erupted, the supreme authority of the emperor became increasingly abused by military faction bureaucrats. A fuss was raised about Japan being in a state of national emergency, facilitating the militarization of Japanese society. This type of loss of function of the parliament and authoritarian inclination were against the words of the Meiji Constitution, or at least its spirit, which had advocated constitutionalism. Thus, Ishii claimed, the supreme authority of the emperor and the mystical authority behind it became highlighted, which provided a pillar of defense for the arbitrary conduct of the military faction and bureaucrats.

Ishii, however, continued to say that, even though the emperor might have been de facto nullified, he still had retained the authority legally stipulated by Article 1 of the Meiji Constitution and, therefore, it was in the name of the emperor's will that the end of the Pacific War was declared. To be sure, because the emperor's will had no legal bearing unless assisted by ministers of state, it cannot be said that the decision to end the war was solely that of the emperor. But had the emperor not attended the court conference to decide the end of the war or not expressed his wishes, it would perhaps have been impossible to overpower the "fight to the end" advocates and leave the final decision to the emperor. The participation of the emperor, who had wished to end the war, in the conference to decide the end of the war made it possible to end the war. Thus, Ishii pointed out that Emperor Showa's participation in that conference was the last glow of the Meiji Constitution's Article 1. In conclusion, he said:

> While it is beyond doubt that Emperor Showa's personal will power and the mystical majesty behind it played a major role in deciding to end the war, legally speaking, we must say that the stipulation of Article 1 of the Meiji Constitution played a critical role.

The last piece that I wish to introduce is a well-known remark that, in May 1935 in the midst of the Emperor-as-Organ Theory Incident, Makino Nobuaki, Lord Keeper of the Privy Seal, shared with US Ambassador to Japan Joseph Grew, who was very moved by it. Makino said to Grew:

> Japan has a guardian that is incomparable to anything other countries have and that is the Imperial Court. Because the emperor is absolutely supreme and he always makes the last decision all the time, Japan is never imperiled by military authoritarianism, communism, or any other ideology. (Joseph Grew, *Ten Years in Japan: A Contemporary Record Drawn From the Diaries and Private and Official Papers of Joseph C. Grew, United States Ambassador to Japan, 1932–1942*. Japanese translation, Ishikawa

Kin'ichi, *Tainichi junen*, Mainichi Shimbunsha, 1948; Chiku-mashobo, 2011)

Reviewing the remarks left by Shiga, Ishii, and Makino, it might be said that it was this Emperor-as-Organ Theory Incident that led Emperor Showa to his decisions at the February 26 Incident as well as at the end of the war. At the same time, it can also be said that those who took issue with the Emperor-as-Organ Theory might have succeeded in reforming the interpretation of the constitution and political organ but never succeeded in changing the operation of the constitution or the national polity.

* * *

Recommended Readings for Deeper Understanding

Ienaga Saburo. "Tenno Kikansetsu" [Emperor-as-Organ Theory] in *Kokushi daijiten* [Great Dictionary of National History] Vol. 9. Tokyo: Yoshikawa Ko-bunkan, 1988.

The most concise explanation of the theory as a school of thought in constitutional law.

Mitani Taichiro. "Tenno kikansetsu jiken no seijishi-teki imi" [Politico-Historical Meaning of the Emperor-as-Organ Theory Incident] in his *Kindai Nippon no senso to seiji* [War and Politics in Modern Japan]. Tokyo: Iwanami Shoten, 1997.

Using historical documents that Miyazawa Toshiyoshi (see below) could not get hold of, Mitani defined the Emperor-as-Organ Theory Incident as "a legal and bloodless coup d'état by which the national polity reformed the political organ, which was followed by the February 26 Incident, an illegal and bloody coup d'état." An extraordinary work.

Miyazawa Toshiyoshi. *Tenno kikansetsu jiken* [Emperor-as-Organ Theory Incident]. Tokyo: Yuhikaku Publishing, 1970.

As its subtitle, *Shiryo wa kataru* [As Historical Documents Testify], indicates, it is a classical and detailed study in full utilization of official documents and newspaper materials that were available at the time of writing.

Toriumi Yasushi. "Tenno kikansetsu mondai" (Emperor-as-Organ Theory Incident) in *Kokushi daijiten* [Great Dictionary of National History] Vol. 9. Tokyo: Yoshikawa Kobunkan, 1988.

The most concise explanation of the incident as a major incident of Japan's political history.

Yamamoto Shichihei. *Showa Tokyo monogatari* [Tale of Tokyo in the Showa Period]. Tokyo: Yomiuri Shimbunsha, 1990.

It contains a number of original observations and comments on the Emperor-as-Organ Theory Incident, during which the author was a junior high school student. The author later became a commentator well known for his wide versatility and sharp observation.

Lecture 7

February 26 Incident and the Ultranationalist Movement in the Showa Era

Tsutsui Kiyotada

Origin of the Ultranationalist Movement in the Showa Era

The origin of the ultranationalistic (*cho-kokkashugi*) movement in the Showa Era, which saw its peak at the February 26 Incident, dates back to the mid-Taisho Era.

The Rice Riots erupted in 1918 (7th Year of Taisho); to deal with them, martial law was declared. This means that in just a little more than ten years after the first declaration of martial law during the Hibiya burnings incident of 1905, mobs arose again and set off another large scale riot. During the intervening years, in the midst of the First Constitution Protection Movement, mobs surrounded the Diet building in 1913, causing the resignation of the Katsura Taro cabinet. And it was the political association Rosokai that people who witnessed those riots with their own eyes established, putting their individual ideological inclinations aside.

Centered around Mitsukawa Kametaro and Okawa Shumei, the Rosokai was a unique association composed of both later-day right-wingers and leftists. Mitsukawa, one of the group's core members, had closely associated with researchers of boat-dwelling people and the destitute as well as with organizations aiming at the liberation of Asia, such as the Committee on Elimination of Racial Discrimination. As he got acquainted with Tomizu Hirondo, who was well known in those days for his advocacy of the Russo-Japanese War, Mitsukawa felt repulsed by Tomizu's imperialistic attitudes and insistence on the suppression of radicals. The main theme of Mitsukawa's thought was salvation of the poor in Japan and international liberation of the oppressed. These egalitarian attitudes toward people inside and outside of Japan were the core of Mitsukawa's philosophy, which had been backed up by nationalism. Nationalism in this instance can be interpreted as something that guaranteed activities to be realistic and well-grounded.

In 1919, the Rosokai's two key members—Mitsukawa and Okawa—founded the Yuzonsha in order to promote an egalitarian and statist movement that had a different vector from leftwing anarchism or communism. Believing that a new movement needed a new leader, it was decided to call Kita Ikki back from Shanghai. Okawa made the boat trip to Shanghai himself to invite Kita.

Although (along with Mitsukawa and Okawa) Kita, at first was an emerging socialist active around the socialist association Heiminsha's circle, he later devoted himself to the revolutionary movement in China together with Miyazaki Toten and Song Jiaoren. After experiencing a setback of the revolutionary movement, Kita was laying low in Shanghai. In China in those days, following the Okuma Shigenobu cabinet's Twenty-One Demands on China, the territorial issue of the Shandong Peninsula, which the Chinese people believed that Japan had snatched from Germany through the Treaty of Versailles, led to the rise of an anti-Japan movement called the May Fourth Movement. Kita was startled to find that his former comrades in the revolutionary movement were playing leading roles in the May Fourth Movement.

Seeing how resentful the Chinese people were of Japan, which they said was dominated by "rich feudal lords," Kita was determined to re-construct Japan "from the bottom of its soul." He discussed the means for the reconstruction in his treatise, *Kokka kaizoan genri taiko* ([An Outline of the Principles of State Reorganization], which was later re-named *Nippon kaizo hoan taiko* [An Outline Plan for the Reorganization of Japan]). Kita was still writing this treatise when Okawa arrived in Shanghai. The two instantly hit it off and talked the whole night through. Okawa brought back home a copy of *Kokka kaizoan genri taiko* with him, which, together with its sequel, he secretly published in Japan. Kita returned to Japan by the end of that year and, with the completion of the "trinity" of Kita, Okawa, and Mitsukawa, the Yuzonsha began full-fledged activities.

What, then, was written in Kita's *Nippon kaizo hoan taiko*? Its fun-damental philosophy was to make Japan an egalitarian society resorting to the supreme authority of the emperor. First in order was a coup d'état under the emperor's name, followed by suspension of the constitution for three years, dissolution of both houses of the Imperial Diet, and dec-laration of martial law over the entire territory. During those three years, all the privileged institutions such as the House of Peers and the peerage system would be abolished, along with all the laws that oppressed free-dom of speech, such as the Security Police Law, Press Regulations, and Publication Regulations. Private ownership of properties would be per-mitted only for a limited amount of time, but land would be publicly owned without exception. In order to correct the inequality in land-lord-tenant relations, the establishment of landed farmers would be pro-moted, a ministry of labor would be established to improve treatment of workers, and the right to education would be guaranteed to children.

And the ultimate goal of the *Taiko* was, after implementing the egal-itarian reforms within Japan, for the Japanese nation to liberate Asian peoples who were under unfair colonial rules, such as India, so as to end the world domination by Britain and the United States and, thereby, to realize an international egalitarian society. It can be said that the very essence of the philosophy of the Yuzonsha—that is, the philosophies of

123

Kita and Mitsukawa—was this connection of domestic egalitarianism with international egalitarianism. And the Yuzonsha philosophy corresponded to the egalitarianism the masses in Japan had demanded through such forms as the Hibiya incendiary riot, the First Constitution Protection Movement, and the Rice Riot. Thus, this philosophy was able to affect Japan in subsequent days.

It was the Asahi Heigo Incident in 1921 that manifested this influence most evidently. A youth by the name of Asahi Heigo demanded Yasuda Zenjiro, head of the Yasuda Zaibatsu (financial clique), to build "a hotel for poor workers." When Yasuda rejected the demand, Asahi abruptly stabbed Yasuda to death and then killed himself then and there. Judging from the death note left by Asahi, it was obvious that he had been under the influence of Kita's *Nippon kaizo hoan taiko*.

After this incident, young officers of the Imperial Japanese Army grew greatly affected by Kita's philosophy. Because World War I had been the first total war in the world's history, introducing all kinds of new weapons such as armored tanks, airplanes, and poison gas and resulting in an unprecedented number of casualties, the anti-war, peaceful mood became widespread all over the world after the war and the conclusion of the Washington Naval Treaty.

It was in this mood that large-scale arms reductions for both the army and the navy were carried out twice in Japan. A total of 96,400 military personnel, including some 3,400 officers and 93,000 non-commissioned officers and soldiers, were released from service. In other words, a large number of professional soldiers became jobless all of a sudden without sufficient severance compensation.

Moreover, under the global expansion of pacifism, some military officers working in military-related public offices in those days had to wear civilian clothes so that they would not be harassed during their commute. Officer training schools were downsized with fewer and fewer applicants. In short, the time of suffering for the military had arrived. For young military officers, who had begun to worry that "their very presence itself had become unacceptable to the Japanese nation." Under these circumstances the *Taiko* was like a book of revelation. Kita Ikki's philosophy that "Japan has an important, world historical and civilizational mission" and particularly the idea that "the military must play a central role in helping Japan accomplish these civilizational missions by promoting egalitarian social reforms in Japan around the emperor and launching the liberalization of Asia" were widely accepted by young officers as their long-searched-for purpose of life.

The first young officer who drew close to Kita was Nishida Mitsugi, who later became Kita's right-hand man. Subsequently, young military officers visited Kita for meetings one after another by way of Nishida's introduction. To a young officer named Suematsu Tahei, Kita stressed that "it is only the uncorrupted soldiers that could save today's Japan, particularly young officers like yourself." Thus, a movement of young military officers who were influenced by the *Nippon kaizo hoan taiko* was started gradually toward the end of the Taisho Era.

Evolution of the Ultranationalistic Movement in the Showa Era

While the general election system was realized toward the end of the Taisho–early Showa eras, marking the beginning of two-party politics in Japan, election campaigns grew extremely fierce. This led to the rampancy of illegal activities to raise campaign funds, and these activities became increasingly conspicuous. Also, because opposition parties, in an attempt to topple the government, constantly tried to look for scandals within the government party, particularly concerning its leaders, cases of suspected political corruption surfaced one after another. Furthermore, because the party that won the election and, therefore, became the government party exercised strong control on the bureaucracy, particularly the home ministry that administered elections, political appointee governors, chiefs of police stations, and all the way down to policemen in *koban* (street corner mini-stations) were all replaced every time there was change of government. This gave the impression that the neutrality of the administration was gravely compromised. As a result, the Japanese nation's trust in party politics was seriously damaged. Then came the storm of the Great Depression of 1929; Japan entered a period of the worst economic conditions in modern history packed with economic recession, deflation, unemployment, and desperate job hunting. The devastation in rural areas was particularly grave—so grave that many families had to sell their daughters to survive. In contrast, the over-privileges of the zaibatsu became all the more conspicuous. To remedy this inequity, voices demanding a "complete breakthrough at one blow" became stronger.

Meanwhile, internationally, the racial discrimination in the United States manifested by the enactment of the Immigration Act of 1924 caused "national indignation" among the Japanese people. When Japan was blocked from attaining the goal of 70 percent of the tonnage allotted to the United States at the London Naval Conference (1930) to follow up the Washington Naval Treaty, some segments of the Imperial Japanese Navy and ultranationalists began to harbor strong anti-British/anti-US sentiment.

The Soviet Union established the Comintern in 1919 as a headquarters for the world communist revolution, and the Japanese Communist Party was founded as its local charter in Japan. From the viewpoint of the Japanese government, this meant that Japan now faced the fear of "indirect invasion." Moreover, when the Soviet Union expanded its concessions in Manchuria and north China by military power through the Sino-Soviet conflict of 1929, officers of the Kwantung Army interpreted that action as an increased military threat from the Soviet Union. At the same time, the Kwantung Army was exposed to a bad precedence that a fait accompli made through military power could be internationally recognized.

Furthermore, in China, Chiang Kai-shek launched the Northern Expedition, advancing the Kuomintang army from south to north to unify China. As a result, conflicts with Japan's rights and interests in China emerged, sensitizing the Japanese sense of crisis about its concessions in Manchuria. Subsequently, the Kuomintang government began its Revolutionary Diplomacy that ignored existing unequal treaties as a matter of course. From the Japanese viewpoint, this constituted the unilateral abolishment of the treaty that Japan had traditionally maintained with China. Relations between the two countries rapidly deteriorated.

Under these circumstances, the central Yuzonsha figure Kita Ikki deepened his relations with young officers, while Okawa Shumei, an establishment elite, became closely associated more with field officer-class higher ranking officers.

In January 1930, Lieutenant Colonel Hashimoto Kingoro of G2 of the Imperial Japanese Army General Staff Office returned home from Turkey. Having witnessed the reform in Turkey by Kemal Atatürk that was modeled after the Meiji Restoration, Hashimoto founded the Sakurakai (Cherry Blossom Society), a secret society within the Imperial Japanese Army, declaring, "In order to accomplish the ultimate goal of reconstructing the state, we would not hesitate to use military force." The Sakurakai's ideological leader was Okawa Shumei. Although Okawa and his associates schemed a coup d'état in March 1931 (6th Year of Showa), with the aim of establishing a cabinet led by the then War Minister Ugaki Kazushige, it fell through. This became known as the March Incident.

In August 1931, a meeting called the Goshikai was convened. Among the participants were young military officers of the Kita/Nishida groups; members of the Ketsumeidan (League of Blood), a group of youths from rural villages and urban low-lying areas that had been impoverished since the Great Depression; and members of the Aikyojuku, a group of rural youth gathered around Tachibana Kozaburo. It was a meeting to discuss an action plan for the "complete breakthrough at one blow" or an "Imperial Color revolution" within Japan that Lieutenant Colonel Hashimoto Kingoro and his associates had schemed to carry out when the Kwantung Army started a certain action in order to improve the situation in Manchuria.

And it was at the October Incident that an abortive attempt at the above plan was carried out. As in the case of the March Incident, too, however, it is unknown how much feasibility the plan actually had. Although Hashimoto and his associates were confined when the scheme was disclosed, they were only lightly punished. But this incident made young officers of the Imperial Japanese Army realize that higher, field-officer ranked members of the Sakurakai were only interested in fulfilling their lust for power. The young officers broke away from the Sakurakai.

Meanwhile, the Kwantung Army launched the Manchurian Incident and continued to conquer more territories in Manchuria, upon which public opinion in Japan shifted in a different direction from the days of the Washington/London Naval Treaties.

In February to March of 1932 (7th Year of Showa), members of the Ketsumeidan assaulted dignitaries of the political and business circles (the League of Blood Incident). Subsequently, young officers of the Imperial Japanese Navy, cadets of the Imperial Japanese Army Academy, and members of the Aikyojuku started the May 15 Incident, in which Prime Minister Inukai Tsuyoshi was assassinated and important institutions such as the official residence of Makino Nobuaki, Lord Keeper of the Privy Seal, the headquarters of the Seiyukai and the Bank of Japan, as well as several electrical transformer substations were raided.

The trial on the May 15 Incident commenced in 1933, and it was widely covered by the mass media. As a result, images of sincere young military officers, who stood up together with peasants and other underprivileged people to destroy such privileged classes as corrupted party politicians, the zaibatsu, and bureaucrats in order to bring relief to the disadvantaged, were transmitted day after day. The courtroom became a stage for advertisement of the Showa Restoration movement. Petitions for reduced sentences poured in daily, unmarried young officers were introduced to women volunteering to be their brides, magazines ran articles on excursions to the birthplaces of these officers, and even phonograph records were produced (which were later banned). The protagonists of the May 15 Incident were treated as if they were some kind of stars. Such outright support for the assassination of a prime minister and subversive acts in the metropolis gave the impression of a revolt of the masses. It goes to show how widespread and widely supported was the argument of ultranationalists' movements since the days of the Yu-zonsha.

While civilian youths and young naval officers among the participants of the Kyoshikai thus took action, young army officers under the influence of Kita and Nishida refrained from joining them. This was because they had had a ray of hope for reform of impoverished domestic conditions by the appointment of Lieutenant General Araki Sadao to minister of war toward the end of the previous year.

Strife within the Imperial Japanese Army

Traditionally, there had been two major factions within the Imperial Japanese Army: the Choshu faction formed around Yamagata Aritomo and passed on to Terauchi Masatake, Tanaka Giichi, and Ugaki Kazushige (originally from Okayama Prefecture) versus the Kyushu faction centered around Uehara Yusaku, Masaki Jinzaburo, and Araki Sadao. Of the two, the Choshu faction and its successor Ugaki faction were dominant in the Taisho–early Showa Era, monopolizing personnel and other important properties of the army.

Against this background, the three most promising cadets of the 16th class of the Imperial Japanese Army Academy, Nagata Tetsuzan, Obata Toshiro, and Okamura Yasuji, got together in the German resort of Baden-Baden and concluded a pact among the three of them on reconstruction of the Imperial Japanese Army. Tojo Hideki, too, joined this pact in later days.

Upon returning to Japan, those three attempted to organize several groups. In the end, they established the Issekikai. It was decided at this Issekikai that, based on the lessons from World War I, the Imperial Japanese Army had to be reorganized to be able to fight a total war and cope with the Manchuria/Mongolia problem. It was also decided that, because the current Choshu-Ugaki faction would be incapable of such reorganization, the Issekikai should back Araki and Masaki as the central figures in the army. Thus, the Issekikai members achieved rapport with the Kyu-shu faction. Young army officers led by Kita and Nishida had also be-come closer to the Kyushu faction centered around Araki, who had been critical of the Ugaki faction's close association with party politics. When Araki was appointed to war minister in December 1931, therefore, the senior officers of the Kyushu faction, mid-level staff officers affiliated with the Issekikai, and the group of young army officers placed high hopes on the new war minister.

These high expectations notwithstanding, while War Minister Araki forced through a thorough purge of the Ugaki faction and the promotion of the Kyushu faction, he was unable to realize measures to relieve rural agricultural/mountain/fishing villages from miserable economic condi-tions because they were curbed by Finance Minister Takahashi Koreki-yo and others. Such measures were the very thing that the young military officers had zealously expected of Araki.

In January 1934, after losing public support, Araki resigned as war minister. Araki appointed Hayashi Senjuro, whom Araki considered to be his comrade, as his successor. Learning that the Imperial Court held Araki and Masaki in very low esteem, however, Hayashi started activi-ties to drive them out. Around the same time, the group around Nagata Tetsuzan and Tojo Hideki also quickly dropped their support of Araki and started to drive him out.

Thus emerged a conflict between two factions within the Imperial Japanese Army—the Imperial Way Faction (Kodoha), a group of senior army officers affiliated with the Kyushu faction, including Araki and Ma-saki, and young army officers who wished to put Araki and Masaki at the head to reform the army and the national government; and the Control Faction (Toseiha), a group of mid-level staff officers centered around Nagata with an aspiration to remake Japan into a country with high de-fense capabilities.

When Nagata became director of the Military Affairs Bureau of the Ministry of War in March 1934, the conflict between the two factions grew all the more fiercer, culminating in the Imperial Japanese Army

Academy Incident in November 1934. Isobe Asaichi and Muranaka Koji, who were identified as the masterminds behind this coup attempt, were arrested by the military police and divested of their commissions. It appeared that War Minister Hayashi chose to side with the Toseiha.

The duo of War Minister Hayashi and Director of the Military Affairs Bureau Nagata continued to demote officers of the Kodoha from the mainstream of the Imperial Japanese Army one after another and, in July 1935, they sacked Masaki, the central figure in the Kodoha, from the post of Inspectorate General of Military Training. Angered by this action, Lieutenant Colonel Aizawa Saburo of the Kodoha cut down Lieutenant General Nagata Tetsuzan in August of the same year, killing him (known as the Aizawa Incident). It was through this intensification of the conflict between the two factions within the Imperial Japanese Army that the February 26 Incident erupted.

February 26 Incident

The February 26 Incident was an attempt at recovery from the brink of defeat by the beleaguered Kodoha faction. The plot of this coup d'état was to assassinate Prime Minister Okada and Finance Minister Takahashi Korekiyo to topple the Okada government, annihilate all those who were likely to recommend someone who was not the faction's choice to succeed as prime minister, including the elder statesman Saionji Kinmochi, Lord Keeper of the Privy Seal Saito Makoto, Grand Chamberlain Suzuki Kantaro, and former Lord Keeper of the Privy Seal Makino Nobuaki, and assassination or arrest opposition forces within the army, including Inspectorate General of Military Training Watanabe Jotaro. After elimination of these obstacles, the coup conspirators aimed at encouraging a person of their choice to visit the Imperial Court and to help him form a pro-Kodoha interim government. Even if this scheme fell through, the conspirators would have been satisfied as long as their action could awaken politicians and rouse the Japanese people.

How, then, did matters actually unfold during this coup attempt?

Among the schemed assassination attempts, a brother-in-law of Prime Minister Okada was mistaken for the prime minister and killed, Makino was able to escape, and the plan on Saionji was aborted. Other than these, nevertheless, most of the planned direct actions were successfully carried out. As for their plan to suggest the formation of a Kodoha-friendly cabinet to the emperor, the young military officer who had been put in charge met War Minister Kawashima Yoshiyuki and handed him their requests, which Kawashima acted upon. General Masaki consulted with Admiral Kato Hiroharu of the Imperial Japanese Navy, whom Masaki had been close to from before, and Prince Fushimi Hiroyasu, Chief of Staff of the Imperial Japanese Navy, who had been sympathetic with the Kodoha, and agreed that Prince Fushimi would visit the Imperial Court to suggest the formation of the Hiranuma Kiichiro cabinet to the emperor.

Thus, in the morning of February 26, things were going quite well for the rebelling young officers. But when Kido Koichi, chief secretary of the Home Ministry, decided at an early stage that the basic political stance of the emperor would be to "not permit the resignation of any incumbent cabinet members whatsoever," and the emperor thus rejected suggestions on a new cabinet from Prince Fushimi and War Minister Kawashima one after another as well as the request for the en masse resignation of the cabinet submitted by Prime Minister ad Interim Fumio Goto late in the evening, the outcome of the coup d'état was more or less determined.

The overthrow of the Okada cabinet, by far the greatest goal of the coup d'état plan, fell through because the emperor adamantly rejected repeated suggestions from members of the imperial family who had been taken in by the young officers' maneuvering. Senior officers, including Ishihara Kanji, chief of operations of the Imperial Japanese Army General Staff Office and operations officer of the Martial Law Headquarters, who had been sympathetic with the revolting young officers, got together for consultation at the Imperial Hotel deep in the night of February 26. When the suggestion to connect the Kodoha with the

Troops deployed to suppress the rioters during the February 26 Incident (Photo courtesy of Kyodo News)

Imperial Japanese Army General Staff Office based on this consultation was rejected and when the request for the imperial pardon was also rejected on February 28, the coup d'état was doomed. On February 29, the coup d'état was suppressed.

Young military officers who joined the coup were imprisoned and executed. Although Kita Ikki and Nishida Mitsugi were not the central figures in the coup attempt, having been informed of the plan immediately before the incident, they were nevertheless sentenced to death as collaborators. In light of Kita's scheduled trip to China in March to explore ways to improve strained Sino-Japanese relations through talks with Zhang Qun, foreign minister of the Nationalist government and Kita's comrade during the Xinhai Revolution, his was quite an unreasonable sentence.

After the February 26 Incident, the Kodoha's influence became decidedly weaker in the Imperial Japanese Army. In its place, the Ishihara faction (Manchurian faction) led by Ishihara Kanji rose rapidly, playing an instrumental role in the blocking of the Ugaki cabinet and the formation of the Hayashi Senjuro cabinet in the ensuing year. With the formation of the Hayashi cabinet as its apex, however, the downfall of the Ishihara faction began; when the Second Sino-Japanese War erupted, Ishihara himself was demoted. The strife between the Ishihara faction and such army leaders as Tojo Hideki continued after this. On the eve of the Pacific War, officers who had been affiliated with the Toseiha under Nagata Tetsuzan such as Tojo, Muto Akira, and Tominaga Kyoji, were appointed to key positions in the Imperial Japanese Army. Nevertheless, there was no solidarity among them comparable to that of the earlier Toseiha, and it is not appropriate at all to call them the Toseiha. It seems more appropriate to describe them as former members of the Toseiha.

As for the Kodoha, while it had been totally deprived of its influence in the army, because Konoe Fumimaro, the ace politician in the 1935–45 period, had been closely associated with the Kodoha, it had been able to retain a certain influence among the upper echelon of Japanese politics. More concretely, Araki Sadao and Yanagawa Heisuke became cabinet members who, during the Pacific War, formed a united front against Tojo Hideki's military faction with Yoshida Shigeru and other pro-Britain/US politicians. And when the war was over, Obata Toshiro joined Prince Higashikuni's cabinet.

In addition, the following things can be said: Even though the early Showa period's ultranationalistic movement as a political movement suffered failure and setback from the February 26 Incident, the egalitarian philosophy at the heart of this movement survived the Incident to be passed on to later days in a variety of ways.

In the 1935–45 period, a number of egalitarian-motivated measures were carried out one after another, from the improvement of conditions of tenant farmers and the creation of landed farmers, to the establishment of such institutions/systems as the Ministry of Health and Welfare (creation of healthcare centers and the maternal and child health handbook), the National Health Insurance System, the Employees Pension Scheme, the Food Control System, and the restriction on dividends—all of which were connected to democratization in the postwar days such as dissolution of the zaibatsu and agrarian reform. In other words, it can be said that the equalization of Japanese society had been continuously promoted throughout the wartime and postwar days.

The February 26 Incident profoundly influenced the people who were engaged in the above reform activities. Many of the bureaucrats who carried out these measures were categorically called "reforming bureaucrats," and many of them had read Kita Ikki's books, including Kishi Nobusuke, who had been under strong influence of Kita since he had met Kita in the Taisho era. Therefore, it is possible to say that, even though the young military officers themselves had failed politically, in the long run, their demands were partially realized during the war and continued to be substantiated after the war.

And in the face of these egalitarian inclinations, the pro-Britain/pro-US orientation was, both domestically and internationally, deemed to protect the privileged *ancien regime* and, therefore, it had to suffer the waning of its influence. What was internationally perceived as a contrast between "Britain and the United States as privileged colonial powers" and "Asia as a weak, subjugated region" corresponded, domestically, to strife between "pro-Britain/pro-US senior statesmen and other privileged classes like the zaibatsu" and "underprivileged and subservient classes." Elder statesman Saionji and Lord Keeper of the Privy Seal Makino were representative "pro-Britain/pro-US" figures, and it was these people who became the target of the harshest attack from such perceptions as "wily vassals surrounding the emperor." In those days, there was no argument that was stronger than "liberation of Asia under colonial rule" and "overthrow of the pro-Britain/pro-US over-privileged surrounding the emperor as enemies of people in destitution." And this perception became one of the forces that led Japan to the Pacific War.

For those like Kita who aimed to fundamentally reconstruct Japan and liberate Asia in response to anti-Japan movements in China, which had been provoked by Japan's Twenty-One Demands and concessions in the Shandong peninsula, a war against Britain and the United States in cooperation with China might have been predictable. But it must have been unthinkable for them for Japan to wage a war against Britain and the United States while fighting China at the same time. And this is where the ironic fate of Japan's ultranationalistic movement in the early Showa era lay.

*   *   *

Recommended Readings for Deeper Understanding

There still is no good overview of the history of ultranationalistic movements in Showa Japan, and the following two remain the basic documents to rely on: Baba Yoshitsugu, "Waga kuni ni okeru saikin no kokka shugi naishi kokka shakai shugi undo ni tsuite" [On Recent Statist and National Socialist Movements in Japan] in *Shiho kenkyu hokokushoshu* [Research Department, Ministry of Justice], Vol. 19, No. 10, 1935, and Saito Saburo, "Uyoku shiso hanzai jiken no sogoteki kenkyu—Ketsumeidan jiken yori 2.26 jiken made" [Comprehensive Study on Right-Wing–Related Criminal Cases—From the League of Blood Incident to the February 26 Incident] in Imai Seiichi and Takahashi Masae, eds., *Gendaishi shiryo 4: Kokka shugi undo I* [Contemporary Historical Documents 4: Statist Movement I], Tokyo: Misuzu Shobo, 1963. Saito's treatise was also published as a report of special researchers on political thought included in *Shiso kenkyu shiryo tokushu dai-gojusan-go* (Criminal Affairs Bureau, Ministry of Justice, 1939) as well as a part of Shakai Mondai Shiryo Kenkyukai, ed., *Dai-isshu shakai mondai shiryo sosho* [Series on Documents on Social Problems, Vol. 1], Tokyo: Toyo Bunkasha, 1975.

Another must read is Imai Seiichi and Takahashi Masae, eds., *Gendaishi shiryo 4-5-23 Kokka shugi undo 1–3* [Documents on Contemporary History 4-5-23: Statist Movements 1–3], Tokyo: Misuzu Shobo, 1963–74.

Hashikawa Bunso. *Showa nashionarizumu no shoso* [Aspects of the Showa Nationalism]. Edited and commented by Tsutsui Kiyotada. Nagoya: University of Nagoya Press, 1994.

A classic of the analysis of the ultranationalist movement in the early Showa era. Also essential for an understanding of the era is Hashikawa Bunso, *Ajia kaiho no yume: Nippon no hyakunen, 7* [Dream of Liberation of Asia: Japan's 100 Years, No. 7]. Tokyo: Chikumashobo, 2008.

Karita Toru. *Showa shoki seiji/gaiko kenkyu—Jugatsu jiken to seikyoku (zoho kaiteiban)* [Study of History of Politics and Diplomacy in Early Showa—The October Incident and Political Situation (enlarged and revised edition)]. Tokyo: Ningen no Kagakusha, 1989.

A basic study of the October Incident.

Kita Hiroaki. *Ni-ni-roku jiken zen kensho* [Comprehensive Verification of the February 26 Incident]. Tokyo: Asahi Shimbunsha, 2003.

Highly reliable study on Kita's incident based on the court record of the February 26 Incident that the author discovered, including the text of the sentences of the trial.

Kita Hiroaki. "Ketsumeidan jiken go-ichi-go jiken—Saiban kiroku kara yomitoku" [League of Blood Incident and May 15 Incident—Deciphering Court Records] in *Kaimei showa-shi—Tokyo saiban made no michi* [Deciphering Showa History—Road to Tokyo Trials], edited by Tsutsui Kiyotada. Tokyo: Asahi Shimbunsha, 2010.

First book to read to grasp the current status of studies on the League of Blood Incident and the May 15 Incident. It is written in this treatise that basic historical documents on the League of Blood Incident are stored at Tokyo District Public Prosecutor's Office, but they might have been transferred to the National Achieves of Japan. It should be confirmed where they are stored and if they are open to the public.

Kita Ikki. *Kita Ikki chosakushu 1–3* [Writings of Kita Ikki 1–3]. Tokyo: Misuzu Shobo, 1959–72.

A basic work for the study of Kita. Because its volume 3 contains pieces that were not written by Kita, meticulous verification of the texts included should be conducted on this compilation. Kita's first book, *Kokutairon oyobi junsei shakai shugi* [National Polity and Authentic Socialism] is published as *Kokutairon oyobi junsei shakai shugi jihitsu shuseiban* [National Polity and Authentic Socialism Modified by Hand], edited by Hasegawa Yuichi, C.W.A. Szpilman, and Hagiwara Minoru, Kyoto: Minerva Shobo, 2008. Hagiwara Minoru's *Kita Ikki no "kakumei" to "Ajia"* [Kita Ikki's "Revolution" and "Asia"] (Kyoto: Minerva Shobo, 2011) is an excellent study on Kita Ikki.

Mitsukawa Kametaro. *Sangoku kansho igo* [After the Triple Intervention], edited and commented by Hasegawa Yuichi, Tokyo: Ronsosha, 2004.

Memoir of Mitsukawa Kametaro, one of the central figures in the ultra-nationalistic movement from the Rosokai/Yuzonsha days through Showa. A vivid sketch to revive a movement in an era. A must read.

Publications on Mitsukawa include: Takushoku Daigaku Soritsu Hyaku-nenshi Hensanshitsu, ed., *Mitsukawa Kametaro—Chiiki, chikyu jijo no keimosha* [Mitsukawa Kametaro—Enlightener on Regional and Global Situations], Tokyo: Takushoku University, 2001; Mitsukawa Kametaro, *Ubawaretaru Ajia—Rekishiteki chiiki kenkyu to shisoteki hihyo* [Asia Deprived—Historical Area Studies and Philosophical Critique], Tokyo: Shoshi Shinsui, 2007; Hasegawa Yuichi, C.W.A. Szpilman, and Fuke Takahiro, eds., *Mitsukawa Kametaro nikki: Taisho hachi-nen–Showa ju-ichi-nen* [Diary of Mitsukawa Kametaro: From 8th Year of Taisho through 11th Year of Showa], Tokyo: Ronsosha, 2010; and Hasegawa Yuichi, C.W.A. Szpilman, and Imazu Toshimitsu, eds., *Mitsukawa Kametaro shokanshu—Kita Ikki, Okawa Shumei, Nishida Mitsugi rano shokan* [Correspondences of Mitsukawa Kametaro—Letters of Kita Ikki, Okawa Shumei, and Nishida Mitsugi], Tokyo: Ronsosha, 2012.

This is a field in which remarkable advances have been made in recent years. The most recent studies in this area include: Hasegawa Yuichi, ed., *Ajia shugi shiso to gendai* [Pan-Asianism Philosophy and Contemporary Time], Tokyo: Keio University Press, 2014, and C.W.A. Szpilman, *Kindai Nippon no kakushinron to Ajia shugi—Kita Ikki, Okawa Shumei, Nishida Mitsugi rano shiso to kodo* [Reformist Arguments and Pan-Asianism in Modern Japan—Thoughts and Actions of Kita Ikki, Okawa Shumei, and Nishida Mitsugi], Tokyo: Ashi Shobo, 2015.

Miyata Masaaki. *Eibei sekai chitsujo to Higashi Ajia ni okeru Nippon—Chugoku o meguru kyocho to sokoku: 1906–1936* [Anglo-American World Order and Japan in East Asia—Collaboration and Rivalry over China: 1906–1936]. Tokyo: Kinseisha, 2014.

An exceptionally good study on the history of the Imperial Japanese Army in the Showa era. It accurately criticizes the proliferation of books that contain inadequate empirical evidence. A must read on this subject. However, it includes portions in critique that appear to be exaggerated.

Okawa Shumei Zenshu Kankokai, ed., *Okawa Shumei zenshu 1–7* [Complete Works of Okawa Shumei 1–7]. Tokyo: Okawa Shumei Zenshu Kankokai, 1961–74.

A basic collection for the study of Okawa. As academic works on the subject, Otsuka Takehiro, *Okawa Shumei—Aru fukko kakushin shugisha no shiso* [Okawa Shumei—Philosophy of a Restorative Reformist], Tokyo: Kodansha, 2009, and Karita Toru, *Okawa Shumei to kokka kaizo undo* [Okawa Shumei and the State Reconstruction Movement], Tokyo: Ningen no Kagakusha, 2001 are recommended.

Tsutsui Kiyotada. *Ni-ni-roku jiken to sono jidai* [February 26 Incident and Its Time]. Tokyo: Chikumashobo, 2006.
First book to anatomize the structure of the February 26 Incident as a coup d'état. It proposes to divide the involved young military officers into a "reconstruction-oriented faction" and an "emperor-oriented faction." It also clarifies the components of the coup d'état plan and reveals, for the first time, the critical importance of the engineering of the "reconstruction-oriented faction" and the measures taken in response by the secretary-general of the Lord Keeper of the Privy Seal Kido Koichi.

Tsutsui Kiyotada. *Ni-ni-roku jiken to seinen shoko* [February 26 Incident and Young Military Officers]. Tokyo: Yoshikawa Kobunkan, 2014.
A decisive work on the study of the February 26 Incident. This book reveals the advances the study on this issue has attained. Based on the *Showa Tenno jitsuroku* [The True History of the Emperor Showa], which was published later, the author applied revisions for the second printing.

*Studies and historical documents on this issue and on this period are too numerous to comment on all of them. Readers are encouraged to refer to the Study History and Bibliography attached to the author's 2014 publication above.

Lecture 8

The Marco Polo Bridge Incident
From the Signing of the Tanggu Truce to the Failure
of the Trautmann Mediation Attempt

Iwatani Nobu

Signing of the Tanggu Truce

On May 31, 1933, a ceasefire agreement was signed in Tanggu, Hebei Province, China, between Major General Okamura Yasuji, Vice Chief of Staff of the Kwantung Army, and Lieutenant General Xiong Bin, Council Member of the Beiping branch of the National Military Council. It was the so-called Tanggu Truce, by which the Kwantung Army would withdraw north behind the line of the Great Wall, while establishing a demilitarized zone to the south of the line, with security forces replacing the Chinese Army in maintaining order. The truce brought an end to a string of incidents starting from the Manchurian Incident, and tensions relieved between China and Japan. From the signing of the Tanggu Truce to the end of 1933, various remedial measures were discussed, such as the withdrawal of the Kwantung Army and the requisitioning of administrative power within the theater of war. In the following year, practical matters were discussed, including direct trains, mail, and tariffs between

China and Manchukuo. Concrete results came about one after another.

In January 1935, a goodwill speech advocating "no threat, no invasion" China policy was made by Minister of Foreign Affairs Hirota Koki. Even Chiang Kai-shek recognized the sincerity of the speech, remarking that Sino-Japanese relations were grounded on the principle of equality. On the basis of that, each country's legation to the other was promoted to the status of embassy. With this, the amicable atmosphere between China and Japan reached its apex.

Indeed, judging from diplomatic relations, a spirit of goodwill was the underlying tone of the relationship between the two countries at the time. However, if one looks local military activities, the trend toward a scheme to separate North China from the rest of the country had already become evident from around the autumn of 1934. Disturbing developments began to be seen in Chahar Province, with an incident taking place in Zhangbei at the end of October in which a group of soldiers led by a staff officer of the Japanese China Garrison Army were detained. The Kwantung Army took advantage of the incident to establish a foothold from which it could interfere in affairs in North China and Inner Mongolia, forcing the Chinese side to admit the right of free travel by Japanese persons in Chahar, as well as forcing Chinese troops to withdraw to the west of the Great Wall line. At the same time as Foreign Minister Hirota's speech, a clash broke out along the border between the Chahar and Jehol (Rehe) Provinces concerning the borders of Manchukuo. The Kwantung Army used this so-called First East Chahar Incident as a pretext to expand the demilitarized area.

In addition, Chiang Kai-shek, while responding positively to Hirota's speech, was wary of the machinations of the Japanese in Chahar Province and directed Song Zheyuan, chairman of the province and leader of the 29th Army, to make preparations against Japanese acts of provocation. Chiang had correctly understood where problems were developing behind the goodwill mood. namely, the extent of the contradictions between China and Japan expanded from the issue of the recognition of Manchukuo into the greater questions of Chinese sovereignty and equal relations between the two countries.

Scheme to Separate North China

In May 1935, Colonel Sakai Takashi, Chief of Staff of the Japanese China Garrison Army, took advantage of the absence of Army Commander Umezu Yoshijiro to investigate who was to blame for a series of invasions into Jehol by anti-Japanese, anti-Manchukuo armed groups and the assassinations of several pro-Japanese newspaper publishers. Sakai paid a visit to He Yingqin, acting chairman of the Beiping branch of the National Military Council, and demanded the withdrawal of Kuomintang institutions from Hebei Province, the dismissal of Yu Xuezhong, chairman of Hebei Province, and the transfer of the Yu Xuezhong Army (Northeast Army) and the Central Army outside of the province. The Chinese side persisted in rejecting the actual signing of an agreement, and instead voluntarily informed the Japanese side of its implementation of the actions, resulting in the so-called Umezu-He "Agreement."

Around the same period, another incident occurred, this time in Zhangbei of Chahar Province. Japanese special service agents were illegally detained. In response, Major General Doihara Kenji, dispatched from the Kwantung Army, met with Qin Dechun, deputy of Song Zheyuan, demanding the withdrawal of the 29th Army (led by Song), which was responsible for defending the area, to south of the Great Wall, as well as the expulsion of anti-Japanese organizations from Chahar Province. As a result of this Doihara–Qin Dechun Agreement, the 29th Army, with its strong anti-Japanese sentiment, was moved out of Chahar Province into Hebei Province, switching places with the Yu Xuezhong Army, which had been responsible for defending the Beiping (now Beijing) area. The army later became one of the actors in the Marco Polo Bridge Incident with the Japanese army.

Around this period, Chiang Kai-shek was starting to feel a positive response to his policy of "first internal pacification, then external resistance (An nei rang wai)." As a matter of fact, he made it a principle of that policy that "if a conflict should come to pass with Wo (derogatory expression for Japanese people in Chinese), putting down the Communists will serve to political cover against Japan." In the process of cleaning up the Communists, the Central Army was sent to the heretofore semi-independent provinces in the southwest of China, such as Sichuan, Guizhou, and Yunnan, enabling the country's unification in both name and reality by the end of 1935. In addition, monetary reforms started to get on track, and the country's transportation network developed remarkably. Above all, the smooth progress in the development of national defense and the reform of the military in preparation for a fight with Japan served as the opportunity for Chiang to shift his policies toward Japan into a more active resistance. His diary entry at the end of 1935 illustrates his confidence. He wrote: "Our central effort this year was cleansing the Communists, and that has already been seven-tenths successful. Next year, we will be able to concentrate on resisting against Japan." In November 1935, an assassination attempt was made on Wang Zhaoming, also known as Wang Jingwei, head of the Executive Yuan, who was responsible for negotiations with Japan, in which he was attempting compromise. The next month, Chiang took over Wang's post as the leader of the Executive Yuan, clearly strengthening the hardline position of China against Japan.

As for Japan, "The three principles by Hirota" (*Hirota Sangensoku*) produced by Foreign Minister Hirota were hammered out at the end of 1935, enumerating the following demands: (1) the suppression of anti-Japanese elements in China, (2) tacit recognition of Manchukuo and economic cooperation with it, and (3) a common front against the spread of communism. That meant that even the Japanese Ministry of Foreign Affairs started to favorably treat the scheme to break off North China by the Japanese Army on the ground. The recognition of Manchukuo had already become a pending issue between China and Japan in early 1935, but Japan's demand grew ever bolder by the end of the year. On the Chinese side, Wang Zhaoming, who had attempted compromise with Japan, receded into the background, with Chiang Kai-shek, who had converted his stance to active resistance against Japan, coming to the fore. Because of that, the relationship between China and Japan reached the point where neither side could pull back.

In the autumn of 1936, the Chengdu Incident, in which sever-

Soldier of the 29th Army defending the Marco Polo Bridge (Source: Yang Kelin and Cong Hao, *Zhongguo kangri zhanzheng tu zhi* [Illustrated History of China's Anti-Japan War], Hong Kong: Cosmos Books, 1992)

al Japanese were killed or wounded over a dispute about the reopening of consulates, and the Beihai Incident in Guangdong Province, in which another Japanese was murdered, occurred. After those incidents, China and Japan attempted to remedy the situation through diplomatic relations. From the outset, neither side had any room to make compromises, and it was another incident—this time the Suiyuan Incident—that put a stop to all negotiations outright.

The Suiyuan Incident involved the incursion of the Inner Mongolian Army, with assistance from the Kwantung Army, into Suiyuan Province, and its repulsion by the army of Fu Zuoyi, chairman of the same province. At this time, Chiang Kai-shek had resigned himself to limited war with Japan—although not an all-out war—and had directed preparations for an outbreak of war. The incident caused a complete rupture in negotiations between the two countries, and the successful repulsion of the Inner Mongolian Army that had been supported by Japan ended up uplifting the anti-Japanese sentiment in China. Also, the Xi'an Incident that immediately followed the Suiyuan Incident forced Chiang to make accommodations with the Communist Party of China, which was focused on resisting Japan, meaning that China had no other choice in the end but to reject the option of negotiating with Japan for improved relations. Japan, too, was forced to recognize the emergence of China as a consolidated nation-state unified through the events of the Xi'an Incident, as well as the existence of Chiang Kai-shek as a strong leader, and the fact that the target of burgeoning Chinese nationalism was Japan.

The Eve of the Marco Polo Bridge Incident

It is not true that tensions continued to mount after that, directly leading to the breakout of the Marco Polo Bridge Incident, without any negotiations. In fact, the year 1937 opened with an unexpected sense that tensions might actually be alleviated. In the Ministry of Foreign Affairs, Sato Naotake, who desired that negotiations between China and Japan be held on an equal footing, became the new foreign minister. Also, within the Imperial Japanese Army General Staff, Ishihara Kanji, who opposed the policy to separate North China, assumed the position of chief of the First Bureau (operations) of the Army General Staff. The China Action Plan (*Taishi Jikkosaku*) and the Third Administrative Policy toward North China (*Daisanji Hokushi Shori Yoko*) were issued after policies were reevaluated following the Xi'an Incident and clearly rejected the separation scenario.

Because of the changes taking place in Japan, even China saw some changes as well. Chiang Kai-shek conferred with Japanese Ambassador Kawagoe Shigeru, who was visiting him in a courtesy call while the former was rehabilitating from the Xi'an Incident, and told him that there was no change in China's diplomatic stance. Thanks to the progress in its monetary reform, the enhancement of its national defenses, and the mounting spirit of unification nationwide, China was gaining confidence that it could get along as a unified state without negotiating with Japan. In fact, it was Japan rather than China at this time that was starting to feel pressed to negotiate.

After the Suiyuan Incident, a respite in tensions existed between the central governments of the two countries. However, starting around June 1937, unsettling rumors began to spread around North China that

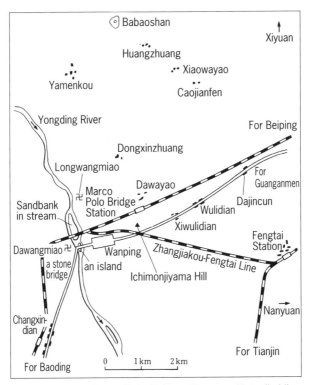

Vicinity of the Marco Polo Bridge (Source: Hata Ikuhiko, *Rokokyo jiken no kenkyu* [Studies of the Marco Polo Bridge Incident], University of Tokyo Press, 1996)

could not be quelled. The China Garrison Army defending the area around Beijing and Tianjin had boosted the number of its forces starting in June of the previous year. One reason for that was to deal with the incursion of the Communist Party into Shanxi Province; another was to restrict the Kwantung Army's interference in the actions of the China Garrison Army in dealing with the North China question. More barracks for the stationed soldiers were needed to house the increased number of soldiers, and the China Garrison Army stationed them in Fengtai, where the British military had previously camped. The area leased by Japan was in close proximity to the location of a company of the 29th Army. Moreover, there was no place in Fengtai suitable for military exercises, with the nearest such place being some six kilometers away in the vicinity of the Yongding River, across which the Marco Polo Bridge was constructed, and right next to the walled town of Wanping, where a battalion of the 29th Army was stationed. As the China Garrison Army conducted exercises continuously at the end of June to the north and west of the bridge, tensions in the area slowly mounted. Martial law was proclaimed in Beiping on June 26, with rumors starting to spread in July that Japan was about to take military action.

At the time, the area around Beiping was defended by the Chinese 29th Army (led by Song Zheyuan), with the 37th Division (led by Feng Zhian) stationed in Beiping, the 38th Division (led by Zhang Zizhong) in Tianjin, and the 132nd Division (led by Zhao Dengyu) in Hejian. On the Japanese side, the 1st Battalion of the 1st Regiment of the China Garrison Army (led by Mutaguchi Renya) was stationed in Beiping, the 2nd Battalion of the same regiment in Tianjin, and the 3rd Battalion (led by Ichiki Kiyonao) in Fengtai. At the time, the Japanese China Garrison Army was carrying out repeated exercises in preparation for inspection from July 9 to 16.

The Marco Polo Bridge Incident

The Marco Polo Bridge Incident took place at around 10:40 p.m. on July 7, 1937. On that day, Colonel Shimizu Setsuro, commander of the 8th Company of the 3rd Battalion, was carrying out night field maneuver exercises in a wasteland near the banks of the Yongding River. When the first stage of the exercise ended around 10:40 p.m., two shots were fired from what was believed to be the vicinity of the embankment being defended by the 29th Army. A roll call was held among the members of the 8th Company gathered there, and one soldier was found to be missing. The head of the company reported that fact to battalion commander Ichiki, who then relayed the information to regimental commander Mutaguchi. Asked his opinion whether troops should be moved to the Marco Polo Bridge, Mutaguchi concurred, ordering Ichiki to mobilize troops toward the bridge and to negotiate with the Chinese regimental commander. Soon after that, the missing Japanese soldier returned to his post, but there was a delay in getting that message to the battalion. The main forces of the battalion were lined up at Ichimonjiyama Hill. It was judged from reports from scouts sent out that the Chinese definitely had a confrontational attitude.

Meanwhile, in Beiping, attempts were being made, mainly by Japanese special service agents, to contact the Chinese to send a joint Sino-Japanese investigative team to the walled town of Wanping near the Marco Polo Bridge to look into matters. That means that a resolution through negotiation was sought at the outset. The Chinese responded that no troops were to be stationed outside the town wall, but again shots were heard around 3:25 a.m. the next morning in the vicinity of Longwangmiao. At 4:20 a.m., Ichiki asked the regimental commander for permission to attack, and Colonel Mutaguchi gave him the green light. At 5:00 a.m., Ichiki advanced toward the Yongding River between Longwangmiao and the railway line. Avoiding attacking the interior of the town, he ordered preparations to shoot at the Chinese troops stationed outside the town wall. The defending Chinese side attempted to hold back the advance of troops led by Colonel Ichiki, but open fire began on both sides. The time was 5:30 a.m. on July 8, 1937.

The fighting between the two sides subsided after about two hours. On the ground, both sides withdrew on July 9, with a ceasefire agreement signed at 8:00 p.m. on July 11. As of that moment, the situation seemed to have settled down as a localized incident.

On July 11, the day the ceasefire was signed, a cabinet meeting was held in Tokyo, at which it was decided at 6:30 p.m. to issue an order to dispatch two mixed brigades from the Kwantung Army as well as the Chosen (Korea) 20th Division to North China. From the outbreak of the incident, Imperial Japanese Army General Staff First Bureau Chief (in charge of operations) Ishihara Kanji and others had tried to prevent the escalation of the situation out of concern that it would affect preparations for war against the Soviet Union. As time progressed, though, the strength of the hardliners gradually grew, and they advocated resolving pending issues by delivering a blow to China. Especially when it was reported that the Chinese Central Army was advancing north, even Ishihara, who had supported keeping the incident localized, came to believe that sending a certain number of troops was unavoidable for the protection of Japanese residents in Beiping. However, as news of the local ceasefire agreement was relayed, the mobilization of troops from mainland Japan was called off.

Meanwhile, on the Chinese side, skeptics felt from the outbreak of the incident that Japan was acting in a premeditated fashion, so Chiang Kai-shek ordered Song Zheyuan to defend the area at all cost. Chiang also ordered the Central Army to advance north. Although Chiang was still unable to ascertain whether Japan was just attempting to make a local provocation or whether it was scheming to start an all-out war, he believed that a peaceful resolution was only possible by negotiating in the presence of the Chinese Central Army, showing that they were always ready to attack. However, the Japanese interpreted the advance north by the Central Army as the Chinese making active preparations for war. The mutual distrust caused each side to fall into a negative spiral of misreading the other's moves. In the same way, the Chinese central government confirmed its conviction that war was inevitable, having decided to advance the Central Army that was being kept at the Henan-Hebei provincial border to Baoding in Hebei Province. That was based on the misinformation received the day after the ceasefire that the Japanese would make a full-scale offensive on July 15.

Escalation of the Situation

Another issue facing the Chinese government leaders was their inability to control over the 29th Army that was responsible for the situation on the ground. That army was primarily composed of troops from northwest China, and not under the direct control of the central command. Accordingly, its commander, Song Zheyuan, did not necessarily adopt the same line of thinking as the central command, in part to maintain his base of support represented by the army. Chiang Kai-shek, for his part, did not know how much he could really trust Sung. There were also problems with the sharing of information between the central command and the army on the ground; indeed, Chiang did not find out about the July 11 ceasefire until the 23rd.

As for the Japanese China Garrison Army, a letter from the Emperor reached the commander on July 14 expressing his apprehensions about the escalation of the situation, spurring efforts to swiftly produce results in the form of an agreement without getting "carried away" with the provocation. Also, attitudes softened in the Chinese 29th Army as well, with the leaders of both sides on the ground signing the details of the ceasefire agreement on July 19. However, illegal shots were fired from the Chinese side on July 19 and 20, causing Japanese to doubt the efficacy of the agreement.

The Chinese representative during negotiations with the Japanese China Garrison Army was Zhang Zizhong. However, the Chinese 29th Army was divided between hawks such as Commander Feng Zhian of the 37th Division and doves such as Zhang, who was involved in the negotiations. Agreements signed by the doves were repeatedly broken by the hawks. Song Zheyuan, while making Zhang carry out negotiations, also privately kept in contact with Feng. In the afternoon of July 24, the Japanese conducted talks with Song, but it turned out that he was not aware of the detailed contents of the agreement, nor had his orders been conveyed. On July 25, the Langfang Incident broke out, with the shooting of signal corps members repairing military-use electrical cables. From that day forward, the attitude of the Japanese on the ground hardened, and an ultimatum was issued demanding the retreat of the 37th Division. The Japanese also requested central command for active troop reinforcements. The Imperial Japanese Army General Staff Office responded accordingly. The next day, the Guanganmen Incident occurred in which Japanese troops trying to enter the city walls of Beiping to protect Japanese residents there were attacked. The China Garrison

Army advised the Japanese central command to allow it to attack the Chinese Army in the Beiping-Tianjin area. The Imperial Japanese Army leaders decided to assign the China Garrison Army the new duty of attacking the Chinese army. They also decided to mobilize army divisions in mainland Japan and deploy troops.

As far as that was concerned, Hashimoto Gun, chief of staff of the Japanese China Garrison Army—who had opposed the escalation of the situation up to that point—said, "the real decision" to exercise force "came at the time of the Guanganmen Incident." In the same way, in the Japanese central command, Kawabe Torashiro, the section chief for war leadership in the Imperial Japanese Army General Staff, who had been cautious about expanding the situation, also said later that the decision to exercise military force came when the Langfang and Guanganmen Incidents broke out. As Lieutenant Colonel Nishimura Toshio, who was working in the operations section of the Army General Staff at the time, said later, the Sino-Japanese War could be said to "begin anew with the Langfang Incident."

At 2:00 a.m. on July 28, 1937, Song Zheyuan received the following notice: "The army is directed to take independent action at this juncture. All the troops within the city walls of Beiping are hereby advised to withdraw immediately so as not to let the war damage spread there." The Japanese China Garrison Army initiated a full-out attack in North China at 8:00 a.m., and Song withdrew from Beiping on the night of the same day.

The Battle of Shanghai

The 29th Army was sent flying with the initiation of a full-scale offensive in North China, and the Japanese army began crossing North China moving southward. The Chinese, fearing that the Japanese would advance as far as Wuhan, wanted the major battleground to be in the lower reaches of the Yangtze River in Central China. Starting at the end of July, Chiang Kai-shek arranged for the purchase of gasoline and communications equipment in Shanghai, and ordered elite troops (Jiao dao zong dui) trained with the latest German military equipment to assemble along the southern bank of the Huangpu River. Tensions in Shanghai were rising on account of the Oyama Incident (of August 9) in which Lieutenant Oyama Takeo and another member of the Imperial Japanese Navy Land Forces were murdered. The Chinese central command decided to encircle and attack the Japanese forces. Based on that order, Zhang Zizhong deployed his troops to the vicinity of Jiangwan and Pengpu. Also, a Supreme War Council was established on August 11, and a secret meeting was held of the Central Standing Committee of the Kuomintang on August 12, at which it was decided that "[we] recognize that a state of war has begun as of today." Sporadic skirmishes began the following morning, developing into a continuous state of war from the evening of August 13. In response, Zhang Zizhong informed Chiang Kai-shek on August 14 that attacks would start at 5:00 p.m. With localized skirmishes expanding to protracted fighting over broad areas, China and Japan thus finally plunged into a full-scale, all-out war.

After the war, Zhang Fakui, who was in charge of the operations of the Chinese military in Shanghai, recalled that the first shot fired in Shanghai had been from the Chinese side. In that way, the battle of Shanghai had been meticulously prepared. Accordingly, the Japanese military experienced hardships when fighting in that city, with as many as 20,000 troops killed or injured in the first two months. Also, the number of Chinese troops outnumbered that of Japan, creating difficulties for the latter. At the beginning of the Battle of Shanghai, Japan only had 5,000 troops from the Navy Land Forces stationed in the city, making it difficult for them to sufficiently protect the Japanese residents of the city. Although the Imperial Japanese Army issued orders for troops to be dispatched to Shanghai, Ishihara argued that it would be cheaper to evacuate the residents of Shanghai when in danger and compensate them later than to wage war, maintaining his negative stance toward sending troops.

At the end of September 1937, the number of casualties in Shanghai exceeded that of the battle in North China, and Ishihara, chief of the First Bureau of the Imperial Japanese Army General Staff Office, was replaced by Shimomura Sadamu, who transferred the main battleground to Central China. Shimomura formulated the policy of taking aggressive action that would inflict a decisive blow on the enemy. His idea went beyond confining Japanese military action to protecting Japanese residents, aiming to go further and strike the main force of the enemy so as to end the war. Here, the policy of non-expansion was effectively discarded at last, and an active policy adopted. The 10th Army landed in Hangzhou Bay in a pincer assault against the Chinese, thus shifting the advantage in the fight toward the Japanese side. By the middle of November, Japan reached the Suzhou-Jiaxing line. Although the Japanese vice chief of staff had originally adopted a cautious attitude, having ordered the main bulk of the troops to remain in the vicinity of Shanghai and directing the 10th Army to be careful about unnecessary expansion, such as pursuing Chinese troops toward Nanjing, he finally gave in to repeated advice and requests by the local military command and decided to attack Nanjing.

The Trautmann Mediation Attempt

Around this time, efforts began in earnest to mediate peace through a third country, with Japan restraining itself from attacking the Chinese capital Nanking for the time being. The Imperial Japanese Army General Staff Office was particularly concerned about the prolongation of the war and displayed a positive attitude toward making peace. On November 5, the German ambassador to China, Oskar Trautmann, relayed the seven conditions of the peace to Chiang Kai-shek, having been requested by Japan. Chiang rejected Japan's proposals at first, for the following reasons, among others: (1) the war was not going so bad for China at the time, (2) a conference of the Nine-Power Treaty nations was currently being held in Brussels, and (3) China was waiting for a response from the Soviet Union about whether it would enter the war against Japan.

Thereafter, however, the war started to go against China and the Brussels conference was concluded without any concrete results. Also, no answer was received from the Soviet Union, so Chiang reconsidered the matter as December 1937 began. Around that time, many Chinese leaders felt the need for a ceasefire in order to regroup, and moves began to be made exploring the formulation of a concrete response to Japan.

Meanwhile, on the Japanese side, the Imperial Army General Staff Office tried to draw a conclusion from different opinions in the government. At the beginning, attempts were made to conclude a peace after preparing a full-fledged attack on Nanjing, but the operation progressed relentlessly, resulting in a situation where the leaders of the operation were unable to keep up with the course of the war. On December 13, when the former capital Nanjing actually did fall, the Japanese army on the ground, which had striven to foster a pro-Japanese administration in China, suddenly shifted its position to a rejection of the Nationalist government. Also, items were added to the conditions for peace partially out of support from public opinion in Japan.

On December 26, the conditions for peace relayed again to the Chinese side included demands for reparations and were consequently difficult for China to accept. Numerous discussions were made aiming at a response by the January 10 deadline that Japan had set. However, the Chinese did not formulate their response by the original deadline, having asked the Japanese for more details, so the date was pushed back to January 15. Also, Japan told China that while the response ought to be a clear one, it was all right to question specific details about particular problems as long as there was a general attitude favoring reconciliation.

Wang Zhaoming, Zhang Qun, Kong Xiangxi, and others started working on drawing up a response along with specific counterarguments, and many people advocated peace at the Supreme National Defense Council as well. However, Chiang Kai-shek, who was at the front, ordered the counterarguments to be excised. In the end, the verbal note passed on by China as its response was hardly any different from that of January 10. Although China was in the midst of reviewing the proposal and thus unable to form a final conclusion, the Japanese side took it that China had adopted a strategy of procrastination, so it announced on January 16 that "henceforth, the Imperial Government will no longer deal with the Nationalist Government." In response, China told Trautmann that it would reject any conditions conveyed to it by Japan, thus cutting off official peace negotiations.

*   *   *

Recommended Readings for Deeper Understanding

Hata Ikuhiko. *Rokokyo jiken no kenkyu* [Studies of the Marco Polo Bridge Incident]. Tokyo: University of Tokyo Press, 1996.

One of the most highly detailed investigations of the Marco Polo Bridge Incident that uses both Japanese and Chinese historical records to explore the incident from a variety of perspectives. It has been designed to focus on the incident while also attempting an understanding of the background developments leading to it. It also contains an appendix with major books for further reading and an annotated bibliography, making it extremely useful to get a grasp of research trends and the location of historical resources.

Kitaoka Shin'ichi and Bu Ping. *"Nitchu rekishi kyodo kenkyu" hokokusho dainikan: Kin-gendaishi-hen* [Report of the "Sino-Japanese Joint Historical Studies," Vol. 2, Modern and Contemporary History]. Tokyo: Bensei Publishing, 2014.

The fruit of joint historical research by Japan and China between 2006 and 2009. One gets an understanding of the differences in perspectives and perception between the two sides through a comparative read.

Uchida Naotaka. *Kahoku jihen no kenkyu—Tanku teisen kyotei to Kahoku kikika no Nitchu kankei 1932-nen–1935-nen* [Studies of the North China Incident—The Tanggu Truce and Sino-Japanese Relations during the North China Crisis, 1932–35]. Tokyo: Kyuko Shoin, 2006.

An elaborate piece of empirical research treating the period from the signing of the Tanggu Truce to the eve of the Marco Polo Bridge Incident. It also uses Chinese historical records made public in Taiwan. Having drawn fully upon both Japanese and Chinese historical resources, this is clearly a work that required much exertion.

Usui Katsumi. *Shinpan: Nitchu senso—Wahei ka sensenkakudai ka* [Revised Version: The Sino-Japanese War—Peace or an Expansion of the Front Line]. Tokyo: Chuokoron Shinsha, 2000.

Provides an outline of the events from the signing of the Tanggu Truce to the end of the war in a concise, comprehensive, and balanced manner. New historical material is included that was not found in the previous 1976 edition, making it an entirely different book. Still, the old version is full of useful references, and it would be interesting to read both versions and compare them.

Yamada Tatsuo et al., eds. *Nitchu senso no kokusai kyodo kenkyu* [Joint International Research on the Sino-Japanese War]. Vols. 1–5. Tokyo: Keio University Press, 2006–14.

The fruit of joint research by scholars from Japan, the United States, China, and Taiwan. It deals with a broad variety of themes, including military, political, economic, social, and cultural matters, as well as international relations and the governments cooperating with Japan. The five volumes are as follows, in order: *Nitchu senso no gunjiteki tenkai* [Military Developments in the Sino-Japanese War], *Chugoku no chiiki seiken to Nihon no tochi* [China's Regional Governments and Japan's Rule], *Nitchu sensoki Chugoku no shakai to bunka* [Chinese Society and Culture during the Sino-Japanese War], *Kokusai kankei no naka no Nitchu senso* [The Sino-Japanese War within International Relations], and *Senjiki Chugoku no keizai hatten to shakai henyo* [Chinese Economic Development and Social Change during the War]. A perfect tome for a deeper understanding of the Sino-Japanese War, as it presents the current level of research and issues of interest.

The Deepening Quagmire of the Sino-Japanese War and the Declaration of a New Order in East Asia

Tobe Ryoichi

Japan's Declaration of "Not Dealing with the Nationalist Government"

On January 16, 1938, after declaring that it would "not deal with the Nationalist government," the Japanese government broke off the mediation efforts by Oskar Trautmann, the German ambassador to China. Two "plot threads" are believed to have led to that.

The first was the aim of making the Japanese nation ready for a long-term war. After the Marco Polo Bridge Incident, the military conflict between China and Japan, first described as the "North China Incident," started to take on the nature of a full-scale war after the second Shanghai Incident, and began to be known as the "China Incident" in Japan. Around that time, the government and the military in Japan debated whether or not to declare war formally. The conclusion of the debate was the decision to put off the declaration. If war were to be declared, international law would permit such positive benefits as the blockading of Chinese coastal ports. But it was determined that the disadvantages of a war declaration would outweigh the advantages, because the US Neutrality Act would come into force, making it difficult for the country to import munitions. China also decided not to formally declare war on Japan. Accordingly, the Sino-Japanese War, until the Pacific War (the Great East Asian War), was not a "war" according to international law.

That legal fiction also affected the Japanese nations's consciousness. As long as the situation was treated as an "incident," it was quite difficult to shake the optimistic view that events would be resolved easily. Both the government and the military were deliberating making a declaration at some opportune time so as to encourage a shift in the nations's consciousness. When the Trautmann mediation attempt collapsed, making it unavoidable that the "incident" would persist for a long time, it was taken as the perfect opportunity for the government to make its declaration. In doing so, the government wanted to make the nation accept the prolongation of the war and to instill a true wartime consciousness.

The other plot thread was the mounting argument toward not recognizing the Nationalist government. After the fall of the capital Nanjing, the sentiment grew stronger in Japan that the war had been won, and that it was thus natural to force surrender terms on China. The first-ever Imperial Conference since the Russo-Japanese War (1904–05) took place on January 11, 1938, at which the following policy was decided: if China did not accept Japan's terms, the current government (i.e., the Nationalists) would not be dealt with as a partner. Japan should rather urge the Chinese to establish another new central government to replace the Nationalist government, and forge more desirable diplomatic relations with that one.

The existence of two plot threads leading to the January 16 declaration by the Japanese government is reflected in the vagueness of the phrase "not dealing with the Nationalists." If the aim were to make the nation accept the prolongation of the war, the main point of the declaration would not necessarily have been the statement of not recognizing the Nationalist government. The phrase "not dealing with" suggests that while current peace negotiations may be halted for the time being, they may be restarted at some future date if that government would change its attitude. However, when the vagueness of the statement was criticized at the Imperial Diet and elsewhere, Prime Minister Konoe Fumimaro and Minister of Foreign Affairs

Landing forces of the Japanese Imperial Navy, wearing gas masks, after the Second Shanghai Incident (Source: Suzuki Sadakichi, *Shina jihen shashincho–Showa 12-nen Koto kaisen hen* [Collection of China Incident Photographs–Hudong Battle], 1938)

Hirota Koki publicly ruled out the possibility that peace negotiations would ever be held at all with the Nationalist government, adding that the war would continue until that government was "eliminated." In that way, the phrase of "not dealing with" the Nationalist government came to mean "not recognizing" it, rigidly restricting the freedom of Japan's policy of dealing with the "incident."

Imperial General Headquarters and the Japanese Military on the Ground

Before the Marco Polo Bridge Incident of July 7, 1937, the Imperial Japanese Army had seventeen divisions, but in the subsequent six months, the number was increased by seven to twenty-four. The supply of weapons and ammunitions could not keep up with the mobilization of these newly created divisions as well as those already established, so in February 1938, the Imperial General Headquarters (*Daihon'ei*) decided not to implement aggressive operations for the time being. However, a large-scale operation ended up being launched in response to appeals from

161

the military on the ground: the Suzhou Operation of April 1938.

The Imperial General Headquarters had been established in November of the previous year—the first time that had happened since the Russo-Japanese War. The aim is said to have been to apply brakes on the actions of the Japanese army on the ground, which was in hot pursuit of the routed Chinese army stampeding in flight. Although the Imperial General Headquarters endeavored to control the Japanese army on the ground by asserting its authority, it was unable to stem the army's galloping march. Succumbing to the pressure of the army on the ground, the headquarters ended up having to order the capture of Nanjing. The Imperial General Headquarters was unable to resist the pressure of the army on the ground in the case of the Suzhou Operation as well.

The Suzhou Operation was triggered by the following events. As troops belonging to the Japanese North China Army (2nd Army) were advancing south along the Jinpu Train Line connecting Tianjin and Pukou (lying opposite Nanjing on the north bank of the Yangtze River), some of them met a large group of Chinese forces northeast of Suzhou in Taierzhuang, finding themselves in a disadvantageous situation separated from the front line. Although the Battle of Taierzhuang was nothing more than a tactical retreat by the Japanese army, China played it up as its first major victory since the beginning of the Sino-Japanese War. The Japanese North China Army learned about the gathering of a huge number of Chinese troops (some 400,000), and attempted a pincer attack that would encircle and destroy the Chinese army from the north and south, in cooperation with Japan's Central China Expeditionary Force. It lacked, however, the necessary number of troops to carry out the plan, and the Chinese army was able to flee by evading the encircling Japanese army, although the strategic Chinese stronghold of Suzhou fell in mid-May. Some elements of the Japanese army ignored the restraints ordered by the Imperial General Headquarters and pursued the Chinese army, getting close to the city of Zhengzhou, but Chiang Kai-shek forestalled an attack on the city by breaking open the embankments of the Yellow River. While the advance of the Japanese army was thus checked, several million Chinese were victims of the ensuing flood waters.

As the territory occupied by the Japanese army expanded in size, an effort was made to establish a new government in China for the maintenance of public order and the reconstruction of the areas under Japanese control. In December 1937, the Provisional Government of the Republic of China was established in Beijing, and the Reformed Government of the Republic of China was created in March of the following year in Nanjing. However, both governments were weak, being merely assemblages of old-style politicians of the warlord era, and thus stumbled in gaining support of the people. Furthermore, there were no signs of an abatement of resistance by the Nationalist government (the Chiang Kai-shek government) that had relocated to Chongqing. One member of the Japanese military compared the Chongqing government with those set up in Beijing and Nanjing, likening the comparison to the difference between a hanging temple bell and a hanging paper lantern. In other words, the Beijing and Nanjing governments were hardly substantial.

While those events continued to unfold, Prime Minister Konoe, between the end of May and June 1938, resorted to the reshuffling of the cabinet to change the direction of policy. The foreign, finance, and army ministers were replaced. Also, although a Liaison Conference between the Imperial General Headquarters and the Japanese government had been set up to align strategies of politics and war when the Imperial General Headquarters was established the previous November, Konoe did not convene it since February 1938. At the time of the Trautmann mediation attempt, the conference members debated intensely about the peace terms and the pros and cons of continuing the attempt. Ever since then, sharp differences in opinion existed between the government and the Imperial General Headquarters. Konoe disliked debate. In addition, he decided to use the five-minister conference instead of the Liaison Conference, for determining important policies regarding the Sino-Japanese War. In other words, he tried to pursue the leadership of the war through a conference consisting of himself, the foreign minister, the finance minister, the army minister, and the navy minister, keeping the military supreme command (the Army General Staff and the Naval General Staff) out of the loop.

The Five-Minister Conference and the Ugaki Peace Attempt

The five-minister conference deliberated three options as policies to resolve the "incident," as follows. The first option was to unite the Provisional Government of the Republic of China, the Reformed Government of the Republic of China and the Mongolia-Xinjiang government that was to be set up some time in the future, thereby creating a new central government, with which new diplomatic relations would be made. The second option was to place an outside influential figure at the top of the new central government who was not connected to the three governments. The third option was to include an "apologetic" reformed Nationalist government as a constituent element of the new central government. The five-minister conference did not necessarily prioritize the three options clearly. Various schemes were conceived and carried out to realize one or more of the three options, creating a tangled situation where they competed with each other.

One of the schemes was the move toward peace known as the Ugaki Peace Attempt, which began in the latter part of June 1938 with a meeting between the Japanese consul in Hong Kong, Nakamura Toyoichi, and Qiao Fusan, secretary to Kong Xiangxi, head of the Executive Yuan. The newly appointed Japanese foreign minister Ugaki Kazushige, who was actively involved in the peace effort, had access to information about the Chinese position via several routes. Those included one through Ogawa Heikichi and Kayano Nagatomo (members of the China Confederation), both of whom had links with Jia Cunde, another secretary to Kong Xiangxi, and another through Kamio Shigeru (adviser to the *Asahi Shimbun*), who had contacts with one of Chiang Kai-shek's advisers, Zhang Zhiluan, chief editor of the *Ta Kung Pao* newspaper. On the basis of such information, Ugaki demanded the resignation of Chiang

Kai-shek as a condition for peace. His vision was that Chiang's resignation would be regarded as an apology by the Nationalist government, after which it would be included as a constituent member of the new central government. This vision can be interpreted as Ugaki's toleration or acceptance of the fact that members of the Nationalist government would in effect constitute the main core of the new government. While being grounded in the third option of the five-minister conference, the Ugaki Attempt sought to avoid the restriction of "not dealing with the Nationalist government."

The Chinese, however, did not accept Japan's demand for Chiang's removal. There was also strong opposition to Ugaki's peace attempt from both the Japanese government and the Imperial Japanese Army. Prime Minister Konoe also did not seem to support him. Ugaki's attempt thus ended in failure, and he abruptly left his post at the end of September 1938. This exemplifies the strong resistance in Japan to modifying the "not dealing with the Nationalists" policy.

At the same time, the first option of the five-minister conference failed to make headway owing to the weakness of the three governments set up by Japan in China and their mutual antagonism. As for the second option, the Kuomintang doyen Tang Shaoyi, the man suggested as the candidate for the "influential outsider," was assassinated by Chong-qing-side terrorists, around the same time that Ugaki resigned. Thereafter, the list of candidates was whittled down to the warlord politician Wu Peifu, who continued negotiating with Japan in fits and starts. In the end, Wu died at the close of 1939 from disease.

Meanwhile, the Japanese military, in the midst of the Ugaki peace attempt, was carrying out large-scale operations on the Chinese battlefield. The 11th Army assigned to Japan's Central China Expeditionary Force was organized as the main force in the military operation launched against the city of Hankou in June 1938. Despite being plagued by the stiff resistance of the Chinese army, terrible road conditions, unbearable heat and infectious diseases, the Japanese army continued its way west along both banks of the Yangtze River, finally capturing the triple cities of Wuhan (Hankou, Hanyang, and Wuchang). At around the same time, the Japanese 21st Army succeeded in landing at Bias Bay (now Daya Bay) east of Hong Kong, occupying Guangzhou. From the north, then, Japan occupied the major port cities of Tianjin, Qingdao, Shanghai, and Guangzhou, while capturing the major political and military centers of Beijing, Nanjing and Wuhan in the interior. Nevertheless, with Chongqing as its capital, the Nationalist government continued its resistance. Also, Japan's military capacity practically reached its limit, as its hands were full just trying to hold on to the vast territory that it had occupied. From that point on, it became harder for Japan to pursue large-scale military operations in China.

Attempts at a Political Solution

If resolving the "incident" through military power had reached a breaking point, then other means—namely, political or diplomatic—had to be used to achieve the same end. Cooperating with Germany and Italy was considered as the diplomatic means toward resolution. Tying up with Germany had the aim of preventing the Soviet Union from intervening in the Sino-Japanese War, and warning it against aiding the Chiang Kaishek government. Tying up with Italy, meanwhile, would check Britain, restraining it also from aiding the Chiang government. Moreover, it was expected that protecting British interests in China could induce Britain to take steps toward mediating peace between China and Japan. Japan's policy of cooperating with Germany and Italy eventually led to moves to reinforce the Anti-Comintern Pact, Japan's alliance with those two countries.

The attempt at peace made by Japan toward Wang Jingwei, also known as Wang Zhaoming, can also be understood in the context of a resolution through political means. The effort began with meetings among Dong Daoning, former head of the Japan Section in the Asia Department of the Chinese Foreign Ministry, his superior Gao Zongwu, former head of the same department, on the Chinese side, and Nishi

Yoshiaki, head of the Nanjing Office of the South Manchuria Railway (or *Mantetsu*), and Matsumoto Shigeharu, Shanghai bureau chief of Domei News Agency, on the Japanese side. It then was expanded to include two members of the Imperial Japanese Army, namely, Kagesa Sadaaki, section chief of military affairs in the Ministry of War, and Imai Takeo, head of the China group of the Army General Staff Office. In

Wang Jingwei (left) and Chiang Kai-shek (right) at the time of the Manchurian Incident

February 1938, Dong Daoning secretly visited Japan, and Gao Zongwu did the same the following July, both with the aim of directly confirming Japanese intentions. Later, Mei Siping, former head of Jiangning Experimental Prefecture, took the place of the sickly Gao in contacting and negotiating with Matsumoto. When Matsumoto subsequently fell ill, his role was taken over by Inukai Takeru, a parliamentarian in the Imperial Diet. In November, Kagesa and Imai traveled to Shanghai along with Nishi and Inukai, where they signed a peace-related agreement with Gao and Mei.

The original purpose of that peace effort was to organize a peace faction within the Chongqing government by rallying opponents to Chiang Kai-shek's policies of resisting Japan, and then to use their pressure to force Chiang out of office. The person regarded as the leader of the anti-Chiang peace faction was Wang Jingwei. Having considered it impossible over time to force Chiang out of office, however, Wang changed tack, leaving Chongqing to start up a third political force not beholden to either Japan or the Chongqing government, and carrying out a peace movement that would try to redirect that government toward peace. The government and the military in Japan had high expectations that more influential politicians and generals of the Nationalist government's anti-Chiang faction would follow Wang and leave Chongqing, making this "conspiracy" effective in weakening Chiang's rule over China. However, this was not the case for the actual players on the ground trying to realize this peace attempt.

In mid-December, Wang secretly escaped Chongqing and arrived in Hanoi. In concert with that, Prime Minister Konoe issued a declaration calling for the recognition of Manchukuo by China, China's signing of the Anti-Comintern pact, the stationing of Japanese troops in China, facilitating economic cooperation between China and Japan, and access to natural resource development in China by Japan, adding that Japan would demand neither reparations nor territory from China. However, the declaration failed to mention the point—agreed upon in advance—that Wang had emphasized the most: the pullout of Japanese troops from China.

In March 1939, Wang's safe house in Hanoi was attacked by Chongqing terrorist organizations. Although Wang survived, his right-hand man was killed. Until then, Wang had been considering the possibility of European exile, but he radically changed his position after the incident. Going beyond just carrying out peace activities as a third force, he came up with the new policy of setting up a peace government in Nanjing, that is, inside an area occupied by the Japanese army. Some have considered that his change in policy was due to pressure from the Japanese side, but a look at documents left by the Japanese parties involved implies that it was Wang himself who made the determination. Wang had envisioned a scenario in which the demonstration of a sound relationship between his government and Japan would push the Chongqing government toward peace. However, his plan was also fraught with the risk of his government just ending up as a puppet government used by the Japanese for managing the occupied territories. Nishi, upon learning of Wang's policy shift, criticized it as having deviated from the original intent, and thus distanced himself from the attempt.

A War to What End?

On November 3, 1938, Prime Minister Konoe announced that the purpose of the Sino-Japanese War was to establish a "New Order in East Asia." That idea consisted of the establishment of a relationship of a "mutually assisting link," in which the three countries of Japan, Manchukuo, and China would cooperate with each other over a broad spectrum, including politics, economics, and culture. It also would aim for "the establishment of international justice, the achievement of joint anti-Communism, the creation of new culture, and the union of economies." In addition, it called for participation even by the Nationalist government in the construction of the New Order, adding that Japan would not reject that possibility as long as the Nationalist Party's "guiding policies" were renounced and it "replace members of their leadership."

The aim of Japan's declaration of a New Order in East Asia was to clarify the purpose of the war. Why did it feel the need to demonstrate that at this juncture? The reason was that most Japanese did not understand why the country was continuing to fight the war with China. However, given the overly abstract and vague nature of the concept declared as the purpose of the war, it is doubtful whether it was sufficient to convince the Japanese of the time why the country was still at war with China.

While the declaration was a domestic appeal to clarify the purpose of the war, it was also addressed to China. After the fall of the triple cities of Wuhan and of Guangzhou, Japan expected that the Nationalist government in Chongqing would renounce its policy of resisting Japan, deposing Chiang Kai-shek and reorganizing itself. That was based upon the third option of the aforementioned five-minister conference. However, no subsequent change was seen in the anti-Japanese stance of the Chongqing government. A month and a half after the declaration, only a few influential politicians followed the lead of Wang Jingwei in leaving Chongqing, amplifying disappointment on the Japanese side.

Wang Jingwei tried to gain Japan's approval for his plan to establish a peace government in Nanjing, but neither the Japanese government nor military were completely in accord with it from the outset. His plan, although it was interpreted to be in line with the second option of the five-minister conference, was in competition with the rival Wu Peifu plan. Thereafter, after various twists and turns, Wang finally established a central government in Nanjing at the end of March 1940, professing itself to be the legitimate government of China, and describing it as a "return to the capital" of the Nationalist government.

The Japanese government, though, did not extend recognition to the Wang government immediately. The reason was the ongoing peace process with the Chongqing government known as Operation Kiri, undertaken because of disillusionment over the Wang government's weakness. The Japanese involved in the effort were Suzuki Takuji, attached to the China Expeditionary Force, Imai Takeo, staff member of the same force, and Usui Shigeki, chief of the 8th Section of the General Staff. They met with Song Ziliang, from the Zhejiang Financial Clique and brother of Soong Mei-ling (Madam Chiang Kai-shek), through whom negotiations were made with the Chongqing side. Both Prime Minister Konoe, who had again assumed the premiership, and Emperor Hirohito held high expectations for that peace effort being advanced by the military, as it seemed likely that an agreement realizing peace would be reached through a tripartite meeting in Changsha among Chiang Kai-shek, Itagaki Seishiro, chief of staff of the China Expeditionary Force and former War Minister, and Wang Jingwei. In time, however, it became evident that the aim of the Chongqing government in Operation Kiri was to carry out a plan to check Japan and sow confusion (in fact, Song Ziliang was a sham, and really an intelligence operative from Chongqing). In November 30 of the same year, Japan signed the Sino-Japanese Basic Treaty, finally recognizing the Wang government, but only after Operation Kiri had been halted.

The process of negotiation leading up to the conclusion of the Sino-Japanese Basic Treaty was protracted, placing a heavy burden on the parties involved. As Japan was demanding enormous privileges across a broad spectrum, Gao Zongwu and Tao Xisheng, who had been partners in Wang Jingwei's peace moves from the beginning, privately separated themselves from the Wang camp and disclosed the contents of the negotiations with Japan to the media. After that, the Wang side continued to resist Japan's demands, but in the end was overpowered. Because it foresaw a weak Wang government and the receding possibility of reaching peace with the Chongqing government, the Japanese side felt that it had to secure as many privileges as possible, both out of military necessity in a long-term war of endurance, as well as for the occupation. In that way, the Wang government—the territory over which it ruled in effect being occupied by the Japanese military—suffered excessive interference and monitoring from the occupying Japanese forces and from Japanese advisers. It could not achieve the actual results of peace that would let it win support from the residents under its control.

Limits to the Military

After conquering Hankou and Guangzhou, the Japanese military was unable to implement any further large-scale offensives. As stated above, the resolution of the "incident" was left primarily up to political and diplomatic measures. Militarily, the policy of "security first" was hammered out. Unless a serious necessity arose, the Japanese military would not consider expanding the area of occupation in China, but instead concentrate on maintaining stability in the areas already under its control.

Of course, that does not mean that military operations in China ceased. Whenever the Chinese would show signs of mustering their forces for attack, the Japanese would forestall their attempt and strike back—winning in most cases. The Japanese military would attack places where Chinese forces were concentrated, ousting them from those areas. Still, due to limitations of troop numbers, the Japanese would not occupy those areas, so they would normally return to their original garrisons when the operation was over. Whenever the Japanese would pull back to their original stations, the Chinese troops that had been kicked out would simply come back. The Chinese military would then trumpet it loudly as a victory, saying that they had "repelled" the attack by the Japanese. Such battles occurred repeatedly. According to one member of the Japanese military, the Chinese armies were like flies that kept on swarming around you no matter how many times you swatted them away.

In December 1939, the Chinese army initiated a series of large-scale counteroffensives over the entire front line in north, central, and south China—the so-called Winter Offensive. The Japanese had no inkling that the Chinese would be able to launch simultaneous attacks along such a long front, and moreover be able to sustain it for so long (some forty days). In some cases, certain Japanese units were in danger of collapse because of the Chinese onslaught, and Japan only repelled the Chinese after having sustained many casualties. The Japanese military was forced to realize that it had misjudged the situation, having mistakenly believed that Japan had weakened China to the point of no recovery in the Hankou and Guangzhou operations.

However, the only earnest, full-scale counteroffensive ever made by the Chinese was this Winter Offensive of 1939. Though the Chinese soldiers had done well fighting in normal battle as regular army and made effective guerrilla actions, it was unable to inflict enough heavy damage on the Japanese to drive them to defeat. Meanwhile, the Japanese won almost every battle they fought, but that was not enough to force the Chinese into submission. It is often said that despite Japan's occupation of a broad swathe of territory, it only controlled "points and lines" in actuality, meaning that it was constantly plagued by the limitation of having too few soldiers. Depending on the area occupied, Japan was sometimes unable to maintain public order as it would like, and suffered from guerrilla attacks quite a few times. The Sino-Japanese War had thus reached a stalemate situation, with neither side being able to win, but neither side losing either.

As of December 1939, the number of Japanese Army troops dispatched to China had reached some 850,000 (twenty-five divisions). The number of war dead on the Japanese side up to the beginning of the Pacific War exceeded 185,000, with the injured numbering 325,000. The count of victims on the China side was far more than that. The Sino-Japanese War had become Japan's largest-scale war in history to that point, with the largest number of victims as well. Even having sent so many soldiers and having sacrificed so many victims, Japan could still not win the war.

Before long, Japan started to view the Sino-Japanese War not as one between just China and Japan, but rather as something that was only resolvable as part of a political tectonic shift worldwide. The breakout of the World War in Europe in September 1939, along with Germany's rapid string of victories in the western front in May 1940 and later, created the sense of the arrival of such a shift. To take advantage of the excellent opportunity represented by that shift, and to use it to resolve the Sino-Japanese War, the Japanese government and military transferred their focus of interest from the battlefields of China to Southeast Asia, where Western colonies lie.

* * *

Recommended Readings for Deeper Understanding

Hata Ikuhiko. *Nitchu sensoshi* [History of the Sino-Japanese War]. Tokyo: Kawade Shobo Shinsha, 1961; reprinted new version, 2011.

The author is one of the writers contributing to "The Road to the Pacific War" (see below). Highly evaluated as a pioneering piece of research into the military aspects of the Sino-Japanese War, this book has been reprinted many times.

Hatano Sumio and Tobe Ryoichi, eds. *Nitchu senso no gunjiteki tenkai* [Military Developments of the Sino-Japanese War]. Tokyo: Keio University Press, 2006.

The second volume of the "Joint International Research on the Sino-Japanese War," five volumes of which have been released so far. As the title says, it is a collection of essays focusing on military aspects of the war. The topics explored are not merely strategy and tactics as well as operations and battles, but also such things as morale, weapons and organization.

Iechika Ryoko. *Sho Kaiseki no gaiko senryaku to Nitchu senso* [The Diplomatic Strategy of Chiang Kai-shek and the Sino-Japanese War]. Tokyo: Iwanami Shoten, 2012.

Making full use of the opened diaries of Chiang Kai-shek and other historical materials from China, this book is a lucid analysis of Chiang's diplomatic strategy toward Japan before and after the Sino-Japanese War.

Kitaoka Shin'ichi and Bu Ping. *"Nitchu rekishi kyodo kenkyu" hokokusho dainikan: Kin-gendaishi-hen* [Report of the "Sino-Japanese Joint Historical Studies," Vol. 2, Modern and Contemporary History]. Tokyo: Bensei Publishing, 2014.

A publication of reports released in 2010. Although the Sino-Japanese War is not the only topic treated, it is interesting to read and compare the juxtaposed essays written by Japanese and Chinese researchers about Sino-Japanese relations in various periods in the modern era leading up to Japan's defeat in the war.

Liu Jie. *Nitchu sensoka no gaiko* [Diplomacy during the Sino-Japanese War]. Tokyo: Yoshikawa Kobunkan, 1995.

An empirical piece of research examining peace efforts during the war by linking them with their visions of postwar Sino-Japanese relations. As it contains criticisms of Tobe's research (see below), it is worth reading both works and comparing them.

Military History Association, eds. *Nitchu senso no shoso* [New Perspectives of the Sino-Japanese War (Sixty Years After)]. Tokyo: Kinseisha, 1997.

A collection of essays published in commemoration of the 60th anniversary of the breakout of the Sino-Japanese War. The essays are distinctive—inquiring into such matters as the wartime economy and administration of the occupied territories, as well as the connection of third-party countries to the Sino-Japanese conflict.

Military History Association, eds. *Nitchu senso sairon* [The Sino-Japanese

War Revisited (Seventy Years After)]. Tokyo: Kinseisha, 2008.

An edited collection of essays released in commemoration of the 70th anniversary of the breakout of the Sino-Japanese War. The essays exploring such new areas as intelligence and propaganda are of great interest. It also contains reliable research on the Nanjing Incident.

Research Section into the Causes of the Pacific War, the Japan Association of International Relations, eds. *Taiheiyo senso e no michi* [The Road to the Pacific War], Vol. 4. Tokyo: Asahi Shimbunsha, 1963; newly bound version, 1987.

The pioneer of empirical research relating to the Sino-Japanese War. A must-read book that is now considered a classic.

Tobe Ryoichi. *Pisu fira—Shina jihen wahei kosaku no gunzo* [Peace Feelers: Portraits of the Players in the Peace Efforts in the China Incident]. Tokyo: Ronsosha, 1991.

An empirical exploration of the actual processes of Japan's policy-making surrounding peace initiatives.

Usui Katsumi. *Shinpan: Nitchu senso—Wahei ka sensen kakudai ka* [Revised Version: The Sino-Japanese War—Peace or an Expansion of the Front Line?]. Tokyo: Chuokoron Shinsha, 2000.

The most compact and reliable study of the Sino-Japanese War. Whereas the previous edition (1976) emphasized developments after the breakout of the war, the new version treats the history leading up to the war in detail as well.

Lecture 10

The Nomonhan Incident and the Japanese-Soviet Neutrality Pact

Hanada Tomoyuki

Conflict along the Manchukuo-Soviet Border

Soviet-Japanese relations in the 1930s were influenced by military and diplomatic history. Ever since the Manchurian (Mukden) Incident (of September 18, 1931) and the founding of Manchukuo thereafter, incessant disputes continued between Japan and the Soviet Union as well as Manchukuo and the Soviet Union about ensuring rights and interests in Manchuria and Mongolia. During this period, according to the records in *"Senshi sosho: Kanto Gun (1)* [Military History Collections on the Imperial Japanese army and navy during the Pacific War: Kwantung Army (1)]," that were compilations of the National Institute for Defense Studies (Japan Ministry of Defense), there were 152 skirmishes along the Manchukuo-Soviet border between 1932 and 1934, 176 in 1935 (including the Battle of Khalkhyn Temple), 152 in 1936 (including the Changlingzi Incident), 113 in 1937 (including the Kanchazu Island Incident), 166 in 1938 (including the Battle of Lake Khazan, or the Changkufeng

Incident), and 159 in 1939.

Such military clashes between Japan and the Soviet Union were reflected in the Japanese Imperial National Defense Policies revised in June 1936 (11th Year of Showa) in which the United States and the Soviet Union were depicted as theoretical enemies (along with the Republic of China and the United Kingdom). Also, according to the Standards of National Policies determined by the four-minister conference (held among Japan's prime, foreign, army, and navy ministers) in August of the same year, military preparations to the north were "to be used to counteract military strength that could be utilized by Russia in the Far East," and "to enhance Japan's military strength in Korea so that it would be sufficient to deal a blow to the Soviet Union during the first stages of a war." In other words, in order to respond to the heightened military threat of the Soviet Union and the Mongolian People's Republic, it was determined that the basic military strategy would be the first-strike principle and short-term military operations. In addition, there was movement in the international political environment where Japan, Germany, and Italy moved to sign the Anti-Comintern Pact, starting in the summer of 1938, to strengthen their military alliance against the Soviet Union and the United Kingdom. Domestically, the clash between the Japanese Army and Navy regarding strategy directions surfaced (the so-called Anti-Comintern Pact reinforcement issue).

Meanwhile, turning the aspect of the Soviet Union's military and diplomacy in the 1930s shows that it was the time when a hardline strategic posture toward Japan came to be solidified. Militarily, the Communist Party leadership and military leaders of the country demonstrated a strong sense of caution toward the Manchurian Incident and the subsequent establishment of Manchukuo. On account of that, they paid great attention to the defense of the Far East in order to prepare for a military incursion by the Kwantung Army, making heavy troop reinforcements and improving the technical capacity of the Special Red Banner Far East Army, based on the Second Five-Year Plan. Also, the Soviet army (Workers' and Peasants' Red Army) incrementally modernized itself through the large-scale construction of military infrastructure in the Far East region.

At the same time, in the diplomatic relation during the meeting in December 1931 between People's Commissar for Foreign Affairs Maxim M. Litvinov and Japanese Ambassador to France Yoshizawa Kenkichi (Foreign Minister starting the next month), Soviet delegation proposed the conclusion of a nonaggression pact between the two countries. Japan, however, did not respond to the proposal for about one year. In the end, Japan refused the proposal in December 1932, when it became unnecessary for the two countries to sign a treaty, as both were participants in the Kellogg-Briand Pact (the Pact of Paris, or the General Treaty for Renunciation of War as an Instrument of National Policy).

Furthermore, a look at the international political environment shows that the Soviet Union, in order to avert the crisis of a pincer attack against its eastern and western borders, not only strengthened its own military capacity but also forged collective security in East Asia. It did so by creating military alliances with the Republic of China and the Mongolian People's Republic as a military and diplomatic strategy to counter the anti-Communist, anti-Soviet camp based on the Anti-Comintern Pact that was signed in November 1936 by Japan and Germany. In particular, the Sino-Soviet Nonaggression Pact concluded in August 1937 stated that the Soviet Union would extend aircraft support and weapon provision to the Republic of China, thereby indirectly heightening the level of tension within Soviet-Japanese relations. Those moves were linked to the "thorough expansion" of a united people's front promoting anti-Fascism as advocated at the 7th Comintern held in July 1935, as well as Stalin's criticism, made at the 18th Communist Party Convention held in March 1939, of the noninterference and appeasement policies by the United Kingdom, the United States, and France toward the Fascist powers.

Both Japan and the Soviet Union greeted May 1939 amidst such a tense military and diplomatic background between the two countries.

The Momentum toward the Nomonhan Incident

The battle widely described in Japan as the Nomonhan Incident and generally known in Russian and Mongolia as the Battle of Khalkhyn Gol was an intense, modern battle that took place between the Japanese-Manchurian army on one side and the Soviet-Mongolian army on the other over a roughly four-month period between May and September 1939. As the two different names suggest, it was a regional conflict fought in the area around Nomonkhan Bürd Oboo, a grave-mound of a Tibetan Buddhist holy priest, located along the eastern bank of the Khalkhyn Gol, or the Khalkha River, that formed the frontier area between Manchukuo and the Mongolian People's Republic. The main cause of the battle is believed to have been the clashing perceptions between Japan and the Soviet Union about the Manchurian-Mongolian border, with the Japanese-Manchurian army regarding the Khalkha River as the border and the Soviet-Mongolian army regarding a line some 20 kilometers east of the river as such.

Until now, the Nomonhan Incident, owing to the influence of judgments of the International Military Tribunal for the Far East, also known as the Tokyo Tribunal of War Criminals, has been seen as a devastating one-sided defeat on the Japanese side. It had been believed that the Kwantung Army, having ignored the non-expansionary policies of the central Army General Staff, "crossed" the Manchurian-Mongolian border, inciting and expanding the conflict, and being defeated in a counterattack by the mechanized Soviet army. However, the fruits of research in recent years have revealed that a high number of military casualties were suffered on both sides. According to Grigory F. Krivosheev, former professor at the Russian Academy of Military Sciences, the number of Soviet casualties increased significantly, partly because of the declassification of historical documents and archives after the collapse of the Soviet Union, and is now thought to be 25,655 men. That greatly exceeds the number of casualties on the Japanese side, shown to be in the vicinity of some 18,000 to 20,000 men in an analysis by the modern Japanese historian Hata Ikuhiko.

The Nomonhan Incident is said to have been triggered by the Manchurian Army, which was in charge of border garrisons. The Manchurian army repeatedly rolled back the "cross-border actions" made by the Mongolian army cavalry on May 11 and 12, 1939. The strategic direction of the Kwantung Army at the time was heavily reflected in the Principles for the Settlement of Soviet-Manchurian Border Disputes ordered by General Ueda Kenkichi, commander of the Kwantung Army, in which it was clearly stated that illegal actions by the Soviet Union would be dealt with "only by resolute and thoroughgoing punitive actions." In order to accomplish that objective, the intention was also clearly indicated that not only was it permissible to make temporary incursions inside Soviet territory and/or to lure Soviet troops inside Manchukuo territory and detain them there, but also to advance troops across the border in order to search for and destroy Soviet troops that had come across the frontier. Moreover, it was written that the "defense commander," stationed where national borders were indefinite, could voluntarily and independently certify the border so as "to prevent the needless incitement of entanglement." Along the Manchurian-Mongolian border, it was Lieutenant General Komatsubara Michitaro, commander of the 23rd Division, who was assigned to that duty. In recent research, Professor Kuromiya Hiroaki of Indiana University has been attempting to validate the theory that Komatsubara had been a spy for the Soviets. The lieutenant general had been the Japanese military attaché to Russia in the late 1920s, where, Kuromiya points out, he was trapped in a "honeypot" (i.e., a case of sexual entrapment). The theory is that Komatsubara then began to provide the Soviets with Japanese intelligence, which led to the debacle of the Japanese-Manchurian army when he was its operational commander during the Nomonhan Incident. There is no definitive proof of that, however.

On the other hand, the leadership of the Soviet Communist Party and military perceived the Nomonhan Incident from the beginning to be an "organized violation of the border" by the Japanese-Manchurian army against the Mongolian People's Republic. One hardly hears debate anymore—as was common in the former Soviet era—asserting the authenticity of the Tanaka Memorial, a forged document from 1927 outlining Japan's strategy to take over the world. However, regardless of the debate about the document's authenticity, the thought pattern still seems to exist today that links the strategic intent of the forged document to the embodiment of Japan's militarism and its subsequent path to the Pacific War. Also, some link it to Operational Plan No. 8-B, drawn up by the Kwantung Army General Staff in 1938, thus explaining the Nomonhan Incident as a military incursion planned by the Japanese-Manchurian army. (In contrast to Plan A, which had proposed a military strike against the Soviet Union across the northern and eastern borders, Plan B proposed massing troops along the western frontier, then initiating an invasion.)

Division commander Komatsubara, so as to deal with the cross-border incursion of the Mongolian army into the eastern bank of the Khalkha River, attempted to realize the intent of Kwantung Army Commander Ueda by dispatching a search party led by Lieutenant Colonel Yaozo Azuma to obliterate the Mongolian army. General Ueda also ordered the mobilization of the 1st Battalion of the 64th Infantry Regiment, which formed the main body of the search party. In response, the Soviet-Mongolian army carried out a new attack, advancing as far as the right bank area of the Khalkh River at one point. On May 21, Komatsubara sent in a detachment led by Colonel Yamagata Takeo with orders to attack and smash the army that had advanced. In the battle, which was the first of the Nomonhan Incident both sides were compelled to make huge sacrifices.

Because of the tense situation in the Far East, the leaders of the Soviet Communist Party and the Soviet military decided to send General Georgy K. Zhukov, deputy commander of the Belorussian Military District, there. According to the revised, enlarged version of the memoirs of Marshal Zhukov, made public after the collapse of the Soviet Union, he declared military support for the Mongolian People's Republic based on the obligations outlined in the Soviet-Mongolian mutual support protocol signed on March 12, 1936. Also, in his account of the affair that was interspersed with his analysis, he said:

> The Japanese government made the determination to stir up international public opinion by describing its own act of aggression as a "border conflict," so as to cover up its real objective of violating the border of the Mongolian People's Republic. I decided not to undertake operations using a large army at the beginning of the military action, but rather to send in special-mission forces, reinforcing them later as needed depending on the development of military maneuvers. I did so, as I had hypothesized that the Red Army would be able to call off the attack in its initial stages in case the troops got caught in fierce counterattacks, allowing the Red Army to withdraw into its own national territory.

Zhukov, newly appointed commander of the 57th Special Corps, ordered the Far East reinforcement of the territory in preparation for an attack against the eastern bank of the Khalkha River. In addition, he realized an extensive buildup involving three rifle divisions, two tank brigades, three mechanized (armored car) brigades, four artillery brigades, and six aviation regiments. The strength of the Soviet-Mongolian army along both banks of the river was thus gradually beefed up, with Soviet aircraft frequently crossing the river and taking action.

The Conflict Escalation of the Nomonhan Incident

After the sneak bombing attack made by the Japanese bomber aircraft on the Tamsk (Tamsag-bulak) Airbase late on the night of June 27, 1939, the Nomonhan Incident expanded beyond the "punishment" of border incursions across the Manchurian border to develop into a full-scale battle between the Japanese tank brigade led by Lieutenant General Yasuoka Masaomi and the Soviet-Mongolian army. Another battle broke out at Bain Tsagan Hill on the west bank of the Khalkha River.

According to primary historical sources from the Russian State Military Archive (*Rossiiskii Gosudarstvenni Voennyi Arkhiv*, or RGVA) publicly declassified after the collapse of the Soviet Union, on July 12, 1939, after the fighting at Bain Tsagan Hill, a telegram jointly signed by People's Commissar of Defense Kliment Y. Voroshilov and Boris M. Shaposhnikov, Chief of the General Staff of the Red Army, was sent to the Far Eastern Front Group Command Headquarters (commanded by General Grigori M. Shtern). The telegram contained rigorous criticisms of the strategies applied to the operation, saying that it was an inadmissible and careless act for the military commanders on the ground to have injected the 82nd Rifle Division—which constituted the main body of the Soviet-Mongolian forces—into the fighting, despite being warned not to do so, and for tank brigades to have been used, among other comments. Moreover, on July 14, when the Soviet-Mongolian troops on the ground were ordered by Grigory I. Kulik, the Soviet Deputy People's Commissar of Defense stationed in Chita base at the time, to retreat from the east bank of the Khalkh River to the west bank, Voroshilov and Shaposhnikov sent another telegram reprimanding him, and ordering an immediate recovery of the original positions.

While the Nomonhan Incident has mostly been researched so far in a way criticizing it as an internal conflict within the Japanese military between the strategic policies of the Army General Staff and those of the Kwantung Army, differences of strategic perception have also been found in defense policy positions within the Soviet military, between the central Red Army General Staff and the military commanders on the ground, concerning how to respond in battle to the Japanese-Manchurian army.

On July 19, the various Soviet units, centered on the 57th Special Corps, were reorganized into the 1st Army Group, with Zhukov appointed new commander. He was given the authority to direct operations in charge of troops on the front, signifying that the Soviet-Mongolian army

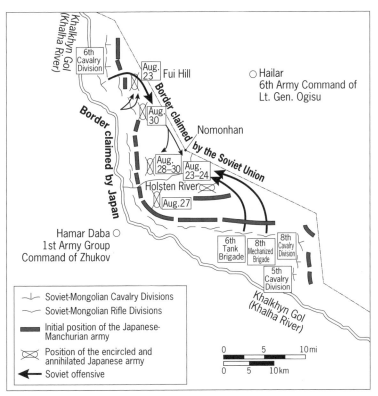

The Nomonhan Incident, August 20 to 31, 1939 (Source: Geoffrey Roberts, *Stalin's General: The Life of Georgy Zhukov*, Random House, 2012)

was preparing for an offensive in August. In the approximately one-month period through mid-August, the 1st Army Group made steady progress in preparations for a large-scale offensive, with the total military force of the Soviet-Mongolian army at more than 57,000 troops. The encirclement and extermination campaign initiated by the Soviets against the Japanese-Manchurian army on August 20 involved attacks in three directions by the 1st Army Group, composed of three groups (northern, central and southern), with catastrophic damage inflicted on the Japanese 23rd Division arrayed along the east bank of the Khalkha River. In recent research, Stuart D. Goldman, scholar in residence at the US National Council for Eurasian and East European Research, has focused on the signing of the German-Soviet Nonaggression Pact (Molotov-Ribbentrop Pact) on August 23 during the course of the August attacks. Goldman's research reveals that the leadership of the Soviet Communist Party and military emphasized the victory at the Far East in advance of the western offensive (in Poland, the three Baltic countries, and Finland) that took place in September and later, from the perspective of the national security of its eastern and western borders.

Adjustment of Soviet-Japanese Relations after the Outbreak of the World War II

Having received a double shock—the defeat in the Nomonhan Incident and the signing of the German-Soviet Nonaggression Pact—Japan's strategic perception about the Soviet Union changed radically, with efforts subsequently being promoted, primarily by the Ministry of War and the Ministry of Foreign Affairs, to neutralize the Soviet Union. The cabinet of Abe Nobuyuki, formed on August 30, 1939, proclaimed the "establishment of independent diplomacy" and began to pursue the adjustment of diplomatic relations with the Soviet Union at the same time it did so with the United Kingdom, the United States, and France, so as to press ahead with nonintervention in the war in Europe and a resolution of the Sino-Japanese War. In response to that, German Foreign Minister Joachim von Ribbentrop, the driving force behind the German-Soviet Nonaggression Pact, proposed the policy of nonaggression among the three countries of Japan, Germany, and the Soviet Union as a countermeasure against Britain, and explored the possibility of Germany's mediating between Japan and the Soviet Union. Also, diplomatic relations between Japan and the Soviet Union were adjusted with the common goal of defeating the United Kingdom, which had continued to support the Republic of China as the behind-the-scenes string puller in the Sino-Japanese War. That was to be done by having Japan, Germany, and the Soviet Union cooperate as the powers of a new order, built primarily by Ribbentrop.

According to the Outline of the Policies on Foreign Measures decided upon by the Abe cabinet on December 28 of the same year, Japan would firmly continue its anti-Communist policy in its stance toward the Soviet Union, while also promoting nonparticipation in the European war and the construction of a New Order in East Asia. It read, "Particularly with the incidents in China, our policy will endeavor to calm down the relations between the two countries and especially maintain security along the border." Also, the outline said that Japan would aim at the resolution of "conflicts along the border through peaceful talks without appealing to force." Accordingly, consideration was to be made of the resolution of various pending problems with the Soviet Union—including general border issues, the conclusion of a trade agreement, a basic treaty on fishing, and rights in northern Sakhalin—so as to calm down relations between the two countries. As far as the signing of a nonaggression pact between the two countries was concerned, the guidelines mentioned that the possibilities for a pact would be explored, predicated on "the renunciation of the Soviet Union's support for China and its halt of military preparations threatening Japan and Manchuria," although saying that Japan would make no formal proposal along those lines.

The new Yonai Mitsumasa cabinet, formed in January 1940, inherited the diplomatic policy line of adjusting relations between Japan and the Soviet Union. Amidst moves by Foreign Minister Arita Hachiro to advance the concept of a New Order in East Asia, Japan made progress on adjusting its relations with the Soviet Union, one power of the New Order. In particular, the rapid victorious advance of the German army across the European front, leading to the fall of Paris on June 14, 1940, pushed Japan to take the initiative in the southern direction (i.e., Southeast Asia). On July 12, 1940, a proposal was advanced at the tri-ministerial conference involving the secretariats of Japan's Army, Navy and Foreign Ministries to strengthen cooperation among Japan, Germany and Italy, according to which Japan and Germany would cooperate to maintain peace with the Soviet Union. The same proposal added that if a state of war should come to exist between either Germany or Japan, on the one hand, and the Soviet Union, on the other, not only would the other country not assist the Soviet Union, but also make consultations about what measures ought to be taken in the event of a threat from that country.

The Second Konoe Cabinet and the Unrealized Vision of a Quadripartite Entente

Japan's foreign policy direction—namely, the conception of a New Order in East Asia by Foreign Minister Arita and the adjustment of Soviet-Japanese relations—was succeeded by the tripartite diplomacy furthered by the Second Konoe Fumimaro cabinet that was formed on July 22, 1940, with Matsuoka Yosuke as foreign minister. As far as relations with the Soviet Union were concerned, the so-called Ogikubo Talks that had preceded the formation of that cabinet called for the signing of a Japanese-Manchurian-Mongolian Frontier Inviolability (Nonaggression) Pact that would be valid for five or ten years, as well as for the "enhancement of military preparedness" during that period "that would be invincible against the Soviet Union." The gist of those talks was reflected in the Imperial Headquarters Government Liaison Conference held on the 27th of the same month, when guidelines were laid forth "to deal with current affairs in line with changes in the world situation," with an appeal for reinforced political ties with Germany and Italy appended by a passage calling for a dramatic adjustment of relations with the Soviet Union.

In the Article 5 (the so-called Soviet exclusion clause) of the Tripartite Alliance concluded by Japan, Germany, and Italy on September 27, 1940, there was no clear mention of an antagonistic attitude toward the Soviet Union. On account of that, the Japanese Ministry of Foreign Affairs drew up a proposal for guidelines adjusting relations between Japan and Russia on October 3. That is thought to reflect Foreign Minister Matsuoka's proposed conception of a four-power entente among Japan, the Soviet Union, Germany, and Italy. According to that proposal, a non-aggression pact would be concluded by Japan and the Soviet Union, after which rights issues would be resolved, such as petroleum and coal in northern Sakhalin as well as fishing in northern seas. It would also include a mutual recognition of the division of spheres of influence between the two countries, with Japan's sphere to extend to Inner Mongolia, northern China, and Southeast Asia, and the Soviet Union's to include the Mongolian People's Republic, Xinjiang, and the Near and Middle East. The new world order would thus be promoted in cooperation with Germany and Italy.

Research in recent years has discussed the historical circumstances behind the concept of a quadripartite entente as a diplomatic development from the Tripartite Alliance, and the possibility of its realization. Miyake Masaki, in his 2007 work, *Stalin, Hitler, and the Vision of a Federation among Japan, the Soviet Union, Germany, and Italy*, has pointed out that Japanese General Takagi Sokichi, chief of research section of the Navy Ministry, already produced a document entitled "The Losses due to Various Foreign Policies," dated August 24, 1939, one year after the German-Soviet Nonaggression Pact was concluded. In that document, he delivered the judgment that the policy of affiliating with Germany, Italy, and the Soviet Union would be the most advantageous for Japan, as opposed to adopting a "policy of isolation and self-direction" or one siding with Britain and the United States. That was an articulation of the alignment of interests, traditionally held by the brass of Japan's Navy, supporting the development of an amicable relationship with the Soviet Union. That contributes to a consideration of the possibility that the Navy brass, which had opposed the Tripartite Alliance, could support a quadripartite entente among Japan, the Soviet Union, Germany, and Italy.

Also, Vassili E. Molodiakov, professor at the Japanese Culture Research Institute of Takushoku University in Tokyo, has written about the possibility of a political and military partnership between the Soviet Union and the Tripartite Alliance, pointing out that the Anti-Comintern

Pact between Japan and Germany itself was inherently anti-British in certain aspects.

Still, the possibility of realizing a quadripartite entente ended with the breakdown of diplomatic negotiations between Germany and the Soviet Union, caused by Hitler's failure to respond to Soviet Foreign Minister Vyacheslav Molotov's "additional conditions" released on November 25, 1940, which were made in response to the contents of the Hitler-Molotov talks held earlier on November 12 and 13. Those conditions were as follows: (1) a demand for the German Army to pull its troops out of Finland, (2) the establishment of Soviet military bases in the areas along both the Bosporus and Dardanelles Straits, (3) recognition of territory from Batumi (Georgia) and Baku (Azerbaijan) south to the Persian Gulf, and (4) Japan's renunciation of its petroleum and coal rights in northern Sakhalin, etc. Also, it was Directive No. 21 (Operation Barbarossa), signed by Hitler on December 18, 1940, which sent the concept of a quadripartite entente among Japan, Germany, Italy, and the Soviet Union into the dustbins of history.

Signing of the Soviet-Japanese Neutrality Pact

Before Foreign Minister Matsuoka's visit to Europe, the Imperial Headquarters Government Liaison Conference on February 3, 1941, issued a draft guideline document proposing negotiations with Germany, Italy, and Russia. Matsuoka had floated the idea of a quadripartite entente among Japan, the Soviet Union, Germany, and Italy. The document is said to have aimed at forcing the Soviet Union to align its policies with those of Japan, Germany, and Italy, thereby adjusting relations among Japan, Germany, and the Soviet Union, for the purpose of forcing the Soviet Union to accept Ribbentrop's proposal for quadripartite entente (German-Soviet negotiations having been broken off at that point) and defeating Britain. The following points were included in the guideline among others: (1) Make the Soviet Union sell northern Sakhalin to Japan via German mediation (or if the Soviet Union failed to agree to that, make it promise to supply 1.5 million tons of petroleum to Japan over the next five years to compensate Japan for giving up its rights in northern Sakhalin); (2) Recognize Japan's status in North China and Inner Mongolia in return for Japan's recognizing the status of the Soviet Union in Xinjiang and the Mongolian People's Republic; (3) Force the Soviet Union to abandon its support for Chiang Kai-shek; (4) Swiftly set up committees for border demarcation and dispute settlement in Manchukuo, the Soviet Union, and the Mongolian People's Republic; (5) Negotiations on fishing would be led toward settlement, but there would be no hesitation to renounce them if necessary in terms of adjusting Soviet-Japanese relations; (6) The Soviet Union to promise to allocate train cars and to discount cargo rates, given that commercial transport between Japan and Germany would increase significantly. In addition, the guidelines stated that the world would be divided into "four great spheres" as part of the framework for the new international order, namely, "the great East Asian sphere, the European sphere (including Africa), the American sphere, and the Soviet sphere (including India and Iran)."

Article 1 of the Soviet-Japanese Neutrality Pact, signed on April 13, 1941, involved definite promises of peaceful amity and the conservation of territorial integrity on both sides (in other words, the mutual respect of territorial integrity and border inviolability on both sides, with the Soviet Union controlling the Mongolian People's Republic and Japan controlling Manchukuo). Article 2 said that neutrality was to be maintained throughout the duration of a conflict if either side were to be the target of military action by a third country. Article 3, then, established the period of efficacy of the treaty to run through April 1946, also stipulating that any notification of the future abrogation of the treaty was to be made a year before the end of that period. Ironically, Article 3 came to have an important significance in 1945 during the final throes of Japan's war.

As for the historical circumstances why the treaty was not a nonaggression pact but rather a neutrality pact, recent research by the Soviet diplomatic historian Boris N. Slavinsky has discovered the documents and archives of Molotov, that were preserved in the Russian Federation Archive of Foreign Affairs, the existence of a top-secret verbal note between the plenipotentiary representatives of the Soviet-Chinese Non-aggression Pact declaring that the Soviet Union would conclude no nonaggression pact with Japan until the time came that the Republic of China and Japan formally normalized their relations.

The concept of quadripartite entente among Japan, the Soviet Union, Germany, and Italy that constituted a basic part of Japanese Foreign Minister Matsuoka's Soviet-Japanese Neutrality Pact went up in smoke on June 22, 1941, on account of the breakout of war between Germany and the Soviet Union, an event that changed world history. Even so, the Neutrality Pact between the two countries served as the only official (diplomatic) route linking the Axis countries and the Allied countries during the years of the Pacific War, while the two camps were at war with each other. In addition, the existence of the pact produced "tranquility in the north" for Japan's Army and Navy, serving as a big historical turning point in Japan's military advance southward.

* * *

Recommended Readings for Deeper Understanding

Goldman, Stuart D. *Nomonhan, 1939: The Red Army's Victory that Shaped World War II*. US Naval Institute Press, 2012. Japanese translation by Yamaoka Yumi, with commentary by Asada Masafumi, *Nomonhan 1939—Dainiji sekai taisen no shirarezaru shiten* (Tokyo: Misuzu Shobo, 2013).

An analysis of the Nomonhan Incident, linking it to European international politics before the outbreak of World War II, and positioning it as a node closely interconnecting the War in Europe and the Pacific War.

Hata Ikuhiko. *Mei to an no Nomonhan senshi* [Brightness and Darkness: History of the Nomonhan Battle]. Kyoto: PHP Institute, 2014.

A comprehensive study of the fruits of the latest research from Japan and Russia. It pays special attention to the way maps were drawn when international borders were being determined between the Soviet Union and Japan, shedding new light on the nature of the Nomonhan Incident as a border conflict.

Hosoya Chihiro. *Ryotaisenkan no Nihon gaiko—1914–1945* [Japanese Diplomacy in the Two World Wars—1941 to 1945]. Tokyo: Iwanami Shoten, 1988.

Chapter 5, *Sangoku domei* (The Tripartite Alliance), and Chapter 6, *Nisso churitsu joyaku* (The Soviet-Japanese Neutrality Pact), are also included in *Taiheiyo senso e no michi* [The Path to the Pacific War] (Vol. 5). A superb treatment of Soviet-Japanese diplomatic history, especially given the restrictions placed on historical documents at the time it was written.

Miyake Masaki. *Sutaarin, Hitoraa to Nissodokui rengo koso* [Stalin, Hitler, and the Vision of a Federation among Japan, the Soviet Union, Germany, and Italy]. Tokyo: Asahi Shimbunsha, 2007.

A look at the Soviet-German proposal to add the Soviet Union to the Tripartite Alliance of Japan, Germany, and Italy, making it a quadripartite alliance. From the perspectives of Japanese and German history, the book carefully analyzes the historical circumstances underlying the plan and the possibility of its realization.

Miyake Masaki et al. eds. *Kensho: Taiheiyo senso to sono senryaku 2—Senso to gaiko, domei senryaku* [Verification: Pacific War and Its Strategy 2—The War and Diplomacy, Alliance Strategies]. Tokyo: Chuokoron Shinsha, 2013.

A collection of reports presented at the international forum on war history research held at the National Institute for Defense Studies (Japanese Ministry of Defense) in 2010. The book is useful for an understanding of various countries' military and diplomatic strategies in World War II, particularly those of the Axis countries. It contains an essay by Vassili Molodiakov on "Soren to sangoku gunji domei" [The Soviet Union and the Tripartite Military Alliance], among others.

Tanaka Katsuhiko. *Nomonhan senso—Mongoru to Manshukoku* [The Nomonhan War—Mongolia and Manchukuo]. Tokyo: Iwanami Shoten, 2009.

A restructuring of the Nomonhan War from the perspective of Mongolian history and pan-Mongolian research. Tanaka points out that the tribal border between the Khalkha Mongols and Barga Mongols transformed into an international border with the emergence of the Mongolian People's Republic and Manchukuo, explaining that the conversion of the tribal to an international border and the resulting conflict that emerged between the sundered tribes became the Nomonhan War.

Tanaka Katsuhiko et al. eds. *Haruha gawa, Nomonhan senso to kokusai kankei* [Khalkh River/Nomonhan War and International Relations]. Tokyo: Sangensha Publishers, 2013.

A collection of reports announced at the international symposia—held at Hitotsubashi University (Tokyo) in 2011 and at the Defense University of Mongolia (Ulaanbaatar) in 2012—on the theme of the Khalkh River/Nomonhan War. It contains several papers written from a variety of perspectives, including Japanese history, Soviet history and Mongolian history.

Terayama Kyosuke. *1930 nendai Soren no tai Mongoru seisaku—Manshu jihen kara Nomonhan e* [The Soviet Union's Policies toward Mongolia in the 1930s—From the Manchurian Incident to Nomonhan]. Sendai: Center for Northeast Asian Studies, Tohoku University, 2008.

A detailed research report on the history of Soviet-Mongolian relations in the 1930s. It reveals the strategic importance that Mongolia's position represented for the Soviet Union.

Tobe Ryoichi. *Gaimusho kakushinha* [Reformists in the Ministry of Foreign Affairs]. Tokyo: Chuokoron Shinsha, 2010.

Traces the trajectory of the reformists within Japan's Ministry of Foreign Affairs, who advocated the "Imperial Way of Diplomacy," centering on Shiratori Toshio, who promoted the tripartite alliance. It thus reveals the historical steps taken in the switch away from the argument regarding the Soviet Union as the main enemy toward the one advocating cooperation with that country in the creation of a new world order.

Slavinsky, Boris. *Pakt o neĭtralitete mezhdu SSSR i IAponieĭ, Diplomatič eskaâ istoriâ 1941–45gg*, English translation by Geoffrey Jukes, *The Japanese-Soviet Neutrality Pact: A diplomatic history, 1941–1945.* (Nissan Institute/RoutledgeCurzon Japanese Studies Series), Japanese translation by Takahashi Minoru and Ezawa Kazuhiro, *Kosho: Nisso churitsu joyaku—Kokai sareta Roshia gaimusho kimitsu bunsho* (Tokyo: Iwanami Shoten, 1996).

A study, written by a historian of Soviet diplomacy, that was one of the first to make use of primary historical materials from the Russian Ministry of Foreign Affairs Official Document Archives after the fall of the Soviet Union. It reveals the historical situation surrounding the Soviet-Japanese Neutrality Pact as viewed from the Soviet side.

Lecture 11

The Path to the Tripartite Alliance of Japan, Germany, and Italy

Takeda Tomoki

Initial Negotiations: From the Signing of the Anti-Comintern Pact to the Talks to Reinforce It

The Anti-Comintern Pact between Japan and Germany was signed in November 1936. Four people were instrumental in the pact's signing: Oshima Hiroshi, military attaché from the Imperial Japanese Army (posted to Germany), intelligence chief Wilhelm Canaris of the German Ministry of War, who was pursuing his own line of diplomatic policy, "Hitler's diplomat" Joachim von Ribbentrop, and German Ambassador to Japan Herbert von Dirksen. While countering the activities of international communism, the pact also was intended to check the Soviet Union militarily. It was colored deeply by the political intentions of Canaris, and it was none other than Oshima who dragged Japan into it (See Tajima Nobuo's *Nachizumu kyokuto senryaku—Nichidoku bokyo kyotei o meguru chohosen* [Nazism's Far East Strategy—The Intelligence War Surrounding the German-Japanese Anti-Communist Agreement], Kodansha, 1997; Miyake Masaki, "Daigosho Nichidoku bokyo kyotei to

Ambassador Oshima at work in the Japanese Embassy in Berlin, 1939 (Source: Carl Boyd, *Nusumareta joho* [Stolen Information], Hara Shobo, 1999)

sonogo" [Chapter 5. The Anti-Comintern Pact between Japan and Germany and the Aftermath] in *Kindai Yurashia gaikoron-shu* [Theories of Modern Eurasian Diplomacy], Chikura Shobo, 2015).

In November 1937, Italy joined the Anti-Comintern Pact as well. The negotiations to reinforce the cooperation among the three countries, based on the pact—the so-called negotiations to reinforce the Anti-Comintern Pact—can also be regarded as the first stage in talks to sign the Tripartite Pact among Germany, Italy, and Japan. The dealings among the three countries started at the beginning of 1938, shifted into full swing by July or so, and continued through sometime around August 1939.

The ideas of Adolf Hitler were influential at the beginning of the first stage of talks. Hitler had been fastening his gaze on expanding Germany's *Lebensraum* to the east, and was focused on weakening Britain's influence in the Far East while also strengthening cooperation with Japan, in the hope that it would aid in containing the Soviet Union. Because of that, Ribbentrop, German ambassador to the United Kingdom, started penning a memorandum to the *Führer* at the end of 1937 proposing closer relations between Germany and Japan. It was delivered to Oshima Hiroshi at the beginning of the following year, 1938. In February 1938, Ribbentrop became German foreign minister, thus laying down the necessary conditions for initiating full-scale negotiations toward an alliance between Germany and Japan.

Japan's Oshima was working in the background as well. Ever since

the Meiji Era (1868–1912), Japan had learned much from
Germany, with the Imperial
Japanese Army especially being full of pro-German supporters. One of the top
pro-German sympathizers
during the Showa Era, which
began in 1926, was Oshima,
who was influenced by his father Ken'ichi, said to have
been the main pro-German
supporter in Japan in both
the Meiji and Taisho Eras
(the latter extending from
1912 to 1926). That led the
younger Oshima both to ad-
mire and respect Germany.
His actions were faithful to
Germany's intentions; Germany itself was groping for
ways to defeat Britain and
expand its *Lebensraum* (See

Oshima Hiroshi shaking hands with Hitler. Rib-
bentrop stands in the center (Source: Carl
Boyd, *Nusumareta joho* [Stolen Information],
Japanese translation by Sakonjo Naotoshi,
Hara Shobo, 1999. Original title, *Hitler's Jap-
anese Confidant: General Oshima Hiroshi and
MAGIC Intelligence, 1941–1945*, University
Press of Kansas, 1993)

Suzuki Kenji, *Chudoku taishi Oshima Hiroshi* [Ambassador to Germany Oshima Hiroshi], Fuyo Shobo Shuppan, 1979).

However, the Japanese government was not in complete agreement
with Oshima's initiative at the outset of the talks. Particularly problematic was whether the new treaty would be targeted at countries other
than the Soviet Union. In other words, there was intense debate domestically whether the new treaty would embroil Japan in a war initiated by
Germany against third countries (i.e., Britain and the United States). On
account of the doubts directed at Oshima, Major General Kasahara
Yukio of the Imperial Japanese Army was dispatched to Germany in Au-

gust 1938, where he received Ribbentrop's private proposal, which he summarily took back to Japan. Japan was then finally able to produce its own proposal on August 26, 1938.

In October 1938, Oshima was promoted to Japanese ambassador to Germany and was given full responsibility over the activities taking place there. However, the communication gap between the actions of Japanese representatives in Germany and the home country failed to disappear. In particular, Minister of Foreign Affairs Arita Hachiro and Navy Minister Yonai Mitsumasa, among others, were wary about having to provide assistance to Germany in the form of military manpower, and were striving to avoid a treaty-based automatic obligation to enter war. Meanwhile, in November 1938, Shiratori Toshio, a diplomat in favor of the alliance, assumed the ambassadorship to Italy, joining forces with Oshima. In January 1939, the Konoe cabinet resigned en masse. The next cabinet was formed by Hiranuma Kiichiro, who retained Arita as foreign minister and Yonai as Navy minister, but intended to force out the ambassadors to Germany and Italy (i.e., Oshima and Shiratori). Debate about the issue thus raged on.

Germany then produced the Gauss proposal in May 1939, which was an attempt to pursue two-pronged negotiations, with the main body of the treaty text to be publicly released, and an exchange of notes (an administrative agreement) between the two governments that could be kept secret if so desired. The battle of words in Japan concerning this proposal was so intense that bitter memories remained long (For the detailed process, see *Showa-shi no tenno* [The Emperor in Showa History], Vol. 21, Yomiuri Shimbunsha, 1974; Takada Makiko, *Nihon no magarikado—Sangoku domei mondai to Yonai Mitsumasa* [Japan's Turning Point—The Problem of the Tripartite Alliance and Yonai Mitsumasa], Keiso Shobo, 1984; Kato Yoko, *Mosaku suru 1930 nendai— Nichibei kankei to rikugun chukenso* [The Groping 1930s—Japan-US Relations and Mid-level Officers of the Imperial Japanese Army], Yamakawa Shuppansha, 1993).

Anti-Communist Diplomacy and the Japanese Foreign Ministry

The mess that Japan's foreign diplomacy found itself in at this time has often been spoken of schematically in terms of the Imperial Japanese Army being the "bad guys" and the Foreign Ministry being the "good guys." What that representation tends to forget, however, is that the anti-Communist diplomacy that preceded the Tripartite Pact during the mid-1930s was being advanced primarily by mainstream members of the Foreign Ministry—Arita, Shigemitsu Mamoru, and others—with an eagerness similar to, and perhaps even stronger than, that of Oshima and the Army. Defensive diplomacy against Communism, which was also being promoted in Germany and Italy around the same period, was being applied widely within the logic that rejected the League of Nations in favor of expansionism: that is, the so-called logic that rejected the Versailles-Washington framework that had governed international affairs since the end of the World War I. Some of the major standard-bearers supporting that logic were the foreign ministries of both Germany and Italy. The same was happening in Japan as well. Starting in the early 1930s, the foreign ministries of the three countries used "anti-Communism" as a conduit through which they contacted with one another, and the roles that the foreign ministries served in building the relations of the three countries were not minor.

Still, the mainstream elements in the Japanese Foreign Ministry resisted removing Britain and France as the targets of the treaty, and avoided the use of force in the first round of negotiations. As far as that point is concerned, the perseverance of Foreign Minister Arita deserves particular notice.

However, there was a group within the mid-level of the Foreign Ministry known as the reformists. In his memoirs, Arita wrote that members of the secretariat class of the Foreign and Army Ministries, and probably that of the Navy Ministry as well, got together in May 1938 to begin exploring, in earnest, the strengthening of cooperation among Japan, Germany, and Italy. On July 30, though, reformist diplomats with connections to Shiratori made an appeal to Foreign Minister Ugaki Kazushige to take a harder line, saying that, "in the end, only war can thoroughly get rid of Britain and resolve the Soviet problem." There also seem to have been hardliners within the European & Asiatic Affairs Bureau of the Foreign Ministry. As of August 1938, Takagi Sokichi of the Imperial Japanese Navy stated:

> What is most regrettable to me is that the bunch of weak-kneed cowards in the European & Asiatic Affairs Bureau of the Foreign Ministry have gone overboard in favor of the hardline argument, saying that "while the Soviets will never rise up, that is precisely why it is diplomatically necessary at this juncture to deal them a blow," while tending to hesitate in carrying out active diplomatic efforts" (Harada Kumao, *Saionji-ko to seikyoku* [Prince Saionji and the Political Situation], referred to as *Harada nikki* [The Harada Diaries] Vol. 7, Iwanami Shoten, 1952).

On January 19, 1939, when the new Hiranuma cabinet drew up its basic policies for negotiating with Germany, Arita presented a compromise proposal saying that the Soviets ought to be targeted as the main country, while adding mention of "third countries," referring to Britain and France; whether or not to give military assistance aimed at such third countries, then, would depend on the situation. Arita made that proposal owing to pressure from such internal ministry forces.

In addition, the Japanese Ministry of Foreign Affairs was strongly conscious of the decline of Pax Britannica during the 1930s, which also had something to do with the discussions in Japan about the death of liberalism and capitalism. At the end of 1938, Shigemitsu, who was the last Japanese ambassador to the United Kingdom before the outbreak of war with the United States and Britain, wrote as follows:

[From now on,] the world that had revolved around Britain will go through a huge change, with the civilization of the future likely to be much different. Having gone through the last world war, the capitalist era—which rests upon the principle of individual freedom that emerged in the French Revolution— will likely become a thing of the past, just like the feudalistic culture that it itself had overturne" (Ito Takashi and Watanabe Yukio, eds., *Shigemitsu Mamoru shuki* [Memoirs of Shigemitsu Mamoru], Chuokoron-sha, 1986, p. 38).

In fact, Shigemitsu's ideas about the changing times were shared by the reformist diplomats of the time, who also rejected the Versailles-Washington framework of the 1920s.

The existence of Germany was impossible to ignore within that perception of the world situation. In a speech made in 1935, Shigemitsu argued that Japan should skillfully utilize the disturbances fomented by Germany in Europe to establish hegemony in Asia. Also, he said that the Anti-Comintern Pact with Germany was a product of the two countries' having sensed a "common interest" in the sense of their cautiousness about Communism even if their military strategies and policies toward Britain and the United States greatly differed (Shigemitsu Mamoru, *Showa no doran* [The Showa Upheavals], Chuokoron-sha, 1952, pp. 186–190).

In addition, even the "Nazi-hating" Togo Shigenori, who was far more pro-British and pro-American than Shigemitsu, said in the early 1930s that he believed that Japan should "take advantage of the takeover of government" by the "far-right party" in Germany, namely the Nazis, and "win Germany to our side" (Togo Shigenori, *Jidai no ichimen* [One Aspect of a Period], Hara Shobo, 1989, p. 89). Although they were opposed to a military alliance with Germany, their psychological state favored trying to use Germany diplomatically.

The Interests of Japan and Germany, and Their Strategic Conflict

To understand the complicated nature of the international situation in the 1930s, though, one must also pay attention to Germany's conduct of its diplomacy toward Asia, which put emphasis on relations with China as well. China, particularly since the time Sun Yatsen was in power (1912–25), had also wanted to actively establish a relationship with Germany. Around the time that the Northern Expedition by the Kuomintang was completed (1927), China and Germany began to step up their contacts with each other through the efforts of Colonel Max Hermann Bauer. Thereafter, the German military advisers to China who came after Bauer—namely, Georg Wetzell and Hans von Seeckt—were both directly and indirectly involved in operations to mop up the Communists in that country. At first, Germany's assistance to China came in the form of a private military advisory organization, but once Hitler seized power, its status was promoted to that of a semi-official military advisory group. However, the measures taken to turn China into the most important Asian partner of the Third Reich were the idea of the traditional German elite, and accordingly clashed with the ideas of Hitler and Nazi Germany, which emphasized drawing closer to the closely united, militaristic Japan of the 1930s (See Bernd Martin, "The Emergence of the 'Fascist' Alliance," *Japan and Germany in the Modern World*, Berghahn Books, 1995).

Also, even when the war between China and Japan did break out, the German advisory group, led by Alexander von Falkenhausen, the successor to Hans von Seeckt, participated on the side of China in its fight with Japan, a signatory of the Comintern Pact. Falkenhausen took part in China's strategic decisions from the start of the war with Japan. During the Sino-Japanese War, strangely enough, the Japanese thus found themselves engaging in battle at times with Chinese soldiers who were trained and being led by Germans, who in effect should have been persons allied with themselves. Japan, naturally, had to lodge grievances with Germany concerning such a situation (See William C. Kirby, *Germany and Republican China*, Stanford University Press, 1984).

In that fashion, Germany carried out its Asian diplomacy at the end of 1937 avoiding an either-or choice between Japan and China, trying to maintain a balance between those countries as the two deepened their conflict. Germany's pluralistic Asian policy thus ended up producing such unforeseen effects. However, once Ribbentrop became German foreign minister in February 1938, the plurality of its diplomacy came to an end, with its policy vis-à-vis Asia swiftly tilting toward Japan. Symbolic of that was Ribbentrop's recognition of Manchukuo, and the recall of Germany's ambassador to China, Oskar Trautmann, in the summer of the same year (See John P. Fox, *Germany and the Far Eastern Crisis, 1931–1938*, Clarendon Press, 1982).

Ribbentrop's hope, though, was not that Japan should be victorious in the Sino-Japanese War, but rather that it serve as a restraining force against Britain in the Far East. During the first stage of negotiations between Japan and Germany, Oshima and Shiratori continued acting in a way that can best be described as ignoring directives, and their dogged counsel to the home country was to make a decision that would abide by the will of Nazi Germany. The five-minister conference had decided to recall both ambassadors if they did not follow their instructions, and the Emperor made them package that decision as a signed memorandum. He did not make a secret of his irritation with the failure of the government to push that decision through, but the government was not so willing to easily share its strategies in China with Germany.

Germany and Italy, exasperated with Japan, concluded the Pact of Steel (the Pact of Friendship and Alliance between Germany and Italy) in May 1939. The pro-German faction in Japan showed its impatience about that, but three months later, on August 23, Germany signed the Nonaggression Pact with the Soviet Union, thus switching from an anti-Soviet to a pro-Soviet policy. That was enough to create doubt in Japan about Germany's attitude toward Britain. With the signing of the

German-Soviet Nonaggression Pact, the Hiranuma cabinet resigned en masse, having made the proclamation that everything in Europe was "messed up beyond all recognition." That meant writing off the first stage of negotiations between Japan and Germany, which themselves had undergone a similar process of getting "messed up." In September 1939, then, war broke out between Britain and Germany, eliminating the ground upon which agreement could be gained for Japan and Germany to move closer to one another, thus cutting off the path toward a tripartite alliance for a time.

The Great War in Europe and the Second Stage of Talks

However, negotiations between Japan and Germany were restarted in July 1940, in what became the second stage of talks. Their pace started to move ahead so quickly, in fact, that neither Japan nor Germany could make the proper adjustments. That was a tribute to the leadership of Matsuoka Yosuke, who had become the new foreign minister of Japan.

One characteristic of the second stage of talks between Germany and Japan was the coolness or indifference of the Germans in response to the active efforts being made by the Japanese government. Japan was entranced by the success of Germany's blitzkrieg actions from the spring of 1940 onward, and the majority of Japanese foresaw that Germany would defeat Britain sooner or later. Since Britain was becoming ravaged through its battles with Germany, approaching the point of collapse, it was natural for Germany not to feel such a great need anymore to form an alliance with Japan.

Nonetheless, after the announcement of the "Outline of Imperial Policy Following the Change in Circumstances," which affirmed the Imperial Japanese Army's demand for political solidarity with Germany and Italy—which was also a condition for the formation of the second Konoe cabinet—Matsuoka was not satisfied merely with leaving the situation at that. He independently forced the Foreign Ministry to prepare a proposal to conclude a military alliance with Germany and Italy against Britain. Based on that, he started to renew the exploration of a proposal with Germany in August 1940, entering into talks in September with German special envoy to Japan Heinrich Stahmer. Though both Shiratori and Oshima had returned to Japan around that time, Shiratori had his differences of opinion with Matsuoka, and neither he nor Oshima were involved in the negotiations anymore. That is how Matsuoka, without any knowledge of what had preceded in earlier negotiations, came to lead the second stage of talks with Germany.

The talks focused on two points: whether or not there would be an inclusion of an automatic obligation for treaty signatories to enter into a war directed at a treaty counterparty, and the possibility of avoiding war with the United States. However, a perusal of the actual text of the Tripartite Pact that was eventually settled upon forces one to conclude that much leeway had been left for a flexible interpretation of those two points.

The resolution of the first point—the automatic obligation to enter a war—was nothing short of muddled. Specifically speaking, the main body of the treaty text contained mention of the automatic obligation, while the protocol and the notes of exchange notes (i.e., the administrative agreement) both left room for an interpretation to be made that the decision to do so could be left up later to the signatory countries. Moreover, a directive had been sent from Berlin immediately before the signing of the pact demanding the insertion of a sentence indicating "military solidarity among the three countries" in the main body of the treaty text, and the deletion of the notes of exchange notes and the other documents. Although the negotiations appeared to be completely deadlocked, things took a sudden turn on the night of September 24, 1940, with Germany having yielded completely to Japan when it finally signed the treaty.

It has been said, furthermore, that the Berlin government did not learn of those last-minute concessions for quite a while. Probably there was some sort of "deception" played by special envoy Stahmer and Eugen Ott, German ambassador to Japan, so as to finalize the negotiations. Ott obtained testimony from Stahmer saying that "there wasn't any time to confer [with Ribbentrop] about the problem" (i.e., the exchanged notes). Also, Matsuoka was high-handed during the negotiations, backed by the fact that the notes of exchange notes were approved at the September 19 Imperial Council in Japan, and used it to justify Japan's demands in the negotiations. Ott said that he and Stahmer were "forced to yield" to Japan on account of that. Communications between Japan and Germany were insufficient indeed (See Hosoya Chihiro's Afterword to the Japanese version of *The Path to the Pacific War*, Vol. 5).

Various interpretations, meanwhile, can also be made concerning the second point mentioned above—the possibility of war with the United States. Still, several written records—notes penned by Matsuoka in August and later, transcripts of the talks with Stahmer, and records of the September 19 Imperial Council—make it clear that Matsuoka was well aware that the increasingly close relationship between Britain and the United States made it difficult for Germany to defeat Britain handily. Matsuoka also knew about the developing closeness between the Soviet Union on one hand and Britain and the United States on the other, making him project a prolonged war in Europe. One can conclude that he did not have such a rosy outlook of events as some people have attributed to him.

On the other hand, Matsuoka was also assertive at this juncture about pressing ahead with policies to implement a southward advance in Asia. According to research by Hattori Satoshi, Matsuoka was aware of the strong possibility of a war breaking out with the United States if Japan implemented the southward advance policy carelessly. For that reason, he believed that the Tripartite Pact would at least create the possibility of restraining Britain, which in turn could check the involvement of the United States. Moreover, he pursued a strategy that would also include the Soviet Union in the treaty, thus forming a quadripartite alliance, thinking that it would amplify the ability to restrain Britain and the United States. However, the core of Matsuoka's diplomacy was the

Tripartite Pact, and not so much the addition of the Soviet Union to it.

If that had been true, the continuity with Arita's idea—that is, avoiding the obligation to enter war while drawing closer to Germany—would have been more apparent, with it becoming clear that Matsuoka had nothing to do with pro-German sentiment. However, that does not signify, naturally, that Matsuoka had made the right judgment (See Hattori Satoshi, *Matsuoka gaiko* [Matsuoka Diplomacy], Chikura Shobo, 2012).

The Tripartite Pact as a Crossroads

On September 27, 1940, the Tripartite Pact among Japan, Germany, and Italy was finally signed in Berlin. It came to be remembered as a momentous day in Japanese diplomatic history, with the attendance of Kurusu Saburo, Japan's then-ambassador to Germany, along with Prime Minister Konoe Fumimaro and Foreign Minister Matsuoka Yosuke. Suma Yakichiro, who was the head of intelligence at the Japanese Ministry of Foreign Affairs at the time, spoke on the radio about how the day represented a historical turning point, not only for Japan, but for the whole world as well. There is little objection, even today, to the assertion that the Tripartite Pact was a crossroads in Japanese diplomacy. Here, we need to look at how this pact was so significant.

The most important point in terms of diplomatic history is the view that the Tripartite Pact was a crossroads in the context of starting the war between Japan and the United States. As has already been written, it is difficult to ascertain whether or not Japan was stipulated to have an automatic obligation to enter war in case Germany engaged in combat with a third country. Moreover, there has been a sharp difference of opinion, even from the beginning, over whether the pact was intended as a means to start war with Britain and the United States, or whether it was intended rather more for avoiding a war with them.

Just as Foreign Minister Arita had done during the first stage of negotiations (between Japan and Germany), Foreign Minister Matsuoka, responsible for handling the second stage, insisted that signing the pact

Matsuoka Yosuke (center) greeting the crowds in Berlin in March 1941, shown together with Hitler (left)

would not automatically require Japan to assist Germany in case that country got involved in a war. In addition, he also strove to prevent the treaty from triggering a war with the United States. However, debates about Matsuoka's diplomacy continue to rage. The points of contention include what specific arguments he used to try to avoid war, how effective such arguments were, and whether or not he was thinking of the plan to involve the Soviet Union in a quadripartite alliance, as mentioned in Lecture 10 (For Matsuoka's enthusiasms for the geopolitics in this process, see Christian W. Spang, "Karl Haushofer re-examined" in *Japanese-German Relations, 1895–1945*).

Still, it is not enough merely to consider the Tripartite Pact as the cut-and-dry result of Matsuoka's grandstanding behavior. As has been seen above, it was also a product of European politics of the 1930s, with its extreme vicissitudes. Moreover, it can also be described as being the outcome of the lineage of anti-communist diplomacy domestically in Japan.

Moreover, the pro-German sentiment of modern Japan is also believed to have been influential during the final stages of the talks. After the Anti-Comintern Pact between Japan and Germany was signed, Prince Saionji Kinmochi, the last surviving *genro*—an elder statesman from the Meiji Era (1868–1912) and considered one of the "founding fathers" of modern Japan—expressed his antipathy toward the pro-German line of thinking, saying,

Somehow, I feel that the Japanese-German Treaty (i.e., the Anti-Comintern Pact) has been utilized by Germany in all aspects, with Japan, if anything, having lost out considerably. Besides, generally speaking, the pro-German sentiment, having its stems in the Meiji oligarchy, and the current Japanese are trying to draw more closely to Britain and the United States." (*Harada nikki* [Harada Diaries], Vol. 5)

Nevertheless, the influence of the pro-German sentiment could even be seen within the Imperial Japanese Navy, which was regarded as a bastion of pro-British and pro-American sentiment.

Germany actually had an influence on the Japanese at quite an early stage, during the Meiji Era Exchanges had also taken place between the Japanese and German navies after World War I, and the Japanese Navy actively learned the latest submarine methods from Germany after the Washington Naval Conference (1921–22). Although Germany was also assertive in transferring technology to Japan, it was the "fleet faction" within the Japanese Navy that took the initiative in that, having bristled at the arms reductions that were imposed by the Washington Naval Treaty. Having lost World War I and being relegated to an abject status in the postwar period, Germany shared a mentality of resistance to the Versailles-Washington framework of international affairs that resonated with the Japanese Navy.

In addition, starting in the late 1930s, several Japanese who had been posted to Germany as military attachés, led by Nomura Naokuni and Kojima Hideo, and also including such men as Endo Yoshikazu, Yokoi Tadao, Kami Shigenori, and Shiba Katsuo, were assigned to the policy planning bureau of the First Section of the Naval General Staff, handling national policy, diplomacy, and the like. In his memoirs, Rear Admiral Inoue Shigeyoshi, who served as chief of the bureau of military affairs of the Navy Ministry, wrote, "The attitude toward the Tripartite Pact, held by everyone from section chief on downwards, was pro-German" (See Kudo Michihiro, *Nihon kaigun to Taiheiyo senso* [The Japanese Navy and the Pacific War], Vol. 2, Nansosha, 1982).

The Ironic Ramifications of the Tripartite Pact

It is impossible for such a huge decision as signing the Tripartite Pact to have ever followed a straightforward script, and that has left much room for various interpretations on the part of the historians who have come later. It is thus difficult to present a definitive version of what happened.

Moreover, the Tripartite Pact that was finally concluded was not even a solid military alliance. Representatives from Italy had to come to Berlin to find out Japan's intentions. With virtually no communication between Japan and Italy, even scholars of the German-Japanese relationship have no qualms in describing it as a "hollow alliance" (See J. M. Meskill, *Hitler and Japan: The Hollow Alliance*, Atherton Press, 1966), the policies of which were "oriented toward 'my old country' first, and characterized by endless friction, jealousy, mutual mistrust, and outright backstabbing" (See Theo Sommer, *Deutschland und Japan zwischen den Mächten, 1935–1940: vom Antikominternpakt zum Dreimächtepakt* [Germany and Japan, between the Powers, 1935–40: From the Anti-Comintern Pact to the Tripartite Pact], Tübingen, 1962; Japanese translation by Kanamori Shigenari, *Nachisu Doitsu to gunkoku Nihon—Bokyo kyotei kara sangoku domei made*, Jiji Press, 1964). Although the three countries did form an alliance, each of them ended up executing World War II independently. Recent research on the history of Japanese-German relations has only reaffirmed the deficiencies of the alliance and the intense strategic confrontations and mutual distrust that lay therein (See Christian W. Spang and Rolf-Harald Wippich, eds., *Japanese-German Relations, 1985–1945*, Routledge, 2006, pp. 13–14).

That being the case, then, perhaps one should say that the Tripartite Pact hardly functioned at all, except for the reality that its conclusion provided the jarring shock that served as the decisive turning point in the path that led eventually to Japan's war with Britain and the United States. Additionally, in December of the following year, 1941, it was Japan itself that ended up starting the war with those two countries. If so, why, in the end, had Japan been so obsessed with the tangled problems of "the automatic obligation to enter war" or "third-party countries" or "avoiding war with the United States"? Even more interestingly, recent study based on the diary of Chiang Kai-shek revealed that Japanese diplomatic gamble of the tripartite alliance prevented Chiang's diplomatic failure from happening (Lu Xijun, *Sho Kaiseki no "kokusaiteki kaiketsu" senryaku 1937–1941: "Sho Kaiseki nikki" kara miru Nitchusenso no shinso* [Chiang Kai-shek's Strategy for International Resolution 1937–1941: Looking into the Layers of Events during the Sino-Japanese War Written in the *Chiang Kai-shek Diaries*], Toho Shoten, to be published in 2016).

When studying the path that led toward the Tripartite Alliance, one must reflect upon the ironic consequences that ensued, as one investigates the history woven by the final decisions made under the leadership of Prime Minister Konoe and Foreign Minister Matsuoka, the complicated nature of international relations that existed in the background, and the varying perceptions and strategies toward foreign countries held by the various Japanese actors.

※   ※   ※

Recommended Readings for Deeper Understanding

The following works are regarded the classics in the study of this field: Taiheiyo Senso Gen'in Kenkyubu (Research Group on the Causes of the Pacific War), The Japan Association of International Relations (JAIR), ed. *Taiheiyo senso e no michi 5: Sangoku domei, Nisso churitsu joyaku* [Path to the Pacific War], Vol. 5: The Tripartite Pact and the Soviet-Japanese Neutrality Pact (Asahi Shimbunsha, 1963, revised version, 1987): Includes Obata Atsushiro, *Nichidoku bokyo kyotei—Do kyoka mondai 1935–1939* [Japanese-German Anti-Comintern Pact and the Issue of Its Reinforcement 1935–39], and Hosoya Chihiro, *Sangoku domei to Nisso churitsu joyaku 1939–1941* [The Tripartite Pact and the Soviet-Japanese Nonaggression Pact 1939–41]. Hosoya refers to the deceptions made at the last moments before the signing of the Tripartite Pact in the section entitled *Shinsoban e no tsuiki* [Postscript to the Newly Bound Version].

Miyake Masaki. *Nichidokui sangoku domei no kenkyu* [Studies of the Tripartite Pact among Japan, Germany, and Italy]. Tokyo: Nansosha, 1975.

Yoshii Hiroshi. *Zoho: Nichidokui sankoku domei to Nichibei kankei* [Enlarged and Revised Edition: The Tripartite Pact among Japan, Germany, and Italy, and US-Japanese Relations]. Tokyo: Nansosha, 1987.

These two scholars recently focused on Matsuoka's diplomacy between 1940 and 1941 in detail:

Hattori Satoshi. *Matsuoka gaiko* [Matsuoka Diplomacy]. Tokyo: Chikura Publishing, 2012.

This book propounds a new theory about the connection between the Tripartite Pact and the arguments made for avoiding the start of a war with Britain and the United States.

Mori Shigeki. "Matsuoka gaiko ni okeru taibei oyobi taiei-saku [Policies vis-à-vis Britain and America in Matsuoka's Diplomacy]," *The Japanese Society for Historical Studies*, No. 421, 1977; "Sujiku gaiko oyobi nanshin-seisaku to kaigun [Axis Diplomacy, and Southward Advance Policy and the Navy]," *The Historical Science Society of Japan*, No. 727, Tokyo: Aoki Shoten,1999; "Matsuoka gaiko to Nisso kokko chosei [Matsuoka Diplomacy and the Adjustment of Japanese-Soviet Relations]," *The Historical Science Society of Japan*, No. 801, 2005.

Mori's detailed individual case studies are also recommendable when it comes to Matsuoka's strategies in his ministerial period. As a treatise on the Imperial Japanese Navy, it is good to start with this book.

Aizawa Kiyoshi. *Kaigun no sentaku—Saiko: Shinjuwan e no michi* [The Choice of the Navy—A Reconsideration: The Road to Pearl Harbor]. Tokyo: Chuokoron Shinsha, 2002.

These two works are presenting research on the Japanese Ministry of Foreign Affairs:

Ishida Ken. *Nichidokui sangoku domei no kigen—Itaria, Nihon kara mita sujiku gaiko* [The Origins of the Tripartite Pact—Axis Diplomacy as Seen from Italy and Japan]. Tokyo: Kodansha, 2013.

Ishida's is one of the rare works discussing the Tripartite Pact from the perspectives of Italy and the diplomatic policy decision-making process. The second and third chapters are recommendable.

Tobe Ryoichi. *Gaimusho kakushinha* [Reformers in the Ministry of Foreign Affairs]. Tokyo: Chuokoron Shinsha, 2012.

A compilation of the author's many years of research on the reformist diplomats. It also contains thought-provoking insights into the Ministry of Foreign Affairs in the 1930s.

The following works deal with the Tripartite Pact and the relationship between Japan and Germany. They are tour de forces that expand the horizons of research on the history of Japanese diplomacy from the aspect of international relations.

Kudo Akira and Tajima Nobuo, eds. *Nichidoku kankei-shi, 1890–1945* [History of Japanese-German Relations, 1890–1945] in three volumes. Tokyo: University of Tokyo Press, 2008.

Miyake Masaki et al. *Kensho: Taiheiyo senso to sono senryaku 2—senso to gaiko, domei senryaku* [Validation: The Pacific War and Its Strategy 2—The War and Diplomacy, Alliance Strategy]. Tokyo: Chuokoron Shinsha, 2013.

*In addition, it should be noted as an aside that many related historical materials can also be found in the *Kokusai kensatsu-kyoku (IPS) jinmon chosho* [Interrogation Records of the International Prosecution Section (IPS)], *Nihon gaiko bunsho* [Documents on Japanese Foreign Policy], *Showa shakai keizai shiryo shusei* [Compilation of Social and Economic Documents of the Showa Era], *Showa-shi no tenno* [The Emperor in Showa History], and *Gendai-shi shiryo* [Materials of Contemporary History].

The New Konoe Order and Reform Bureaucrats

Makino Kuniaki

The Meaning of the New Konoe Order

In a narrow sense, the term "the new Konoe order," in the context of this lecture, refers to the system envisioned by supporters of Prime Minister Konoe Fumimaro, in his second cabinet formed in July 1940. In this system, Konoe and his supporters set various targets to be met in the latter part of the 1940s; these targets were realized to a certain extent. The Konoe order also refers to the movement (the so-called New Order movement) to realize such targets.

Konoe, who was popular among ordinary Japanese, had formed his first cabinet in June 1937. The Sino-Japanese War broke out immediately after he became prime minister. In the summer of 1938, the so-called reform bureaucrats, the Shakai Taishuto (Socialist Masses Party) and mid-level officers from the Imperial Japanese Army tried to create a one-party totalitarian state led by the "new Konoe party," in the fashion of the Nazis in Germany (or perhaps the Communist Party in the Soviet

Union, although that was not publicly declared). That effort failed, however, owing to the opposition of the Home Ministry and existing political parties, with Konoe being pushed out of office in January 1939. World War II broke out in September of the same year, though, and Germany carried out its blitzkrieg allowing it to occupy the bulk of Western Europe from April 1940 onward. In order to cope with such rapid changes in the international situation, a movement grew apace in Japan arguing the need to reform the domestic order. In June 1940, Konoe resigned his post as chairman of the Privy Council, declaring that he would stand at the vanguard of the New Order movement.

The term "new order" was applied to all sorts of spheres of activity at the time, with particular emphasis placed on creating a new political and economic order. The initial aim of the New Political Order was to create a party that would rule in the style of a one-party state and demonstrate strong political leadership. Meanwhile, the original goal of the New Economic Order was to implement a "separation of capital and management," under the principle of putting the public good first. The idea was that by removing those capitalists seeking private gain from corporate management, the corporations would be managed in a way that followed national policy.

Why, then, did the New Order movement pick up strength in 1940, aiming at a new political and economic order?

Historical Background of the New Order

Several factors are commonly cited as the background to the New Order movement: the bogging down of the Sino-Japanese War, Japan's experiences in Manchukuo, the influence of the Nazis, and the sympathy toward socialism on the part of the Imperial Japanese Army, Japanese bureaucrats, and intellectuals. Here, however, a consideration will be made of the background to the New Order—particularly the calls for a New Economic Order—from a slightly different perspective, using the fruits of research by Yamazaki Shiro.

While the Japanese economy swiftly recovered from the Showa Depression thanks to the reimposition of an embargo on gold exports, a big underlying factor was the expansion of government spending through the issue of bonds underwritten by the Bank of Japan. The increase in military expenditures incurred since the Manchurian Incident of 1931 and the establishment of Manchukuo both played a central role in that. Although the expansion in government spending was effective in stimulating the economy when companies were suffering from a low capacity utilization rate and unemployment was high, there was the risk of its setting off vicious inflation when good economic times returned. To clamp down on such government spending and restore the health of government finances, Takahashi Korekiyo, finance minister in the cabinet of Prime Minister Okada Keisuke, forcefully called for a suppress in military expenditures in the 1936 fiscal year budget, but he was met with fierce resistance from the Imperial Japanese Army. Moreover, several economic critics who agreed with the Army's position, including Takahashi Kamekichi and Yamazaki Seijun, also attacked the finance minister from the standpoint of the need to prioritize the expansion of productivity.

In the end, Takahashi Korekiyo was assassinated by a group of young army officers in the attempted coup d'état of February 26, 1936, and the new Hirota Koki cabinet that succeeded the Okada government approved substantial increases in the military budget, which caused governmental spending to expand even further. Since such spending, mainly for military spending, was continued even after the recovery, the economy came to be overheated, creating tightness in markets, which subsequently caused numerous problems that required policy responses in the form of governmental regulation (see chart).

The imposition of economic controls had become inevitable even before the outbreak of the Sino-Japanese War in 1937. The Cabinet Research Bureau, which had been set up in 1935 to enhance the ability of the Cabinet to formulate comprehensive policies, was first reorganized into the Planning Agency in April 1937, then merged into the Cabinet

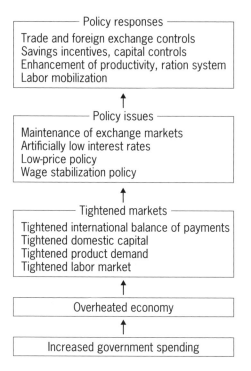

```
┌──────────── Policy responses ────────────┐
│ Trade and foreign exchange controls       │
│ Savings incentives, capital controls      │
│ Enhancement of productivity, ration system│
│ Labor mobilization                        │
└───────────────────────────────────────────┘
                      ↑
┌──────────────── Policy issues ────────────┐
│ Maintenance of exchange markets           │
│ Artificially low interest rates           │
│ Low-price policy                          │
│ Wage stabilization policy                 │
└───────────────────────────────────────────┘
                      ↑
┌─────────────── Tightened markets ─────────┐
│ Tightened international balance of payments│
│ Tightened domestic capital                │
│ Tightened product demand                  │
│ Tightened labor market                    │
└───────────────────────────────────────────┘
                      ↑
┌───────────────────────────────────────────┐
│            Overheated economy             │
└───────────────────────────────────────────┘
                      ↑
┌───────────────────────────────────────────┐
│       Increased government spending       │
└───────────────────────────────────────────┘
```

Developments after the February 26 Incident (Source: Yamazaki Shiro, *Shintei Nihon keizai-shi* [Newly Revised Japanese Economic History], Foundation for the Promotion of the Open University of Japan, 2003)

Resources Bureau in October of the same year to form the new Planning Board (Kikakuin).

To be able to carry out military expenditures in excess of the country's inherent economic strength, Japan had to introduce economic controls, as it was a "have-not" country dependent on the import of a wide variety of resources. One can say that the Sino-Japanese War only aggravated that situation, leading to calls for the establishment of a New Economic Order that would reform capitalistic principles altogether.

Moreover, the increased government spending, carried out primarily to cover military expenditures, created a sort of "bubble economy" that stimulated the motivation for consumers to spend, spurring the expansion of a consumer culture during this period in which ordinary people enjoyed spending their money on tourism, publications, music, and department store purchases. The spread of a consumer culture played a part in the full-mobilization efforts of the government, as people visited shrines associated with former emperors and imperial tombs around the country in the course of their sightseeing, consumed prodigious amounts of war-related reporting, lapped up popular war songs, and bought so-called comfort bags to be sent to soldiers at the front, among other activities. The various events that took place in conjunction with the Imperial 2,600th Year Celebration—held at about the same time as the 1940 New Order movement—were symbolic of the mobilization of the national populace through consumer culture.

The Reform Bureaucrats Make Their Appearance

The bureaucrats active during the period of the New Konoe Order are often referred to as the "reform bureaucrats (*kakushin kanryo*)," but there are various other definitions as well. This lecture will define the reform bureaucrats more narrowly, following the thinking of the scholars Furukawa Takahisa and Shimamoto Minoru, and restrict them to those bureaucrats who were involved in the controlled economy, paying special attention to "the group of bureaucrats in the Ministry of Commerce and Industry plus the Planning Board in 1940 who were involved in the proposal for the New Economic Order," consisting of Kishi Nobusuke, Shiina Etsusaburo, Minobe Yoji, Kashiwabara Hyotaro, Okumura Kiwao, Mori Hideoto, and Sakomizu Hisatsune, among others.

Various reasons have often been cited for the emergence of the reform bureaucrats during the period of the New Konoe Order, such as (1) the support by the military, (2) the structural conflict between Japan's military and political parties and the emergence of a cabinet "expert" organization, and (3) the influence of ideological singularities, Marxism and international socialism, on the reform bureaucrats. In addition to those factors, Shimamoto Minoru's theory—the formation of mutually complementary groups through the confluence of visions—will be introduced here.

Despite the narrow definition of the reform bureaucrats, each of them had disparate histories and orientations. For example, throughout the 1930s, the relatively senior Kishi Nobusuke (forty-four years old in 1940), a bureaucrat in the Ministry of Commerce and Industry who concurrently served as the deputy minister of industrial development in Manchukuo and deputy minister of the Manchurian Affairs Bureau, promoted the rationalization of domestic industries and carried out nationalization policies via business laws, also advancing the industrial development of Manchukuo. Okumura Kiwao of the Ministry of Communications had vociferously called for a shift from a free to a controlled economy during the debates in 1936 over a proposal to bring electricity under state control. Mori Hideoto of the Ministry of Finance advocated the pursuit of a controlled economy domestically after his personal experiences in Manchukuo, and also called for the formation of an East Asian community through the creation of national organizations. On the other hand, Minobe Yoji of the Ministry of Commerce and Industry and Sakomizu Hisatsune of the Ministry of Finance were pragmatic bureaucrats with almost none of the ideological leanings of Okumura and Mori, and both were involved with the practical details of state control of the economy. To implement the state control made necessary by the excessive government spending mentioned above, the pragmatists were responsible for a provisional special-measure law for exports and imports (Minobe) and a provisional financing law (Minobe and Sakomizu).

It was the meeting known as the *Getsuyokai* (Monday Group), which began in October 1939, that brought those bureaucrats and military men together, with their differing histories and orientations. The bureaucrats Kishi, Okumura, Mori, Minobe, Sakomizu and Shiina Etsusaburo were joined with army officers such as Muto Akira (Director of the Military Affairs Bureau of the Army Ministry), Iwakuro Hideo (Chief of Army Affairs Section in the Military Affairs Bureau) and Akinaga Tsukizo (Planning Board examiner). As far as such technocrats as Minobe and Sakomizu were concerned, the ideas of such men as Okumura and Mori provided justification for their state-control efforts, while such ideologues as Okumura and Mori required the administrative abilities of such men as Minobe and Sakomizu to realize their ideas. In addition, the personal network created between the ideologues and technocrats in that way was backed up by such leaders in the Ministry of Commerce and Industry as Kishi and Shiina, as well as such army officers as Muto.

Thanks to such networks, the reform bureaucrats emerged as a single group.

Despite the formation of such a strong network, nevertheless, the Cabinet, the Imperial Diet, and business circles were powerful as well. Had the latter's opinions differed from those of the reform bureaucrats, the bureaucrats would not have been able to put their ideas into action. However, in actuality, Japan's political parties, military, and business world were at odds with each other, and the new political order was being advocated precisely to overcome such differences. Amidst such circumstances, the reform bureaucrats, armed with both ideology and technical ability, rapidly rose to power with the backing of the military, effectively filling the power vacuum.

The Constitution of the Empire of Japan (the Meiji Constitution) had originally incorporated a system of the separation of power so as not to concentrate too much power in individual organizations or persons. For instance, even the status of the prime minister, despite his being the leading minister of state, was considered equal to that of other ministers. Supplementing the separation of powers was the *genro* system (of elderly statesmen who were considered the founding fathers of Meiji Japan), which rendered stability to domestic politics. However, with the successive deaths of the *genro*, the existing political parties lost the trust of the people on account of spreading corruption and internal squabbles. Meanwhile, the military, which was calling for intensified state control to realize the goal of constructing an "advanced military state," was in conflict with the political parties and the corporate world. Both of those developments contributed to the emergence of a power vacuum, with new prime ministers appearing one after another. The persistence of such a power vacuum was one factor for the deepening of the quagmire of the Sino-Japanese War, which worsened Japan's relations with Britain and the United States, driving the country further into international isolation.

And so, people started calling for the creation of a new political order—the creation of a one-party state system—that would be able to exhibit the powerful leadership that could break through that situation. With the launching of the New Order movement, the Shakai Taishuto (of the 1930s) was disbanded. The existing political parties also went so far as disbanding themselves so as to be able to seize the initiative within the New Order movement; eventually, almost all parties were to be disbanded in order to take part in the movement. The conditions were thus met to create a one-party state, formally speaking. In August 1940, Konoe Fumimaro presented a memorandum to Emperor Hirohito via Kido Koichi (Lord Keeper of the Privy Seal of Japan), which emphasized the strengthening of executive power for the purpose of exercising control over a free, unfettered economy "from the standpoint of the overall public good." To do that, the memorandum argued for the need to amend the constitution, or at least to make changes in the way it was administered. The new political order, in the end, aimed to revise the Constitution of the Empire of Japan.

At the same time that Konoe proclaimed the beginning of the New Order movement, the Planning Board initiated the drafting of various basic outlines that would establish its fundamental principles. Akinaga Tsukizo of the Planning Board assigned the drafting of the outlines for the establishment of a New Economic Order to Minobe, Sakomizu, Okumura, Mori and others. That put the reformist bureaucrats in the spotlight, with Mori, Minobe, Sakomizu, and Okumura described as the "Four Devas" (i.e., the big four) under the State Minister Suzuki Teiichi of the Planning Board, and Mori, Minobe, and Sakomizu labeled as the "Three Crows" (i.e., the trio) of the Planning Board. At a roundtable talk of the trio, joined by Kashiwbara Hyotaro of the Ministry of Railways, Mori said, "For the country to do things in a planned way," it had to have "a considerable management capability," and the bureaucrats fulfilling that role had to be "creative engineers," using the Nazi term "Führer" to describe them. The common perception held by those promoting the New Order at the time was that it was necessary to use Nazi-like leadership principles to get around the problems of the separation of powers.

However, the fact that almost all of Japan's political parties had disbanded in order to take part in the New Order movement backfired in the sense of virtually co-opting the existing order, making it difficult at first to construct a new political order based on a one-party state. Moreover, as the ideological right wing attacked the notion on the basis of national polity theory, saying that a one-party state meant to deprive the Emperor of authority, the Imperial Rule Assistance Association (Taisei Yokusankai) was launched in October 1940 not as a political party but as a national organization. Konoe, who became the organization's president, did not announce any platform or declaration but rather simply put forth a vague policy called *shindo jissen* ("the realization of the way of subjects," meaning that everyone should play his or her proper role in serving the country).

A Tangle of Ideals and Practical Demands

Meanwhile, there was intense debate in politics, business world, and journalism concerning the outline for the establishment of a New Economic Order, specifically the issues of separating capital and management, the reorganization of industrial associations, and the reorganization of small and medium-sized corporations. In particular, the issue of separating capital and management necessitated significant changes to the capitalist economy. The argument criticized the way that companies were managed through the pursuit of private gain, in which the owners of capital receive dividend payments. Instead, it advocated the "privately owned, state-run" method to carry out the production required by the state. The book *Nihon keizai no saihensei* [Restructuring the Japanese Economy] (Chuokoron-sha, December 1939), written by Ryu Shintaro, a member of the *Asahi Shimbun* editorial board and also active in the Showa Kenkyukai (Showa Research Association), set up as a think tank for Konoe, was considered the "general information manual" for the principles of the New Economic Order, and became a best-seller at the time. It described the argument for the separation of capital and management as the shift "from profit-oriented to production-oriented"

Konoe Fumimaro delivering an address at the inaugural ceremony for the Imperial Rule Assistance Association (Source: Cabinet Intelligence Bureau, *Shashin Shuho*, NO. 138, October 23, 1940)

management.

While the debate over the New Economic Order was heating up, the Corporation Accounting Controlling Ordinance, drafted primarily by Sakomizu, came into effect in October 1940. The ordinance defined the duty of corporations thus: "the first principle of management is to share the responsibility for the national economy for the fulfillment of national goals." It also decreed that the public good was to be given priority over private gain. Because of the philosophy of putting the public interest first, the ordinance stipulated that both the distribution of profits and salaries be kept at reasonable levels; if the total amount of dividends exceeded 8 percent of owned capital, or if the dividend rate exceeded that of the previous fiscal year, it was necessary to get permission from the competent minister.

The ordinance is said to have been a "perfect" law, without any loopholes, and served to further strengthen the cautionary feelings held by business interests toward the New Economic Order amidst the heated debate over it. The person who actually drew up the ordinance under Sakomizu was Shimomura Osamu, a secretary in the Financial Bureau of the Ministry of Finance, and who later played a big part in the income-doubling plan of Prime Minister Ikeda Hayato after the war. According to Shimomura, the ordinance was not so much designed for the purpose of realizing the principle of separating capital and management as it was to eventually control the total accounting of companies, so as to prevent loopholes from emerging as the various elements or factors affecting prices were on their way to being controlled. In the end, although economic controls were initiated, as mentioned previously, to respond to the various problems arising from excessive government spending, since they were unable to stem the fundamental cause of that spending—namely, the war and the increased military expenditures—more and more controls had to be imposed to keep prices down. It thus resulted in a situation where controls led to more controls, unassociated with any principles.

Arguments against the New Order from the Position of Protecting the Constitution

The New Order movement was met with strong opposition from three quarters: the ideological right wing, which viewed the Imperial Rule Assistance Association as a rejection of direct rule by the Emperor; from party politicians, who felt a sense of repulsion against the rejection of the role of the Diet; and from the business world, which regarded the argument for the separation of capital and management to be "red" (i.e., socialist), among other similar arguments.

One person particularly active at the time in opposition to the economic New Order was Yamamoto Katsuichi, a member of the National Spiritual Cultural Research Center of the Ministry of Education, who was working on "thought guidance" (*namely, a social and educational movement return to traditional Japanese spiritual values, away from such Western ideas as liberalism, individualism, Marxism, socialism, materialism, money-first thinking, etc.*). He had studied under Professor Kawakami Hajime, who was famous as Marxian economist, in the economics department of the Kyoto Imperial University, and adopted a position close to socialism at first. Later, though, while studying in France, he encountered the economic thinking of the physiocrats, who stressed the spontaneous discipline of the market. He also immersed himself in the socialist economic calculation controversy that was raging among Western economists at the time (which dealt with the possibilities of running a socialist planned economy), and came to emphasize market mechanisms through price fluctuations.

Between May and July 1940, Yamamoto, who had gained fame through his denunciations of Okumura Kiwao's plan for the state to control electricity, publicized his criticisms of Ryu Shintaro's *Restructuring the Japanese Economy*, saying that profits were a yardstick of management rationality, and that to suppress them would lead to an inefficient economy. His comments created significant repercussions as a theoretical condemnation of the New Economic Order. Kobayashi Ichizo, the founder of Hankyu Railways and the Minister of Commerce and Industry in the second Konoe cabinet at the time, was also strongly opposed to the New Economic Order, which put him in conflict with his deputy minister, Kishi Nobusuke. Yamamoto's arguments found wide acceptance as a theory with which to counter the New Order movement among such business leaders as Kobayashi, as well as such ideological rightists as Minoda Muneki and Mitsui Koshi, and such party politicians as Hatoyama Ichiro.

The opponents to the New Order attacked the New Economic Order and the Imperial Rule Assistance Association as being contrary to the Constitution of the Empire of Japan. Yamamoto said, "The market mechanism, which prices are determined according to concrete and practical transactions in the market, and, by which the direction of production is determined using prices as the basis of economic calculation, has run through the ages." He added that though "it [the market mechanism] was severely impeded during the final years of the Tokugawa Period (1603–1868)," it was the Meiji Restoration (of 1868) that "consciously revived it and put it on a firm footing again." As far as the New Order opponents were concerned, then, the Imperial Rule Assistance Association could be compared to the shogunate and invade national polity, and reinforcing economic controls was regarded as the abandonment of private property system (the reforms of national polity and private property were targeted by the regulations of the Maintenance of the Public Order Act). The opponents saw the New Order movement as a restoration of the feudalistic *ancien régime* (i.e., the old order) and a counterrevolution to extinguish the fruits of the Meiji Restoration. The opponents to the New Order were defenders of the Constitution of the time, aiming to uphold the Meiji Constitution, which was considered the fruit of the Meiji Restoration.

The End of the New Konoe Order and the Aftermath

Konoe Fumimaro, who was supposed to have been at the center of the New Order movement, instead started to waver in his convictions on account of the criticisms it was receiving. He eventually came to be extremely reluctant toward political and economic reforms. The passage about the separation of capital and management was struck from the guidelines for the establishment of a new economic order, decided upon by the Cabinet in December 1940, with recognition of "an appropriate level of corporate profit," causing the innovative tone of the early days to regress sharply. Meanwhile, the criticisms never let up saying that the Imperial Rule Assistance Association was anti-constitutional. The reorganization of that organization in April 1941 caused it to lose its politicized nature, turning it for all intents and purposes into an auxiliary association aiding the government's prosecution of the war—something far removed from its original intent of creating a new political order. What was left of the movement in the end was a framework for national mobilization, including various individual economic controls, as well as the Imperial Rule Assistance Association transformed into an auxiliary association cooperating with the government.

Between January and April 1941, several of the current and former investigators on the Planning Board who had been involved in drawing up the outline for the establishment of a New Economic Order—namely, Inaba Shuzo, Masaki Chifuyu, Wada Hiro'o, Katsumata Seiichi et al.—were arrested on charges of violating the Maintenance of the Public Order Act, in what is known as the Planning Board Incident (or the Senior Official Group Incident). Meanwhile, Okumura Kiwao left the Planning

Board when Tojo Hideki became prime minister and formed a cabinet in October 1941, becoming the deputy head of the Cabinet Intelligence Bureau. Serving thus as an ideologue during the prosecution of the Pacific War, he never returned to work on controlling the economy. Kishi Nobusuke, who became minister of commerce and industry in the Tojo cabinet, recalled Minobe Yoji from the Planning Board to his ministry, while Sakomizu Hisatsune returned to the Ministry of Finance in 1942 to work on economic controls during the war years. In November 1943, the Planning Board itself was abolished, with its functions integrated with the Ministry of Commerce and Industry and transferred to the Ministry of Munitions. When that happened, Mori Hideoto resigned as a bureaucrat. With all those moves, the network of the reform bureaucrats effectively disappeared.

However, in the cabinet of Admiral Suzuki Kantaro that formed in April 1945, Sakomizu, who was married to the daughter of Admiral Okada Keisuke, was recommended by his father-in-law to become chief secretary of the cabinet, and Akinaga Tsukizo assumed the director of the Cabinet Planning Bureau. Those appointments strongly alarmed Konoe Fumimaro as well as his entourage. Konoe lodged a complaint in the so-called "Konoe's Address to the Throne" to the Emperor, in which he wrote about a "reform movement plotted by a group within the military, and a movement by the so-called the reform bureaucrats taking advantage of that," as well as the threat of a Communist revolution on the part of "left-wing elements" who were manipulating those men from behind. In his diary entry of April 9, 1945, Hosokawa Morisada (Konoe's son-in law) wrote,

> As far as the creation of this cabinet is concerned, Admiral Okada is being controlled by the schemes of the reform bureaucrats, who have coincidentally united forces with the detached group led by Hiranuma Kiichiro to recommend Admiral Suzuki Kantaro. In this cabinet that has been swiftly realized, the reform bureaucrat group—namely, left-wing men from the Army—has fulfilled its

goal, with the Hiranuma group again getting robbed of its rightful share, [adding that] the Akinaga faction looks back and sticks out its "red tongue."

Hosokawa thus viewed the Suzuki cabinet as having been formed by such reform bureaucrats as Sakomizu and Akinaga, by having pushed Okada. Meanwhile, the Army, which was wary that the Suzuki cabinet might be a "cabinet to end the war," welcomed the presence of the ex-reform bureaucrat Sakomizu and cooperated in the formation of the cabinet. As a result, among the people originally involved in the New Konoe Order, it was Sakomizu and the other reform bureaucrats actually involved in its practical workings—rather than the leader of the movement, Konoe himself—who paved the way to ending the war.

The New Konoe Order as the Result of "Systematic Opportunism"

After the war, Sakomizu Hisatsune became critical of the controlled economy. In his memoirs interviewed later, he looked back on his time as the Finance Section chief in the Ministry of Finance, when he was labeled a reform bureaucrat, and said, "Controls are trying to play God. Needless to say, trying to play God is impossible, after all. I keenly felt that the controls were not something that humans could do well." Similarly, Shimomura Osamu, who was involved in the day-to-day workings of the controls under Sakomizu, also rejected the controlled economy after the war ended, arguing that the people's activities ought not to be controlled in accordance with a plan, but said rather that economic growth was possible only as a result of the creative power of the people being set free. Sakomizu, who served as the head of the Economic Planning Agency in the postwar Ikeda Hayato cabinet, argued for the possibility of the plan for doubling the national income using the theory of his former subordinate Shimomura.

The political scientist Maruyama Masao wrote that Sakomizu told him directly that he used to say the following words when he delivered his instructions to the new personnel entering the Ministry of Finance every year:

We officials must be systematic opportunists. We cannot just be plain opportunists, but also need to be capable at the same time of making plans. On the other hand, though, we have to be opportunistic in terms of their mental attitude as well, able to serve any sort of politics. That is why we must be opportunists and good planners at the same time.

One is reminded here of the words of Hashikawa Bunso, whose appraisal was that "Japanese fascism was not abnormal enough to merit the term 'fascism,' but was really nothing more than the abnormal wartime adaptation of modern Japan's traditional bureaucratic system." Indeed, the real situation of the New Konoe Order perhaps was that those bureaucrats known as reform bureaucrats, who bore the burden of the actual New Order, tried to justify their policies through their principles, while responding to reality as "systematic opportunists" as they put various controls into practice when mobilizing the national populace for war. Their opportunistic experiences, then, can be considered to have influenced the postwar policies that increased national income, by not restraining the private interests of the people but instead taking advantage of them.

* * *

Recommended Readings for Deeper Understanding

Furukawa Takahisa. *Showa senchuki no sogo kokusaku kikan* [Comprehensive Policy Organs in the Middle Showa War Period]. Tokyo: Yoshikawa Kobunkan, 1992.

    An analysis of the role played by the comprehensive policy organs during the middle period of the Showa Era war, primarily the Planning Board, taking a detailed look at the thoughts and actions of military men and reform bureaucrats.

Hashikawa Bunso. *Showa nashonarizumu no shoso* [Various Aspects of Showa Nationalism]. Edited by Tsutsui Kiyotada. Nagoya: University of Nagoya Press, 1994.

A collection of essays by Hashikawa Bunso, who focused his gaze on the reform bureaucrats at a relatively early stage. It contains many important treatises enabling one to understand Hashikawa's arguments about Japanese fascism.

Makino Kuniaki. *Senjika no keizaigakusha* [Economists during the War]. Tokyo: Chuokoron Shinsha, 2010.

An analysis of the thoughts and actions of Japanese economists during the Second World War, and their connection with the background of the times. The second chapter, in particular, takes a detailed look at the thoughts of Yamamoto Katsuichi, who was taken up in this lecture.

Makino Kuniaki, Kobori Satoru, and Yamakawa Yukie. *Araki Mitsutaro monjo kaisetsu mokuroku* [Catalog and Outline of Araki Mitsutaro Papers]. Nagoya: Economic Research Center Library, School of Economics, Nagoya University, 2014. (http://www.nul.nagoya-u.ac.jp/erc/collection/araki.pdf)

A catalog and outline of the papers formerly in the possession of Araki Mitsutaro (1894–1951), an economist who served as professor in the economic department of the Tokyo Imperial University, and which are now stored at Nagoya University. The documents include many invaluable resources for an understanding of the actions of the pragmatists among the reform bureaucrats, such as materials from the Institute of World Economy (Sekai Keizai Chosakai), the establishment of which Minobe Yoji and Sakomizu Hisatsune played a big part in, as well as materials from the National Economic Resources Institute (Kokka Shiryoku Kenkyujo), the establishment of which Sakomizu Hisatsune was also involved in.

Maruyama Masao. *Chokokkashugi no ronri to shinri, hoka hachihen* [The Logic and Psychology of Ultranationalism and Eight Other Essays]. Edited by Furuya Jun. Tokyo: Iwanami Shoten, 2015.

Contains many important essays of Maruyama Masao, such as the classic essay on Japanese nationalism research, "Chokokkashugi no ronri to shinri [The Logic and Psychology of Ultranationalism]." His conversations directly with Sakomizu apparently left a big impression on Maruyama, as they appear twice in the book (p. 196 and p. 453).

Minagawa Masaki. *Konoe shintaisei no shiso to seiji—Jiyushugi koku-fuku no jidai* [Ideology and Politics of the New Konoe Order—The Age of Conquering Liberalism]. Tokyo: Yushisha, 2009.

An analysis of the thoughts of the political scientist Yabe Teiji and the constitutional scholar Kuroda Satoru, clarifying why they were connected to the New Konoe Order.

Ruoff, Kenneth. *Imperial Japan at Its Zenith: The Wartime Celebration of the Empire's 2,600th Anniversary*. Ithaca, New York: Cornell University Press, 2010; Japanese translation by Kimura Takehisa, *Kigen 2,600 nen— Shohi to kanko no nashonarizumu*, Tokyo: Asahi Shimbunsha, 2010.

An analysis of the mutual interaction of the pursuit of recreation by the people, the pursuit of profit by railway companies, department stores, and the like, and the attempts of the government to stir up nationalism, in the context of the various events celebrating the 2,600th anniversary of the founding of the Japanese imperial dynasty, held in 1940.

Shimamoto Minoru. "Kakushin kanryo no taito—Koso no goryu ni yoru sog-ohokanteki shudan no seiritsu" [The Rise of the Reform Bureaucrats—The Formation of Mutually Complementary Groups through the Confluence of Visions], *Hitotsubashi Business Review*, Vol. 45, No. 4. Tokyo: Toyo Keizai, 1998.

Uses organization theory to position the reform bureaucrats as a "mid-level group that swiftly rose by threading its way through the existing order during a period of upheavals," elucidating both the process of its rise and its ending.

Shiozaki Hiroaki. *Kokunai shintaisei o motomete—Ryotaisengo ni wataru kakushin undo, ideorogi no kiseki* [Seeking a New Domestic Order—Trajectory of the New Order Movement and Ideology after the Two World Wars]. Fukuoka: Kyushu University Press, 1998.

An analysis of how the orientation toward "reform" by the cooperativist movement and state-control bureaucrats in the Ministry of War as well as economic commentators such as Takahashi Kamekichi, came to be linked to the New Order movement.

Yamazaki Shiro. *Busshi doin keikaku to kyoeiken koso no keisei* [The Material Mobilization Plan and the Formation of the Co-Prosperity Sphere Idea]. Tokyo: Nihon Keizai Hyouronsha, 2012.

A detailed analysis, in chronological order (explicated by fiscal year), of the Resources Mobilization Plan, the plan that was implemented by the Planning Board during the Sino-Japanese War aiming at the prioritized allocation of resources to the munitions industry through materials mobilization and state economic control. It takes the intriguing perspective that the New Economic Order movement was an extension of international movements, including industrial rationalization efforts, which aimed to carry out "the rational reorganization of industries and corporations by thoroughly eliminating non-military 'waste.'"

Lecture 13

From the US-Japan Negotiations to the Outbreak of War

Moriyama Atsushi

The Beginning of Negotiations between Japan and the United States

After the expiration of the Treaty of Commerce and Navigation between Japan and the United States on January 26, 1940, it was possible for the United States to impose economic sanctions on Japan at any time. Japan considered the repair of its relations with the United States as an issue of utmost urgency, given that most of the important resources it needed were imported from that country. However, not only did the United States impose controls on the exports to Japan of such important materials as petroleum, scrap iron, and steel in July 1940, but it also embargoed all exports of aviation gasoline (87 octane and above) in August, as well as scrap iron in September. With Japan concluding the Tripartite Pact with Germany and Italy, its conflict with the United States deepened even further.

It was under such circumstances that negotiations were initiated between Japan and the United States to seek an improvement of relations between the two countries. As they ended up failing and leading to war, both sides have come to view them in a very bad light, as each could only regard them as a conspiracy attempt by the other side to cover up its intent to begin war. The initiation of private diplomacy—which began when Bishop James E. Walsh and Father James M. Drought of the Catholic Foreign Mission (Maryknoll) Society were approached by Ikawa (Wikawa) Tadao, director of the Central Union of Co-operative Societies in Japan—only served to spur that trend on. Even after the war, Kase Shun'ichi, who was the head of the United States Section of the Japanese Ministry of Foreign Affairs when the war began, was consistently critical of the "amateur diplomacy" conducted by Nomura Kichisaburo, Japan's Ambassador to the United States at the time, and Ikawa. It was Shiozaki Hiroaki who, in 1984, raised questions about that trend, pointing out that both Japan and the United States had the incentive, when negotiations started, for bargaining to take place. He thereby opened the way for a new dimension to be added to studies of the history of Japan-US negotiations, which had theretofore been seen in terms of the "victor-loser" paradigm of the history of the bilateral relationship. Since then, no new work of diplomatic history has come out rewriting the general outline of the US-Japan negotiations since 1986, when Sudo Shinji's *Nichibei kaisen gaiko no kenkyu* [Research on the Diplomacy of the Outbreak of War between Japan and the United States] (Keio Tsushin, 1986) was published.

Let us survey the beginning of the negotiations, specifically the draft of a mutual understanding plan between Japan and the United States of April 16, 1941. Although the plan was intended as a springboard for future discussions, Nomura misled the ministry officials back in Japan through his communication manners. Namely, he failed to inform them of the preconditions—that were impossible for the Japanese side to accept—set out in the Outline of Proposed Basis for Agreement Between the United States and Japan, known as "the Hull (US Secretary of State Cordell Hull) four principles" therein were: (1) the territorial integrity and the inviolability of the sovereignty of all nations, (2) nonintervention in internal affairs, (3) equal opportunity of trade, and (4) no alteration to the status quo in the Pacific except for peaceful means. The Japanese government had misread the draft of the mutual understanding plan, believing it to be the actual proposal of the United States, and was wild with joy about the favorable conditions it presented, such as the formal recognition of Manchukuo by the United States, American efforts to counsel Chiang Kai-shek to resolve the Sino-Japanese War, and cooperation by the US government in Japan's acquisition of resources in southeastern Asia.

However, Foreign Minister Matsuoka Yosuke, carrying the Soviet-Japanese Neutrality Pact (signed in Moscow on April 13, 1941) with him on his way back to Japan, was more intent on conducting power diplomacy with the United States. Immediately after returning home, he sulked with talking about the "misdirected" draft of the mutual understanding plan, and went on to sabotage the negotiations with the United States. Japan finally got around to sending its counterproposal on May 12, which was a revision of the draft in a way that rendered the contents even more advantageous for Japan. Nomura, who feared that the negotiations would not succeed, failed to convey the entirety of that proposal to the American side, throwing the negotiations further into disarray. The United States position was made clear in its unofficial proposal of May 31 and the official proposal of June 21, but the desperate Nomura, out of his desire to wrap up the negotiations, failed to relay all of them back to Japan. Even after Japan received the full text of the actual American proposal, the appended oral statement containing negative language towards Matsuoka made the negotiations even more entangled. Right after that, though, on June 22, Germany invaded the Soviet Union, suddenly changing everything.

Outbreak of Ruuso-German War, and Japan's Debate between the "Northern Advance" and "Southern Advance" Positions

The initiation of war between Germany and the Soviet Union undermined the power balance that had underlain the US-Japanese negotiations. If Germany's power were to be absorbed by the Soviet Union, there was no need for the United States to rush into compromising with Japan. On the other hand, if the Soviet Union were to be collapsed by Germany, the power of the Axis countries would grow even more enormous. The United States thus gradually started to shift away from a position of compromising with Japan and toward a hardline policy.

On June 5, Germany notified Japan about its upcoming attack of the Soviet Union through Japanese Ambassador to Germany Oshima Hiroshi. Japan saw that as a golden opportunity, inciting proponents of the argument, primarily within the Imperial Japanese Army, for the advance to the north (i.e., a Japanese attack on the Soviet Union). The General Staff Office of the Army was the main backer of that argument, pressing the Ministry of the Army to mobilize troops, but the ministry was conflicted about whether to be cautious or to go ahead and attack the Soviet Union, with staff holding both positions. More than anything, the reluctance was also related to the policy of advancing to the south, which Japan had been working on since the end of 1940. Japan had attempted to mediate the border conflict between Thailand and French Indochina, thereby trying to enhance its influence on both sides. Both the Japanese Army and Navy wanted to take advantage of that situation and form a military alliance with Thailand and French Indochina, contemplating the acquisition of bases. However, Matsuoka did not put that idea into action, feeling that a southern advance policy would be meaningless without also including a plan to attack Singapore, and asked both the Army and Navy whether they were really ready for war with Britain. Both the Army and Navy had been trying to reconcile their differences about the southern advance policy since the previous year, and were beginning to settle on the position of not treating Britain and the United States separately, as advocated by the Navy. Matsuoka speculated that both the Army and Navy were not up to fighting a war with both Britain and the United States, and continued to fudge the matter.

On account of the unwillingness of French Indochina to extend resources to Japan, as well as the rupture of Japanese-Dutch negotiations, and the sense of oppression stemming from encirclement of Japan by the British-US camp, the Japanese Army and Navy attempted to strengthen relations with the area, even if with just southern French Indochina and Thailand. They thus conveyed their willingness to enter into war with Britain and the United States to Matsuoka, putting the "Acceleration of the Policy Concerning the South" up for a vote at the Liaison Conference between the government and the Imperial General Headquarters on June 25, 1941.

The confirmed report from Ambassador Oshima about the opening of hostilities between Germany and the Soviet Union, cited earlier, complicated the tug-of-war between the Army and Navy, on one side, and Matsuoka, on the other. A new "national policy" was being drawn up simultaneously with the aforementioned southern policy, with the "guidelines for imperial national policy associated with developments in the situation" being determined by the Imperial Council (the council in the presence of the Emperor) on July 2. The "national policy" thus adopted as Japan's policy for the immediate future was the resolution of the Sino-Japanese War and "preparations for forces in both the north and south." The national policy thereby included both arguments, making preparations along both directions: advancing from the south for self-sufficiency and self-defense, and entering into war with the Soviet Union in the north in case the opportunity presented itself. While it was theatrically declared on paper that Japan was "willing to enter war with Britain and the United States," the emphasis through and through was placed on the preparations.

During the process of deliberations, however, Matsuoka insisted on halting the occupation of southern French Indochina and attacking the Soviet Union, sowing confusion in the Liaison Council. The situation was such that even the other non-military officials on the Council, including President of the Privy Council Hara Yoshimichi, were advocating attacking the Soviet Union.

In other words, amidst the battle between the northern advance and southern advance positions, it was tentatively decided upon to occupy southern French Indochina. Japan thus was considering a southern advance only to the extent that it would not lead to a decisive conflict with Britain and the United States.

Despite the inclusion of both arguments—that is, both the northern and southern advances—the reality is that once a national policy gets spelled out explicitly, that fact in itself lends authority to executing such a policy. The supporters of the argument to attack the Soviet Union, primarily the Imperial Japanese Army General Staff Office, used preparations for a war with that country as a pretext for pressing Army Minister Tojo Hideki to mobilize troops. It was decided on July 5 to muster an additional 500,000 troops, in the so-called Kwantung Army Special Maneuvers. The army planned to attack the Soviets by year-end if the Far Eastern Soviet Army pulled out part of their forces by the first part of August. The reduction in Soviet troop strength did not occur as the General Staff Office had anticipated, though, so on August 9, it abandoned its plan of using force by the end of the year, instead moving the focus to the following spring.

In the end, the northern advance argument did not see the light of day, with the state of neutrality between Japan and the Soviet Union continuing to operate until right before Japan's defeat in August 1945, when the Soviet Union unilaterally abrogated the Neutrality Pact. For that reason, traditional historical studies have tended to overlook the influence of that argument on Japan's foreign policy. However, the Soviet Union remained the main enemy as far as the Imperial Japanese Army was concerned, even during the period that the war with the United States was intensifying. The Army only shifted its main target from the

Soviet Union to the United States starting in September 1943, or shortly less than two years since the beginning of hostilities with the United States (Tobe Ryoichi, *Gyakusetsu no guntai* [The Paradoxical Military], Chuokoron-sha, 1998). At that time, the Kwantung Army boasted its largest size ever.

The Imperial Japanese Navy, meanwhile, was extremely alarmed about being pulled toward the north. In comparison with the re-source-rich territories of the south, there were hardly any resources in the north (the oil fields in northern Sakhalin being insufficient to meet the needs of Japan). Invading Siberia would only end up dissipating Ja-pan's national strength. The Navy thus continued restraining the Army's argument of attacking the Soviet Union after the onset of hostilities with the United States.

The Occupation of Southern French Indochina and the Total Embargo on Japan

The turning point that heavily pushed Japan toward war with the United States was the imposition of a total embargo on Japan by the United States, Britain, and the Netherlands. For Japan, which relied almost to-tally on imports for its petroleum, a total embargo meant the complete cutoff of that substance. Naturally, Japan had stocked up oil reserves for emergencies, but it only had enough for two years in peacetime and a year and a half in wartime. The idea thus came to the fore, primarily among the Supreme Command and mid-level officers in the military, of attacking the Dutch East Indies, an oil-producing region at the time, be-fore reserves ran out.

Japan did not think that occupying French Indochina would elicit fierce opposition from Britain and the United States. In "Nihon no taibei kaisen" ["The Outbreak of Japan's War with the United States"] in *Tai-heiyo senso e no michi 7* [The Path toward the Pacific War 7], Tsunoda Jun pointed out that the mid-level officers in the Japanese Navy had ad-vocated Japan's occupation of southern French Indochina so as to in-

243

duce the country into hostilities with the United States. However, Moriyama Atsushi (1998) has described that as being a prime example of *a posteriori* reasoning.

In contrast to the suppositions of the Japanese side, the United States, once it found out about the occupation of southern French Indochina, quickly explored steps to counter it. On July 26, 1941, it launched a freeze of all Japanese assets in the United States. Still, people had already pointed out in the United States that such a total embargo would cause Japan to use military force. For that reason, the US government explained that it was not a total asset freeze per se, but that frozen funds would be released every time it became necessary to settle accounts. On August 1, the United States announced an embargo on the export of petroleum. In addition to an embargo on petroleum exceeding the amount consumed before the Sino-Japanese War, there would also be an embargo on lubricating oil and aviation-use gasoline. Although that meant that Japan's import of other substances should have been possible theoretically, it became a total embargo in the end because the United States did not indicate how payments should be made.

Why did the freezing of assets transform into a total embargo? There has been controversy over that issue ever since immediately after the war, and the controversy has continued to the present day (Arakawa Ken'ichi, "Tainichi zenmen kin'yu kettei no kozo," *Boei Daigakko Kiyo: Shakai Kagaku Bunsatsu* ["Structure of the Decision to Impose a Total Embargo on Japan," *Bulletin of the National Defense Academy: Social Science Volume*, Vol. 72, 1996]). Some argue that the embargo was the firm will of US President Franklin D. Roosevelt, while others say it was pressured by public opinion, although some point out that Roosevelt and Secretary of State Cordell Hull were not aware until September 1941 that the freezing of assets had become a total embargo (Jonathan G. Utley, *Going to War with Japan, 1937–1941*, Fordham University Press, 1985. Japanese translation, *America no tainichi senryaku*, Asahi Press, 1989). With the American decision-making process still wrapped in a "black box" even today, it surely would have been exceedingly difficult at the time to predict a total embargo.

Japanese Prime Minister Konoe Fumimaro was perplexed by the hardline policy of the United States. (He had just reshuffled the cabinet to form the Third Konoe cabinet on July 18, 1941, after the mass resignation of the cabinet, which was done in order to remove Foreign Minister Matsuoka from office, whose presence was one of the factors interfering with the promotion of negotiations with the United States.) He thus announced his idea of holding a US-Japan summit to meet directly with President Roosevelt and attempt to break through the situation. If an agreement were reached at such a summit, Konoe's plan was to immediately ask the Emperor for approval. This was a cunning scheme that would avoid any meddling by the Army. Roosevelt initially expressed enthusiasm about the idea, raising hopes on the Japanese side.

Amidst the complicated situation, with expectations for a breakthrough in the negotiations mixed with anxiety about them breaking off, the Imperial Council held on September 6, 1941 adopted an Outline of the Pursuit of Imperial Policy, saying that war would be launched with the United States if there was no prospect for successful diplomatic negotiations by the first part of October. Emperor Hirohito, however, expressed displeasure with the decision to set a deadline on the negotiations. On the previous day (September 5), he had pressed Chief of the General Staff Sugiyama Gen hard about the overoptimistic expectations regarding the war, and he broke tradition at the September 6 Imperial Council by actually asking a question. Moreover, the Emperor read out loud a *tanka* composed by his grandfather, Emperor Meiji, thus pressing the Supreme Command about its intentions. Hirohito was suspicious that the Supreme Command had ignored prospects for successful negotiations so as to force hostilities to begin. In response to his attitude, both the government and the Supreme Command declared that they were undertaking negotiations in all seriousness. However, it was eventually up to the United States whether the diplomatic negotiations would succeed. The conditions put forward by Japan in the aforementioned Outline of the Pursuit of Imperial Policy were in no way acceptable to the United States.

On the American side, the summit was vociferously opposed by such anti-Japanese hardliners as Stanley K. Hornbeck, chief of the State Department Division of Far Eastern Affairs. Secretary of State Hull was also negative toward any procedure that would let diplomatic matters be decided over his head. The United States was thus inclined toward working out the details with Japan before any meeting between the two sides took place. That put Konoe in a quandary, as he had preferred to bring the negotiations to a successful conclusion by making certain concessions at the negotiating table without revealing any intentions beforehand. Japan thus had no choice but to present the United States with a deliberately ambiguous proposal regarding the withdrawal of its troops from China, hoping to materialize the summit that way. The United States, on the other hand, sent its response to Japan on October 2, in which it demanded definite concessions, adding that it would reject the holding of a summit were the conditions to remain vague. Konoe then was able to put together a concession proposal, having obtained the backing of Foreign Minister Toyoda Teijiro, Naval Minister Oikawa Koshiro, and others. However, Army Minister Tojo was adamantly against the proposal. On October 16, Konoe abandoned the cabinet (i.e., resigned as prime minister). It was assumed that Prince Higashikuni Naruhiko would succeed him, but having a cabinet led by an imperial prince start a war and lose it would compromise the position of the Emperor. The proposal to select Higashikuni was therefore shelved, with Army Minister Tojo given the Imperial command to form the next cabinet.

The Tojo Cabinet and US-Japan Negotiations

Normally one would think that entrusting the formation of a cabinet to the very person—Tojo—who had forced the Third Konoe cabinet to collapse because of his opposition to the withdrawal of troops from China would be an indication of the orientation toward war. However, even if

the US-Japan negotia-
tions had hypothetical-
ly succeeded, they
would have ended up
meaning nothing had
Japan's withdrawal
from China not en-
sued. The only person
who had the power to
make that happen was
Tojo, the current Army
minister at the time.
Such a calculation was
behind the decision to
give him the Imperial

Japanese Ambassador to the United States Nomura
Kichisaburo (left) and Extraordinary Ambassador Kurusu Saburo at the White House on November 17,
1941 (November 18 Japan time), after meeting President Roosevelt (center)

command to form a cabinet. In addition, the Emperor had handed down
another command to "start over from scratch," rendering the decision of
the September Imperial Council invalid. That meant that he ordered a
reconsideration of national policy that was detached from all that had
transpired so far. Though Tojo immediately launched the policy reconsideration, the problem was that the Emperor's command to "start over
from scratch" only applied to the government, and his influence was not
forced upon the Supreme Command. In the end, the Supreme Command
did not change its conclusions one bit. The Imperial Japanese Army
General Staff Office insisted that negotiations with the United States be
broken off and the decision be made to immediately launch war.

After about a week of work on the reconsideration, the options were
narrowed down to three choices: (1) suffer unspeakable hardships and
privations, or avoiding war (2) deciding to launch war immediately, and
(3) pursuing war preparations and diplomatic negotiations simultaneously, then launching war if nothing resulted. At the Liaison Conference
(between the government and the Imperial General Headquarters) on
November 1, 1941, intense debate continued for more than 16 hours,

lasting until the wee hours of the morning. The Imperial Japanese Navy, which had been one of the major advocates of avoiding war in the previous cabinet, changed its position to one of approval under the new Naval Minister Shimada Shigetaro. Suzuki Teiichi, leader of the Planning Board, also changed his position, saying that a prolonged war could be pursued from the aspect of securing resources. Foreign Minister Togo Shigenori and Minister of Finance Kaya Okinori both opposed the war, but were unable to overturn arguments supporting to start a war. The Liaison Conference eventually concluded that diplomatic negotiations would first be attempted, with war with the United States to be started if they failed. It thus took a giant step toward launching the war.

The negotiations were carried out with a contingency position: Plan A (the comprehensive proposal), which included broader concessions than those made by the previous cabinet, and Plan B (the barter proposal, involving the withdrawal of troops from southern French Indochina in exchange for the reopening of trade). Both plans, however, contained elements that would be unacceptable to the United States, so there was little possibility of them succeeding. Also, given that Foreign Minister Togo reprimanded Ambassadors Nomura and Kurusu, who had arbitrarily presented a plan to the United States that was more concessionary than Plan B, and because of his hardline attitude during the deliberations of Plan A (he retracted the approval of Secretary of State Cordell Hull's four principles made by the previous Foreign Minister Toyoda), the assessment of Togo by most historians has been strict (Sudo 1986, Yoshida Yutaka and Mori Shigeki, *Ajia-Taiheiyo senso* [Asia-Pacific War], Yoshikawa Kobunkan, 2007, etc.). In response to that, Moriyama (2009) has repositioned Togo's diplomacy at the beginning of the war from a new perspective, so the question is still open.

The Note from Secretary of State Cordell Hull

On November 26, the United States delivered an informal proposal to the Japanese side: a note from Secretary of State Cordell Hull (called in

Japan the Hull Note, but known by that name only since the war ended). It took a very hard line, presenting four principles, the withdrawal of Japanese troops from China and French Indochina (including police forces), the repudiation of any Chinese government except that of Chiang Kai-shek, and the de-facto repeal of the Tripartite Pact. While Japan had indicated its readiness to make some sort of compromise through its Plans A and B, the American side all of a sudden slapped down new conditions at the last minute. The Hull Note dashed to smithereens any hope that the Japanese side still held about the negotiations with the United States. The extent of the shock can be appreciated by the fact that Foreign Minister Togo, who had been considering resignation in case war started, changed his mind and stayed in his post, charging headlong into war. Also symbolic of the depth of the Hull Note's intolerance is how the British ambassador to Japan at the time, Robert Craigie—reputed as one of the most knowledgeable diplomats in Japanese affairs—wrote later in his recollections that he knew that war was inevitable the moment he learned about the details of the note.

For the faction supporting the start of a war, the Hull Note was almost a blessing, for it made it possible for the nation to unite and face war with the United States. What motivation, then, did the United States have in passing along the Hull Note? Details on how the note was composed have been presented in Sudo's research (1986) and in his later work *Haru noto o kaita otoko* [The Men Who Wrote the Hull Note] (Bungeishunju, 1999). As a matter of fact, Hull is known to have drafted a provisional agreement proposal and sought compromise with Japan until immediately before the actual Hull Note was delivered. Neither Britain nor the United States had finished preparations for war yet, so it was advantageous for them to avoid the crisis that was near at hand (they knew that Japan's Plans A and B were its final proposals on account of their having broken Japanese codes). For that reason, the United States was considering a provisional agreement proposal that if Japan pulled its army out of southern French Indochina, the United States would lift the freeze on Japanese assets and start supplying it

249

with a certain amount of goods (It would be valid for three months). The plan was to hand that proposal to Japan along with the Hull Note, and its contents were shown to the ambassadors and envoys of Britain, China, Australia, and the Netherlands. As far as what was actually written is concerned, the proposal differed somewhat from Plan B, but researchers are still divided over whether or not handing the provisional agreement proposal to Japan would have prevented it from directly launching war on the United States.

In reality, just one day before the Hull Note was delivered, Secretary of State Hull abruptly abandoned the idea of offering Japan the provisional agreement proposal together, meaning that it was only the Hull Note that reached the Japanese. Various theories have been developed on why that happened. In his memoirs, Hull himself wrote that he was tired of the uncooperative attitude of the countries involved, but there is some question about the credibility of those memoirs, which were written after the war, so further examination of the issue is necessary. Countless other factors have also been cited, including (1) the opposition to the proposal by China and Britain, (2) the erroneous report sent by US Secretary of War Henry Stimson saying that Japan was sending huge numbers of troops southward, and (3) Hull's displeasure that China had leaked the contents of the proposal to the press. The first factor is rather unlikely, considering the fact that the United States did not attach so much weight to China's opposition. Also, Britain was not so clearly opposed to the proposal (it got a shock later when it learned that the proposal had been scrapped). Meanwhile, given that both the second and third factors mentioned above are simply circumstantial evidence, they cannot really be described as the "clinching argument" in Hull's decision. Historians will likely continue to debate this matter. In any case, it is definite that the United States had given up on using the negotiations to avoid war, and instead took the option of letting Japan initiate hostilities against it.

The Pearl Harbor Conspiracy Theory and the Code Wars

The Pearl Harbor conspiracy theory holds that President Roosevelt did nothing to prevent Japan from attacking Pearl Harbor although he had gotten wind of it beforehand, in order to use the "back door" of Asia to fight the war in Europe. It had always been dubious that the operation against Pearl Harbor would ever succeed, even during advance map exercises, as it required attack forces to be advanced sneakily toward Hawaii, without being discovered by anybody. In actuality, though, the attack ended up inflicting devastating damage on most of the battleships of the US Pacific Fleet. The attack on Pearl Harbor had been considered impossible in the first place, and was only able to achieve the miraculous success it did because the United States had been focusing its gaze on Southeast Asia instead. However, the conspiracy theory interprets Japan's string of good luck as having been thought up by someone else. The theory, mainly advocated by revisionists, mostly of the Republican Party persuasion, has been repeatedly professed on countless occasions almost since the day the war ended. Still, historical materials have yet to be presented that substantiate it directly. Even so, the reality is that there are still parties on both sides of the Pacific who are convinced that there was some sort of conspiracy.

Naturally, it is true that not just Roosevelt, but also other leaders in the upper echelons of the US government, wanted to "maneuver [Japan] into the position of firing the first shot" (Stimson's diary entry of November 25, 1941, in *Gendaishi shiryo 34: Taiheiyo senso 1* [Contemporary History Materials 34: Pacific War 1], Misuzu Shobo, 1968). However, just because something a person wishes for becomes reality does not mean that that person is the culprit—the two are quite separate matters.

One set of historical materials used as grounds for the plot conspiracy is Japan's diplomatic cables that were deciphered by the United States (Operation Magic). According to that view, the United States was

251

aware that Japan was about to launch hostilities, and also knew that Japan was spying on the movements of the US Pacific Fleet. However, Japan was carrying out intelligence activities against all areas targeted for attack, and the intelligence related to Pearl Harbor was likely lost among the "noise" (Roberta Wohlstetter, *Pearl Harbor: Warning and Decision*, Stanford University Press, 1962. Japanese translation, *Paru Haba*, Yomiuri Shimbunsha, 1987). The Japanese Ministry of Foreign Affairs had not been informed about the attack on Pearl Harbor, so there is no way that the words "Pearl Harbor attack" would have appeared in diplomatic cables in the first place.

At the time, azimuth (direction) detection technology (i.e., monitoring radio signals emitted from ships so as to estimate the position of the transmission source) had already been put to practical use and was widely known. That is why the Japanese carrier battle group maintained strict radio silence and traveled toward Hawaii along northerly shipping routes where there was scant ship traffic. In addition, Japan had embarked on a massive radio deception campaign in the waters around the country in order to obfuscate the carrier battle group's true whereabouts. John Toland, in his book *Infamy: Pearl Harbor and Its Aftermath* (Doubleday, 1982. Japanese translation, *Shinjuwan kogeki*, by Bungeishunju, 1982), cites the lately discovered historical records as the basis of his argument that the United States knew about the position of Japanese taskforce. But, that records (which mentioned that Japanese taskforce was moving southeast from the Marshall Islands) didn't prove their true position and direction.

Also, Robert Stinnett, in his book *Day of Deceit: The Truth About FDR and Pearl Harbor* (Free Press, 2001. Japanese translation, *Shinjuwan no shinjitsu—Ruzuberuto giman no hibi*, Bungeishunju, 2001), presents an argument claiming that the task force had broken its radio silence and was releasing signals, and that the United States had deciphered Japanese Navy coded telegrams even before the war started. As the grounds for those statements are unclear as well, one can only say that his argument falls apart. Thinking about it commonsensically, had the US Pacific Fleet set sail from Pearl Harbor right before the attack, it would not have suffered any damage, and still the United States would be able to take the high road in entering the war (Hata Ikuhiko, *Sutineto 'Giman no hi' no giman* [The Deceit of Stinnett's Day of Deceit] in Hata Ikuhiko, ed., *Kensho: Shinjuwan no nazo to shinjitsu* [Verification: The Riddle and Truth of Pearl Harbor], PHP Institute, 2001).

Sudo (2004) presents a convincing argument concerning this problem. However, as it is impossible to prove that the conspiracy "did not exist," the conspiracy theory will likely be repeatedly bandied about in the future, eventually withering away with time.

* * *

Recommended Readings for Deeper Understanding

Research Group into the Causes of the Pacific War, The Japan Association of International Relations, ed. *Taiheiyo senso e no michi* [The Path toward the Pacific War] Volume 6 *Nanpo shinshutsu* [The Southern Advance]; Volume 7 *Nichibei kaisen* [The Start of the War between Japan and the United States]. Tokyo: Asahi Shimbunsha, 1963.

Volumes 6 and 7 of the *Taiheiyo senso e no michi* [The Path toward the Pacific War] series, the first postwar compilation of primary historical resources. In particular, Volume 7, *Nichibei kaisen* [The Start of the War between Japan and the United States], written by Tsunoda Jun, emphasized the pro-war reasoning on the part of the Navy, which had previously been seen as the "good guys" (i.e., in opposition to the war), affecting those related to the affair who were still living at the time. It was a conspiratorial argument—which had a great impact on later research—that posited that the mid-level naval officers who formed the core of the First Navy National Defense Policy Committee had already decided to launch war against the United States as of June 1941, and pushed for the stationing of troops in southern French Indochina to induce Japan to initiate hostilities against the United States. The problem was that most of the data related to the private (unreleased) historical materials used by Tsunoda were not written down, making them impossible to verify. That failing was largely rectified in the newly bound version published in 1987, but many materials remained private even at that stage.

War History Room, The National Institute for Defense Studies, Japan De-
fense Agency. *Senshi sosho: Daihon'ei rikugunbu daitoa senso kaisen keii*
[War History Series: Sequence of Events Leading to the Start of the Great
East Asia War by the Army Department of the Imperial Headquarters]
Vols. 1–5. Tokyo: Asagumo Shimbunsha, 1973–74.

A compilation drawing upon numerous unpublished and/or private historical materials and testimony. It sheds light on many facts, and demands
perusal. However, one needs to be aware of the fact that the authors are
former members of the Imperial Japanese Army, and therefore are biased to
a certain extent. It is regrettable that many sources are private even today,
and much of the testimony was not set down in writing, meaning that both
are unverifiable.

Miwa Munehiro. *Taiheiyo senso to sekiyu—Senryaku busshi no gunji to
keizai* [The Pacific War and Petroleum—The Military and Economy of Strategic Resources]. Tokyo: Nihon Keizai Hyouronsha, 2006.

Empirically clarifies the sequence of events, both during the war and
after the war, in the petroleum issue that became a factor in the war between Japan and the United States.

Moriyama Atsushi. *Nichibei senso no seiji katei* [The Political Process of
the US-Japan War]. Tokyo: Yoshikawa Kobunkan, 1998.

A work that meticulously verifies, to the fullest extent possible, the policy-making process during the war, making liberal use of newly discovered
materials related to people in the Japanese Imperial Navy, as well as public
historical materials available in the War History Department of what was
then the Japan Defense Agency, among other materials. Keeping its distance
from interpretations tinged with conspiratorial theory and not assigning
blame, it analyzes the special features of the complicated policy-decision
system of the period, using both the "inclusion of both arguments" (i.e., both
the northern and southern advances) concept passed down from Yoshizawa
Minami and developing it further, while adding the new "evasion of decision-making" concept as well.

Moriyama Atsushi. "Kaisen gaiko to Togo gaisho—Otsu-an o meguru kobo"
[Togo Shigenori and His Modus Vivendi] in *Higashi Ajia Kindaishi* [Mod-
ern East Asian History], No. 12. Tokyo: Yumani Shobo, 2009.

An article that takes a look at the diplomacy toward the United States by Foreign Minister Togo Shigenori—which has not traditionally been held in high regard—and reexamines it from the perspective of his reinforcing the control over diplomacy. He points out the possibility that Togo may have engaged in elaborate planning aiming at successfully concluding the negotiations via Plan B.

Moriyama Atsushi. *Nihon wa naze kaisen ni fumikitta ka: "Ryoron heiki" to "hikettei"* [Why Did Japan Decide to Enter the War with the United States?: "Interests of All Sides" and "Evasion of Decision-making"]. Tokyo: Shinchosha, 2012.
    A restructuring of the fruits of Moriyama's two previous works (1998 and 2009) into a book of general interest, more specifically tracing the process that led to the start of the war. He includes new findings, such as reflecting why deadline diplomacy was adopted in November 1941 over the policy of "going through thick and thin to attain one's objective" (or enduring unspeakable hardships for the sake of vengeance, i.e., avoiding war), as well as how Nomura and Kurusu, even after having been reprimanded by Togo, continued trying to reach a compromise by altering Plan B.

Shiozaki Hiroaki. *Nichieibei senso no kiro* [The Crossroads of Japan's War with Britain and the United States]. Tokyo: Yamakawa Shuppansha, 1984.
    Written by Shiozaki, who edited *Ikawa Tadao Nichibei kosho shiryo* [Historical Materials on Ikawa (Wikawa) Tadao and the Japan-US Negotiations] (Tokyo: Yamakawa Shuppansha, 1982) with Ito Takashi, verifying that there was support by both the Japanese and American governments of the persons engaged in the private diplomacy. He proposes the repositioning of the Japan-US negotiations from within international relations.

Sudo Shinji. *Shinjuwan 'kishu' ronso* [Controversy over the Pearl Harbor 'Sneak Attack']. Tokyo: Kodansha, 2004.
    Demonstrates empirically that none of the numerous Pearl Harbor conspiracy theories—which the world is overflowing with—hold water. Though the military section contains several mistakes, the book is a valuable analysis from the position of diplomatic history.

Yoshizawa Minami. *Senso kakudai no kozu—Nihongun no Futsuin shinchu* [Outline of the War's Expansion: The Occupation of French Indochina by the Japanese Military]. Tokyo: Aoki Shoten, 1986.

Explores Japan's policy decision-making process surrounding the question of stationing of troops in French Indochina, looking at it from a standpoint of questioning the war responsibility of Emperor Hirohito, and proposing a concept of "maintaining order by advancing both arguments" (i.e., the northern and southern advances). The book broke new ground by rephrasing the responsibility argument, which tends to fall down the slippery slope of addressing the question of "why" the war started (and assigning blame), into the question of "how" it started.

Lecture 14

Emperor Hirohito's "Sacred Decisions" and the Political Process of Japan's Surrender

Suzuki Tamon

The Role of the Imperial Conferences

Timeline of major events leading up to the end of the war in 1945

June 8	An imperial conference determines the general policy for the upcoming decisive homeland battle.
June 22	The decision to initiate diplomatic talks with the Soviet Union is made at an unofficial imperial conference.
July 27	The Potsdam Declaration is received.
August 6	An atomic bomb is dropped on Hiroshima.
August 9 (midnight)	The Soviet Union enters the war against Japan.
August 9	An atomic bomb is dropped on Nagasaki.
August 10 (12:03 a.m.)	The first imperial conference discusses the Potsdam Declaration *"with the understanding that the said declaration does not comprise any de-*

	mand which prejudices the prerogatives of His Majesty as a sovereign ruler."
August 14	The second imperial conference decides to accept the Allied reply.
August 15 (noon)	A recorded radio broadcast by Emperor Hirohito announces the acceptance of the Potsdam Declaration and the end of the war.

Looking at the above timeline, one is struck by three things: the close timing of the atomic bombs and the Soviet entry, the key role played by the imperial conferences, and the markedly short time in which Japan decided to end its long war.

First, the dropping of the atomic bombings was closely followed by the Soviet entry into the war against Japan, making it difficult to determine the effect of each event on the surrender. Debate still rages as to whether it was the atomic bombs or the Soviet entry that brought about the end of the war. (Asada Sadao, *Genbaku toka no shogeki to kofuku no kettei* [The Shock of the Dropping of the Atomic Bomb and the Decision to Surrender] in Hosoya Chihiro, Iriye Akira, Goto Ken'ichi, and Hatano Sumio, eds., *Taiheiyo senso no shuketsu* [The Close of the Pacific War], Kashiwa Shobo Publishing, 1997). Advocates for the atomic bomb factor argue that the bomb was necessary for avoiding the high casualties of a mainland invasion, while those arguing for the Soviet factor maintain that use of the bomb was unnecessary.

Second, the timeline reveals the clear role played by the imperial conferences (meetings held in the presence of the emperor) in bringing about Japan's decision to surrender. Two such meetings were held to consider surrender, and both times the emperor made decisions that directly affected the political situation thereafter. Given the influence of these decisions, there remains considerable controversy as to why they did not come earlier. Those who view the emperor's decisions as successful praise his political leadership during that time, while those who see the decisions as delayed refer to the blame he should bear.

The third and final point is one that has often been overlooked in analyses of the surrender: Japan's decision to accept the Potsdam Declaration occurred in the remarkably short span of just one week beginning on August 9.

Research in recent years has become increasingly compartmentalized, with new studies analyzing the changing policies of the emperor and the Imperial Japanese Army and Navy at the end of the war. In keeping with the stated purpose of this edited volume, this lecture seeks to introduce to a general audience new directions in research regarding Emperor Hirohito while offering a detailed chronological survey of his role in Japan's decision to surrender. In doing so, it will make use of the *Showa Tenno jitsuroku* [Emperor Showa's Annals], the 12,000-page, 61-volume official biography of Emperor Hirohito made public in 2014. For a detailed, academic study of the full context of Japan's decision to surrender, see Suzuki Tamon, *"Shusen" no seiji-shi 1943–1945* [Japan's Long Road to Surrender: 1943–1945] (University of Tokyo Press, 2011).

Japan's Homeland Defense Strategy and Emperor Hirohito's Anxiety

According to *Showa Tenno dokuhakuroku* [Emperor Hirohito's "Monologue"], there were two reasons for Hirohito's decision to surrender. The first was the possibility of the destruction of the Japanese people resulting from a decisive homeland battle. The second was the possibility that the *kokutai* (Japan's national polity, which includes a ruling emperor) could not be preserved in the event that the legitimizing symbols of the imperial office, the *sanshu no jingi* (the three sacred treasures: the mirror, sword, and jewel), could not be protected.

It is said that on April 7, 1945, Suzuki Kantaro, who just become prime minister that day, was watching the cherry blossoms fall when he suddenly remembered the fall of Rome. Suzuki's long-held belief was that "the entry of the military into the political sphere is the start of the ruin of a country." (Henceforth, all quotes, unless otherwise noted, come

259

from Ministry of Foreign Affairs, ed., *Shusen Shiroku* [Historical Records of the End of the War] (Government Agency Materials Editorial Association, 1996); Eto Jun, general editor, Kurihara Ken, and Hatano Sumio, eds., *Shusen kosaku no kiroku* [Record of Plans to End the War], Vols. 1 & 2 (Kodansha, 1986); Suzuki Tamon, *"Shusen" no seiji-shi 1943–1945* [Japan's Long Road to Surrender: 1943–1945] (University of Tokyo Press, 2011); Suzuki Tamon, "Showa Tenno to Nihon no 'shusen'" [Emperor Showa and Japan's War Termination] in Kitaoka Shin'ichi, ed., *Kokusai kankyo no hen'yo to seigun kankei* [Changes in the International Environment and the Relationship between the Government and the Military] (Chuokoron Shinsha, 2013)).

Indeed, major changes were in store for Japan. Exactly one month later, Germany surrendered on May 7, and US President Harry Truman exhorted Japan to follow. In response, a top-level conference of the "Big Six" (the prime minister, foreign minister, army minister, navy minister, army chief of staff, and navy chief of staff) was convened. While surrender was not discussed, a radical revision of the policy toward the Soviet Union was debated.

The decisive homeland battle was authorized on June 8, 1945, when the imperial conference redefined the objectives of the war, to "upholding the *kokutai* and protecting the imperial lands (i.e., Japan)." Under this new and radically defined rubric, war aims could be successfully achieved merely by preserving Japan's national polity and its territories.

Around this time, Japan was beginning to run out of the oil it so badly needed to sustain the war. The country's supply of aviation-grade gasoline was predicted to last only until September 1945, meaning that Japan could continue its operations until autumn at the very latest. According to the war plans revealed at the June imperial conference, battles for Kyushu and Shikoku were predicted to occur around July and August, with a fight for the Kanto Plain—the seat of the Japanese government—taking place in the early autumn or later. (It was revealed after the war, however, that the US military had been planning to invade Kyushu on November 1.)

On June 13, Emperor Hirohito learned that the naval garrison on Okinawa had fallen. On the same day, he was also informed that plans were being made to move the Imperial General Headquarters to underground tunnels in the town of Matsushiro in Nagano Prefecture. It was perhaps not so much the existence of the Matsushiro Imperial General Headquarters but rather the rapidity of the move there that shocked the emperor at this time. As is well known, the emperor was reluctant to move on account that it might cause anxiety among the Japanese people, particularly those residing in Tokyo.

The next day, Emperor Hirohito recommended that his mother, the Empress Dowager Sadako (posthumously known as Teimei), be evacuated to the small town of Karuizawa, also in Nagano Prefecture. Probably due to extreme stress stemming from these developments, the emperor himself became ill around this time, stricken with repeated bouts of diarrhea and vomiting.

Emperor Hirohito's conditions for surrender are said to have loosened from around this time, as he came to believe that Japan would lose the battle on the mainland. As if to substantiate his view, he also received reports of the poor readiness of the Japanese military from Army Chief of Staff Umezu Yoshijiro and Special Naval Inspector Admiral Hasegawa Kiyoshi. A report about preparations for the Kanto Plain was delayed, which further concerned the emperor.

On June 22, 1945, the emperor called an informal conference at which he suggested that diplomacy be pursued in conjunction with war. At that time, the Soviet-Japanese Neutrality Pact was still in place, and the Suzuki cabinet proposed to the Soviet Union on July 13 that it act as a mediator for peace. Japan's diplomatic overtures proved too late, however, as the Soviets had already agreed to enter the war against Japan. Outwardly, the Soviet Union maintained a noncommittal face toward Japan, using the Potsdam Conference as an excuse for delaying its response.

On July 31, 1945, Emperor Hirohito and Kido Koichi, Lord Keeper of the Privy Seal, met to discuss the transfer of the three sacred treasures.

According to the *Showa Tenno jitsuroku* [The Annals of the Showa Emperor], the plan was to move the sword to the Hida Ichinomiya Minashi Shrine in Takayama City, Gifu Prefecture. The emperor is reported to have said at this time, "Should the worst occur, I shall guard them myself and share their fate." Meanwhile, the US military was expected to make its landing in Japan at any time. August 20 was soon chosen as the date for the evacuation of the empress dowager to Karuizawa (Otabe Yuji, *Shoken kotaigo, Teimei kogo* [Empress Dowager Shoken, Empress Teimei], Minerva Shobo, 2010).

In contrast, the date of the planned move of the Imperial General Headquarters to Matsushiro is unclear. According to the memoirs of Lieutenant Colonel Kobayashi Shinaji, deputy aide-de-camp of the army minister, the plan was to begin transporting items in mid-July and to have the emperor himself make the move after mid-August, but that move was postponed right before it was to take place (Yomiuri Shimbunsha, ed., *Showa-shi no tenno* [The Emperor in Showa History], Vol. 3, Yomiuri Shimbunsha, 1968). Judging from the sequence of events described above, there is a high likelihood that the date of the move to Matsushiro was postponed in conjunction with the start of talks with the Soviet Union on July 13.

"Mokusatsu" and the Potsdam Declaration

On July 26, 1945, Great Britain, the United States, and China released the Potsdam Declaration calling for "unconditional surrender of all the Japanese armed forces." However, whether the declaration also meant the unconditional surrender of the Japanese government is subject to debate even today. For example, some within the Japanese Ministry of Foreign Affairs wondered whether conditions for the surrender of the Japanese government were in fact being proposed, since the Potsdam Declaration also listed conditions such as: "points in Japanese territory ... shall be occupied to secure the achievement of the basic objectives," with "the Japanese military forces ... completely disarmed," and "stern justice . . . meted out to all war criminals."

To Japan, one of the most noteworthy aspects of the Potsdam Declaration was that the Soviet Union had not signed it, a development that was expected to mean that Russia would continue to remain legally neutral. The second item of interest was the fact that it contained no reference to the imperial system, which very much concerned Japan's leading officials. The Americans were in a strong position, having already successfully made the first A-bomb test on July 16, 1945. Some hypothesize that the Potsdam Declaration was premised upon the dropping of the atomic bomb on Japan, but the relationship between the two factors is uncertain at best.

At a press conference held at 4:00 p.m. on July 28, 1945, Prime Minister Suzuki is said reported to have said, "The Government attributed no significant value to it [the Potsdam Declaration]. We will simply *mokusatsu suru* (variously translated as "ignore," "reject," or "kill with silence"). Whether he in fact made such statements, however, is unclear. Recent studies indicate that newspaper reports preceding the conference published on the morning of the same day already stated that "the government will '*mokusatsu*' [the Potsdam Declaration] (*seifu wa mokusatsu suru*)." It is possible that these reports may have been influenced by the Tojo Hideki cabinet's "*mokusatsu*" policy toward the Cairo Declaration of 1943 (Naka Akira, *Mokusatsu*, NHK Publishing, 2000; Hatano Sumio, *Suzuki Kantaro no shusen shido* [The Leadership of Suzuki Kantaro at the End of the War] in The Military History Society of Japan, ed., *Dainiji sekai taisen 3* [The Second World War, Vol. 3], Kinseisha, 1995).

Whatever Suzuki's statements, there is no doubt that Japan was attempting to buy time while waiting for the Soviet Union to make a response. Effectively, however, Japan's "*mokusatsu*" of the Potsdam Declaration not only gave the United States the pretext to drop the atomic bombs, it also gave the Soviets a reason to enter the war.

The Dropping of the Atomic Bombs

At 8:15 a.m. on August 6, 1945, an atomic bomb was dropped on Hiroshima, causing some 140,000 deaths. While President Truman announced that it had been an atomic bomb, Japan, having yet to fully apprehend the nature of the new weapon, labeled it a "new type of bomb." The army and navy both sent teams to Hiroshima to investigate. On the following day, at 7:30 p.m., Army Minister Anami Korechika and Foreign Minister Togo Shigenori conferred for an hour and a half, with Anami implying in an unofficial capacity that he was no longer confident in Japan's ability to wage prolonged war.

At 3:55 p.m. on August 8, 1945, an air-raid warning was issued for Tokyo, which resulted in the evacuation of Emperor Hirohito for the first time to a special air-raid shelter on the palace grounds that had been completed July 29. It is thought that this shelter was chosen as a direct result of the bombing in Hiroshima. While in the shelter, the emperor met with Foreign Minister Togo and expressed further doubt about a mainland battle. "Given the use of this type of weapon, it will become impossible to fight a war when the enemy forces land. It would be wrong to miss the opportunity to end the war in order to secure favorable conditions."

On the morning of August 9, 1945, the special intelligence department of the Imperial General Headquarters intercepted communications from an American base made to a B-29 using an unusual call signal similar to the one used to call the planes that dropped the bomb on Hiroshima (Matsumoto Hidefumi and Yaku Yasuhiro, *Genbaku toka: Mokusatsu sareta gokuhi joho* [The Dropping of the A-Bomb: *Mokusatsu sareta Top Secret Information*], NHK Publishing, 2012). Since Hiroshima, the army and navy had become increasingly cautious of B-29s. At 10:25 a.m., a scramble order was issued to Omura Airfield in Nagasaki, but an atomic bomb was dropped at 11:01 a.m., exploding one minute later (Naoi Kin'ya, *Ten ni mukatte mugen ni nobiru kurokumo* [The Black Cloud

Stretching Infinitely toward the Sky], *Ushio*, Vol. 183, 1974).

The Soviet Entry into the War and the First Imperial Conference

Recent research suggests that Japan had detected signs of a possible Soviet Entry for some time. The Japanese were aware that the Soviets were sending troops to the Far East. Also, on May 24, the Japanese naval attaché in Switzerland had reported the results of the Yalta conference wherein it was decided that the Soviets would assist the British and Americans in defeating Japan if the war had not reached a conclusion within a certain time limit (Okabe 2012, Yoshimi Masato's *Shusen-shi— Naze ketsudan dekinakatta no ka* [A History of the War's End—Why Couldn't a Firm Decision Be Made?], NHK Publishing, 2013).

Although they anticipated a possible Soviet entry, Japan failed to accurately predict its timing. The army remained divided in their forecasts. While Colonel Suenari Shiroki of the Russian Section of the Army General Staff Office predicted that the Soviets would enter the war around August or September, Colonel Tanemura Sako and others hoped it would come sometime after the US landing (Asaeda Shigeharu, *Tsuioku* [Reminiscences], self-published, 1997).

Soviet entry nevertheless became a reality in the first hours of August 9, when the Soviet Army launched a simultaneous attack across the Soviet-Manchukuo border. Leaders of the Japanese Army were shocked to receive radio reports of the Soviet offense, which had occurred much earlier than they had anticipated. The outcome looked bleak: the bulk of the Kwantung Army had been already transferred to the Japanese home islands, and the leaders judged that they would be overwhelmed within three months or so.

As far as the Japanese Army was concerned, it was the Soviet entry into the war that would decide the country's destiny. As he clung to the hope that the Soviets would not take part in the final battle on the home islands, the Army's Deputy Chief of Staff Kawabe Torashiro was inclined to listen to the advice of advisers who thought that such a development was unlikely. He later recalled that he felt like he was being asked "Now what will you do?" after a one-two punch by the atomic bombing and the Soviet entry.

The next 24 hours would prove fateful for Japan. At 10:30 a.m. on August 9, a meeting of the Supreme War Council was held, with two special cabinet meetings convened later that afternoon and evening. By 10:00 p.m., consensus had still not been reached, for at the emergency cabinet meeting held at 6:30 p.m. that evening, Army Minister General Anami Korechika and Navy Minister Yonai Mitsumasa had been unable to come to any agreement.

> Anami: We are losing on the battlefield, but we are not losing the war. The Army and Navy see the situation differently.
> Yonai: I would not say "defeat," but Japan is losing.
> Anami: I do not think we are losing.
> Yonai: There would be no problem if we had some prospect of winning.
> Anami: A decision cannot be reached [by making calculations] with an abacus. At any rate, the protection of the national polity is in danger. It can be protected with conditions. How can we protect it if our arms and legs have been cut off?

Although Anami was planning to continue the war if the national polity could not be assured, his immediate fear was that it would be difficult to preserve the national polity in the event of disarmament and an Allied occupation.

The first imperial conference was held in the wee hours of the morning on August 10, 1945, at 12:03 a.m. Three of its participants—Army Minister Anami, Army Chief of Staff Umezu, and Navy Chief of Staff Toyoda Soemu—argued that at least four conditions had to be met if Japan were to agree to surrender: preservation of the national polity, self-disarmament, domestic prosecution of war criminals, and no occupation by foreign powers. Meanwhile, three other participants—Navy Minister Yonai, Foreign Minister Togo Shigenori, and Chairman of the Privy Council Hiranuma Kiichiro—feared that an insistence on the four conditions could result in a breakdown in negotiations. They argued that the Potsdam Declaration ought to be accepted by Japan with just one condition: preservation of the national polity. Two hours passed with no sign of consensus.

Around 2:00 a.m. on August 10, 1945, Prime Minister Suzuki, who was acting as chairman of the meeting, suddenly rose from his chair and went before Emperor Hirohito, asking for his opinion. On this occasion, the emperor revealed the first imperial decision, wherein he stated clearly that he agreed with the Foreign Ministry's proposal:

> The plans of the Army and Navy Supreme Command have resulted in constant error and missed opportunities. There is talk of a decisive battle on the homeland, but I have been told that fortifications at Kujukuri Beach [east of Tokyo] are delayed and won't come to completion until the end of August. They say that additional troops also have yet to be sufficiently equipped. How could we fight the US military in such a state?

Such was Hirohito's first "sacred decision" (*seidan*). Given the impossibility of a victorious battle on the home islands, the emperor reasoned, the Potsdam Declaration should be accepted with the single *joken* (condition) proposed by the foreign minister.

Early in the morning of August 10, Japan settled on its message to the Allies offering its acceptance of the Potsdam Declaration, "*with the understanding that the said declaration does not comprise any demand which prejudices the prerogatives of His Majesty as a sovereign ruler.*" Around 4:00 a.m., the Foreign Ministry began translating the message into English. It was now four days after the first atomic bomb at Hiroshima, twenty-eight hours after the Soviet Union entry, and seventeen hours after Nagasaki.

An "Unconditional Surrender" with "Conditions"

In the final stages of Japan's surrender, the main issues of contention became the interpretation of the terms *joken* (condition) and *kokutai* (national polity), particularly their different Japanese and English nuances. In particular, the meaning of the phrase *tenno no kokka tochi no taiken* (the prerogatives of His Majesty as a sovereign ruler) proves elusive, even in Japanese. In Chairman of the Privy Council Hiranuma's view of the national polity, for example, those prerogatives were not merely prescribed by the Imperial Constitution but instead transcended it (Hasegawa 2006).

At 12:45 a.m. on August 12, 1945, the United States broadcast the response of the Allied Powers to Japan's proposal from San Francisco. It did not squarely deal with the issue of the emperor's fate but rather stopped at an expression of the position of the Allies. The main points of the Allied response were as follows:

> *From the moment of surrender the authority of the Emperor and the Japanese government to rule the state shall be subject to the Supreme Commander of the Allied Powers who will take such steps as he deems proper to effectuate the surrender terms.*

> *The ultimate form of Government of Japan shall, in accordance with the Potsdam Declaration, be established by the freely expressed will of the Japanese people.*

The Japanese Foreign Ministry took great pains to translate the message into Japanese. As for the meaning of the expression "subject to," contained in the first part of the Allied response, the ministry translated it loosely as *seigen no shita ni okareru mono to suru* (something to be limited under) instead of as *juzoku* (subordinate) or *reizoku* (in servitude), concluding that the authority of the Emperor was not to be trans-ferred to the Supreme Commander of the Allied Powers but rather just restricted. Meanwhile, it did not translate the English phrase "form of government" in the second part of the response as *seiji keitai* (political form) or *tochi soshiki* (governmental organization), but rather as *seifu no keitai* (form of government), as if the government were to be placed under the Emperor.

The Allied offer upset the advocates of the national polity theory, which put the domestic political order at risk of collapse. At 8:40 a.m. on August 12, 1945, the chiefs of staff of both the army and navy reported their opposition to the Allied response to the emperor, claiming that it aimed to make Japan a vassal state and cause the national polity to be changed through the free will of the people.

Emperor Hirohito, though somewhat anxious about allowing Allied occupation on the basis of international agreements, thought that the majority of the Japanese people would not support a change in the na-tional polity if they were able to freely express their wishes. In addition, a telegram arrived at 2:10 a.m. on August 13, 1945 sent by Okamoto Suemasa, the Japanese Minister to Sweden. This telegram provided information about foreign newspaper reports indicating that Japan's statement had been accepted. After receiving the cable, Hirohito ap-pears to have begun to stand firmer in his opinion, even remarking, "I am certain."

Around the same time, some within the army started voicing the need for a coup to preserve the national polity. Army Minister Anami's brother-in-law, Lieutenant Colonel Takeshita Masahiko, presented a plan to top-ranking army officers to "defend" the Emperor and "protect" important officials by taking them into custody. The army also sent a military truck to the Imperial Palace to begin loading baggage for Naga-no.

On the evening of August 13, 1945, US military planes flew over To-kyo dropping flyers printed with both the Japanese proposal and the Allied response and prompting Japan to surrender. At 8:30 the next morning, Hirohito, who had read one, became increasingly worried about a coup. In an extraordinary step, Hirohito quickly summoned Prime Minister Suzuki to order the convening of an imperial conference.

The second imperial conference began at 11:02. Prime Minister Suzuki reported the discussions made at the Big Six council, but the three men opposed to the Allied reply (Anami, Umezu, and Toyoda) persisted in their dissent. It was at this point that Hirohito addressed the council with tears in his eyes:

> There is opposition to the enemies' reply on the part of the chiefs of staff and the army minister. They say it will lead to disturbance in the national polity, but I do not share in their thinking. They say that there is danger in occupation, but I see no malice in the enemy's message. Although I, too, am somewhat anxious, were the war to be continued as is, the country, the people, and the national polity would be totally destroyed, ending in annihilation (*gyoku-sai*) and nothing more.

The main point of contention during this second imperial conference was the interpretation of the Allied reply. In short, because the members of the imperial conference came to see the "unconditional surrender" of the Japanese military with the "conditions" implied by the Byrnes reply as acceptable, surrender at last came to be seen as advantageous. At the same time, the interpretation of the word "condition" became inextricably linked to the question of whether or not the other side could be trusted. Emperor Hirohito's comment that "I see no malice in the enemy's message" indicates that he believed in the good faith of the enemy.

There is debate as to whether Japan's surrender was conditional, but the majority of Japan's political leaders at that time saw it as such and believed that these conditions (*joken*) would have worsen if they did not surrender summarily. It was precisely because the "conditions" accompanying "unconditional surrender" allowed for a range of interpretations that war termination was possible. The degree to which Japan felt it could trust the Allies also affected this outcome. Emperor Hirohito, in particular, felt that America was not acting out of ill will.

The Psychological Factors of Surrender

The author's position is that on the national level, Japan surrendered on account of four factors: a desire to avoid a decisive homeland battle, the dropping of the atomic bombs, Soviet entry into the war, and the existence of terms or conditions (both translated into Japanese as *joken*) accompanying "unconditional surrender." (See Suzuki, *Shusen no sei-ji-shi 1943–1945* [Japan's Long Road to Surrender: 1943–1945]). Meanwhile, for those involved, the process leading to the surrender had developed along a different dimension. In closing, I would like to draw attention to some of the psychological factors that likely influenced Japan's surrender.

On a personal level, most of Japan's politicians and military leaders were operating with little sleep or rest during the seven-day period that started with the entry of the Soviet Union into the war on August 9, with the two "sacred decisions" being made in that span. For example, Army Lieutenant Colonel Takeshita Masahiko, the center of the planned coup, recorded in his diary that he had "not slept for days on end" (The Military History Society of Japan, eds., *Daihon'ei rikugunbu senso shi-dohan kimitsu senso nisshi* [The Secret War Journals of the War Leadership Group of the Imperial Headquarters Army Division], Kinseisha, 1998). Moreover, Prince Takamatsu Nobuhito, one of Emperor Hirohito's younger brothers and a lieutenant colonel in the navy—and the center of Japan's peace movement—wrote, "Although I had predicted the general course of events, the tempo of the final few days has been such that my mind is completely unable to catch up" (Prince Takamatsu Nobuhito, *Takamatsu no miya nikki* [The Diaries of Prince Takamatsu], Chuokoron-sha, 1997).

For politicians and military officers educated in the prewar period when defeat was unthinkable, it was painful to have to choose between continuing the war and surrendering. From the standpoint of the parties involved, unconditional surrender was possible at any time and it was precisely that which they sought to avoid.

Lack of sleep must have negatively affected their ability to think, and the lack of time very likely robbed them of mental space to consider their options. Moreover, they had to make their decisions under time constraints, basing them on erratic information. At such times, people make decisions based on past experiences and current circumstances. Accordingly, the statements made by the emperor and other officials from August 9 onward must be considered within an expanded context that includes a buildup of minor past events. Things that would seem trivial to us today are likely to have seemed very important to those in the middle of that very tense situation.

At the time, Hirohito's "sacred decisions" were seen by some not as a result of the imperial council meetings per se, but rather as an expression of the emperor's feelings toward the military. For example, Deputy Army Chief of Staff Kawabe wrote, "It was an expression of his mounting distrust of the military" (Research Group of the Kawabe Torashiro Papers, eds., *Shosho hikkin* [Always Following Imperial Decree], Kokushokankokai, 2005). It is thus possible to see Emperor Hirohito's decision to surrender as based on his distrust of the military.

During the war, Japan's political leaders were constantly confronted with contradictory information, making it difficult for them to discern that which could be trusted. At the same time, clear-headed thinking is difficult under the particular conditions of war. For these reasons, to understand how Japan decided to surrender, clarifying how things were seen at the time is perhaps more important than ascertaining the actual state of things as they came to be understood later. The "new type bomb," or the atomic bomb, is one important example of this. More research is needed to determine how this and other developments were seen in the final days of the war.

Postscript

My research was supported by the Japan Society for the Promotion of Science (JSPS) Grant-in-Aid for Science Research #70636216. Also, owing to the voluminous number of books referenced, the list below contains only those major books used in my research that were published in 2011 or later. Please refer to my book, *Shusen no seiji-shi 1943–1945* [Japan's Long Road to Surrender: 1943–1945] (University of Tokyo Press, 2011) for a list of reference works from earlier years. Dates and times listed are Japanese local time. For the sake of clarity, the English version of this lecture has been modified by the author.

＊　　＊　　＊

Recommended Readings for Deeper Understanding

Furukawa Takahisa. *Potsudamu sengen to gunkoku Nihon* [The Potsdam Declaration and the Japanese Military State]. Tokyo: Yoshikawa Kobunkan, 2012.

Furukawa Takahisa. *Showa Tenno—'Risei no kunshu' no kodoku* [The Showa Emperor—Isolation of the 'Rational Monarch']. Tokyo: Chuokoron Shinsha, 2011.

Hasegawa Tsuyoshi. *Genbaku, Soren sansen, tennosei, shusen kosaku meiso no seiji bunseki* [The Atomic Bomb, the Entry of the Soviet Union into the War, the Imperial System, and a Political Analysis of the Wavering Plan to End the War] in Inose Naoki, Kikuzawa Kenshu, Kotani Ken, Todaka Kazushige, Tobe Ryoichi, Hasegawa Tsuyoshi, Hara Takeshi, Betsumiya Danro, Mizushima Yoshitaka, and Murai Tomohide. *Jirei kenkyu Nihon to Nihongun no shippai no mekanizumu—Machigai wa naze kurikaesareru noka* [The Mechanism of the Failure of Japan and the Japanese Military]. Tokyo: Chuokoron Shinsha, 2013.

Hasegawa Tsuyoshi. *Anto—Sutarin, Toruman to Nihon kofuku* [Racing the Enemy: Stalin, Truman, and the Surrender of Japan]. Tokyo: Chuokoron

Shinsha, 2006; paperback edition, Vols. 1 & 2, 2011.

Hatano Sumio. *Shusen o meguru shidosha gunzo—Suzuki Kantaro o chushin ni* [The Group of Leaders at the War's End—Focusing on Suzuki Kantaro] in Ryoichi Tobe, *Kindai Nihon no ridashippu* [Leaders at Crossroads in Modern Japan: They Made Decisions, Mistakes, and History]. Tokyo: Chikura Publishing, 2014.

Ito Yukio. *Showa Tenno den* [Biography of the Showa Emperor]. Tokyo: Bungeishunju, 2011; paperback edition, 2014.

Kato Yoko. *Nihongun no buso kaijo ni tsuite no ichi kosatsu* [A study of the Demilitarization of the Japanese Military] in Masuda Hiroshi, ed., *Dainippon teikoku no hokai to hikiage, fukuin* [The Collapse of the Japanese Empire, Repatriation and Demobilization]. Tokyo: Keio University Press, 2012.

Koketsu Atsushi. *Nihon wa naze senso o yamerarenakatta noka—Chushinjiku naki kokka no mujun* [Why Couldn't Japan End the War?—The Contradictions of a Nation without a Central Axis]. Tokyo: Shakaihyoronsha, 2013.

Koshiro Yukiko. *Imperial Eclipse.* Ithaca, NY: Cornell University Press, 2013.

Okabe Noburu. *Kieta Yaruta mitsuyaku kinkyuden—Johoshikan: Onodera Makoto no kodoku na tatakai* [The Vanished Emergency Cable of the Secret Yalta Pact—Intelligence Officer Onodera Makoto's Lonely Fight]. Tokyo: Shinchosha, 2012.

Shoji Jun'ichiro. *Senso shuketsu o meguru Nihon no senryaku 2* [Japan's Strategy for Ending the War, Vol. 2] in Miyake Masaki, Shoji Jun'ichiro, Ishizu Tomoyuki, and Yamamoto Fumihito, eds. *Kensho: Taiheiyo senso to sono senryaku 2* [Verification: The Pacific War and Its Strategy, Vol. 2]. Tokyo: Chuokoron Shinsha, 2013.

Teshima Yasunobu. *Showa senjiki no kaigun to seiji* [The Navy and Politics in the Wartime Showa Years]. Tokyo: Yoshikawa Kobunkan, 2013.

Yamamoto Tomoyuki. *Shusen ka kowa ka—Teikoku rikugun no himitsu shusen kosaku* [War or Peace—The Secret Plans of the Imperial Japanese Army to End the War]. Tokyo: Shinchosha, 2013.

Yellen, Jeremy. "The Specter of Revolution: Reconsidering Japan's Decision to Surrender," *The International History Review*, Vol. 35, No. 1 (March 2013).

Lecture 15

The Occupation of Japan: The International Background behind the Policy of the United States toward Japan

Iguchi Haruo

Research Trends and the Aim of This Lecture

How did Japan succeed in its economic recovery, after being defeated at the end of World War II? Most prior research has focused on the domestic aspects, arguing that the recovery was accomplished by powerful political figures, bureaucrats, and men in the financial and corporate worlds, among others.

Several representative studies of the period of the Allied occupation of Japan are listed below.

Chronological histories of the period in which Japan was occupied by the Allied Powers include two books by Iokibe Makoto, *Senryoki— Shusho-tachi no shin Nihon* [The Occupation Period—The Prime Ministers' New Japan] (Kodansha, 2007) and *Nihon no kindai 6—Senso, senryo, kowa 1941–1955* [Japan in the Modern Age, Vol. 6—The War, the Occupation, the Peace Treaty 1941–1955] (Chuokoron Shinsha, 2013). Meanwhile, a detailed book about the developments on the American side is Michael Schaller's *The American Occupation of Japan: The Origins of the Cold War in Asia* (Oxford University Press, 1987) (Japanese translation, *Ajia ni okeru reisen no kigen—Amerika no tainichi senryo*, Bokutakusha, 1996). Also, excellent books published in recent years include Kusunoki Ayako's *Gendai Nihon seiji-shi 1: Senryo kara dokuritsu e* [Contemporary Japanese Political History, Vol. 1: From Occupation to Independence] (Yoshikawa Kobunkan, 2013) and Fukunaga Fumio's *Nihon senryo-shi 1945–1952—Tokyo, Washinton, Okinawa* [History of Japan's Occupation 1945–1952—Tokyo, Washington, Okinawa] (Chuokoron Shinsha, 2014).

A good book about General Douglas MacArthur is Masuda Hiroshi's *Makkasa* [MacArthur] (Chuokoron Shinsha, 2009).

Aside from those, studies of recent years treating America's occupation policies and the issue of Japan's remilitarization include the following works, which broadly analyze developments both domestic and abroad: Sado Akihiro, *Sengo Nihon no boei to seiji* [Defense and Politics of Postwar Japan] (Yoshikawa Kobunkan, 2003); Nakajima Shingo, *Sengo Nihon no boei seisaku—'Yoshida rosen' o meguru seiji, gaiko, gunji* [Postwar Japan's Defense Policies—Political, Diplomatic, and Military Aspects of the 'Yoshida Doctrine] (Keio University Press, 2006); Kusunoki Ayako, *Yoshida Shigeru to anzen hosho seisaku no keisei—Nichibei no koso to sono sogo sayo* [Yoshida Shigeru and the Formation of Security Policy—The Ideas of Japan and the United States and Their Mutual Interaction] (Minerva Shobo, 2009); and Shibayama Futoshi, *Nihon saigunbi e no michi* [The Path to Japan's Remilitarization] (Minerva Shobo, 2010).

Monographs focusing on the many Americans active in Japan-US relations during the Occupation period include two books by Howard B. Schonberger: *Japanizu konekushon—Kaiun'o K. Sugahara gaiden* [Nisei Entrepreneur: A Political Biography of Kay Sugahara] (alternatively known as *Japanese Connection: A Biography of the Shipping Magnate Kay Sugahara*) (posthumously published, no English edition exists, translated version by Bungeishunju, 1995), and "Aftermath of War:

Americans and the Remaking of Japan, 1945–1952" (Kent State University Press, 1989; Japanese translation, Jiji Press, 1994).

As for political history monographs dealing with the subject of the rebirth and development of Japan's political parties and politics, refer to the following: Fukunaga Fumio, *Senryoka chudo seiken no keisei to hokai—GHQ minseikyoku to Nihon shakaito* [Formation and Collapse of Centrist Governments during the Occupation—The GHQ's Bureau of Civil Administration and the Japan Socialist Party] (Iwanami Shoten, 1997); Nakakita Koji, *Keizai fukko to sengo seiji—Nihon Shakaito 1945 nen–1951 nen* [Rebuilding of the Economy and Postwar Politics—The Japan Socialist Party 1941–1951] (University of Tokyo Press, 1998); Murai Tetsuya, *Sengo seiji taisei no kigen—Yoshida Shigeru no 'kantei shudo'* [Roots of the Postwar Political System—Yoshida Shigeru's 'Policymaking Initiative by the Prime Minister's Office] (Fujiwara Shoten, 2005); and Komiya Hitoshi, *Jiyuminshuto no tanjo—Sosai kosen to soshiki seitoron* [The Birth of the Liberal Democratic Party—Public Elections of the Party President and Organized Party Theory] (Bokutakusha, 2010).

Representative works dealing with the problem of constitutional revision include Koseki Shoichi's *Nihonkoku kenpo no tanjo* [The Birth of the Japanese Constitution] (Iwanami Shoten, 2009) and *Heiwa kenpo no shinso* [Depths of the Peace Constitution] (Chikumashobo, 2015), both on the side of safeguarding the constitution, and Nishi Osamu's *Nihonkoku kenpo wa koshite umareta* [How the Constitution of Japan Was Born] (Chuokoron Shinsha, 2000) and *Nihonkoku kenpo seiritsu katei no kenkyu* [Studies on the Process of Establishment of the Constitution of Japan] (Seibundo Publishing, 2004), both on the side of constitutional revision.

Two must-read books dealing with media-related studies of the Occupation years, including censorship, are Ariyama Teruo's *Senryoki media-shi kenkyu—Jiyu to tosei, 1945* [Studies of the History of Media during the Occupation Period—Freedom and Control, 1945] (Kashiwa Shobo, 1996) and Yamamoto Taketoshi's *GHQ no ken'etsu, choho, send-*

en kosaku [The GHQ's Censorship, Intelligence and Propaganda Activities] (Iwanami Shoten, 2013).

A classic monograph dealing with the process of the shift back to independence from the occupational rule of the GHQ is Hosoya Chihiro's *San Furanshisuko kowa e no michi* [The Road to the San Francisco Peace Treaty] (Chuokoron-sha, 1984).

However, the prior research mentioned above fails to explore the relation between Japan's postwar restoration to international society and the decline of China within postwar international politics. In fact, it is no exaggeration to state that Japan's postwar fate was decided by the Cold War and the state of affairs in China. The following sections of this chapter will explore this view.

Prior to the Outbreak of the War between Japan and the United States

The success of the heavy industrialization of Manchuria depended on the introduction of American capital to the region: such was the analysis of John Paton Davies, Jr., who served as US consul in Mukden (now Shenyang), immediately after the launch of the industrialization of Manchuria by Ayukawa Yoshisuke. Davies later served as a subordinate of George F. Kennan, architect of the postwar containment policy and director of policy planning at the US State Department; he received much respect by Kennan for his wartime stint at the US Embassy in Moscow and his postwar service in the East Asia section of Kennan's Policy Planning Staff.

Ayukawa had developed the idea of getting the United States to give Manchukuo a de facto recognition and then introducing American capital into Manchuria. However, the US consulate in Mukden, reflecting the position of the US government, would not recognize a Japanese version of a modified Open Door Policy (i.e., the idea that East Asian markets would be open to the United States and other countries as long as Japan was in charge). The United States adopted a stricter definition of the

Open Door Policy. Manchukuo aimed to coerce the United States into renouncing its extraterritorial rights as the Sino-Japanese War got bogged down and US-Japan relations worsened.

After Japan concluded the Tripartite Pact with the Axis countries in September 1940, US-Japan relations worsened even further. Once Japan occupied southern French Indochina in the latter part of July 1941, the United States teamed up with Britain and the Netherlands to impose comprehensive economic sanctions on it. Japan was no longer able to import oil, and Japanese assets in those countries were frozen.

US Treasury Secretary Henry Morgenthau, Jr., a Jewish financier, demonstrated some understanding toward exploring a modus vivendi with Japan, while playing a leading role in the policy of applying economic sanctions against the Axis countries, including Japan. He maintained a low profile of appeasement toward Japan, convinced that he could pry Japan away from the Axis alliance. However, US President Franklin D. Roosevelt and Secretary of State Cordell Hull had learned through their access to Operation Magic (the system used by the United States to crack encoded secret Japanese diplomatic cables of which Morgenthau had no knowledge) that Japan had no intention of leaving the Axis, and that it might be planning to launch war on the United States. The United States was not ready for a war with Japan yet, and the majority of American public opinion was against entry into the war against the Axis countries. Under those circumstances, Roosevelt and Hull thus tried to use the modus vivendi proposal to delay war between Japan and the United States by three months—until the spring of 1942— when preparations for war against Japan would be completed, but were unable to present that proposal to Japan.

It was in the middle of such developments that the Japanese Navy launched its surprise attack on Pearl Harbor on December 7, 1941 (December 8, 1941, Japan time). American public opinion shifted dramatically toward supporting the war. Already, the United States had been supporting the war effort (helping Britain and China since the spring of 1941, and the Soviet Union from the same summer), but now it formally became one of the Allies of World War II (in reality, however, the United States had already been frequently clashing militarily with the German Navy in the North Atlantic since September 1941).

The Direction of the Chiang Kai-shek Government

Ever since the Russo-Japanese War of 1904–05, the United States has positioned Japan as a junior partner in East Asia. The only exception was the decade or so from Japan's entry into full-scale war with China in 1937 to the middle of 1947. The junior-partner arrangement did not change even in the late 1960s, when the United States was losing international economic competitiveness and began to fear Japan, which had risen to become the world's greatest economic power second only to the United States, as well as during the mid-1970s, when the United States led by Nixon promoted normalized relations with China at electrifying speed.

Political moves based on the United States' expedient assessments had a major impact on the turning points in Asian history, including Japan's defeat, the Korean War, and the Vietnam War. The opportunistic assessment of the Republic of China by the United States determined Japan's position in international society in the end, on account of the defeat of the Kuomintang in the Chinese Civil War by the Communists and its retreat to Taiwan.

During World War II, the United States had assumed that the Republic of China would be its junior partner in the postwar order of East Asia. For that reason, after Japan's defeat in the war, the United States sought to establish the early stabilization of China by earnestly promoting the realization of a joint government between the Nationalists and Communists, led by the former, in the hope that China would not return to the state of civil war that had existed between the two sides before the Xi'an Incident of 1936. However, the relations between the United States and the Republic of China during the war could hardly be termed close at all. That is evidenced by the United States' recognition of the Soviet demands for rights in China that Stalin made during the Yalta Conference of February 1945, which was not attended by China's leaders.

In the spring of 1944, the Imperial Japanese Army launched Operation Ichi-Go in mainland China, and by the autumn of the same year it had successfully brought the coastal regions of the country back under its control. However, relations between the United States and the Republic of China had grown chilly by that time. The United States, disillusioned by the military strength of the Chiang Kai-shek government, was considering appointing General Joseph Stilwell, who was serving as military advisor (chief of staff) to Chiang, as Supreme Allied Commander in China. The same October, President Roosevelt issued an ultimatum to Chiang saying that American military support to China would be cut off unless it accepted Stilwell's appointment, with Stilwell personally handing Roosevelt's telegram containing that message to Chiang. Chiang, however, lashed back at the Roosevelt administration, and Stilwell was replaced by Roosevelt in the last part of the month. Chiang thus retained his position as Supreme Allied Commander in China, and continued to receive military support from the United States.

Around the same time, the US government, along with the US Army, started to explore giving military assistance to the Communists in Yenan (Yan'an), with the efforts primarily shouldered by the aforementioned diplomat Davies, now based in Chongqing. The United States had been focusing its attention on the successful guerrilla operations of the Communist Party army against the Japanese, and wanted to utilize them, but the assistance was not extended in the end.

When Patrick J. Hurley, who had served as US Secretary of the Army in the Hoover Administration, was appointed as American ambassador to China in 1944, he urged the Chiang Kai-shek government to carry out dialogue and cooperate with the Chinese Communist Party. Those efforts continued even after Japan had lost the war. However, because the US government was afraid that Chiang, in the face of the success of Japan's Operation Ichi-Go, would go ahead and independently make peace with Japan, it was neither able to oust him from his position as Supreme

Allied Commander in China, nor could it modify the Chiang govern-ment's negative stance toward establishing a cooperative relationship with the Communists.

In addition, the United States, envisioning China's becoming one of the five major powers supporting the postwar order, respected the posi-tion of the Chiang government. China was to be a permanent member of the Security Council of the United Nations that started to be organized in the latter half of 1944, and it also was to have occupied a permanent position within the Bretton Woods system (devised by Morgenthau and his aides) that was to be set up after the war, including the International Monetary Fund (IMF) and the International Bank for Reconstruction and Development (IBRD, or the World Bank), both of which were launched around the same time.

Japan's Economic Reconstruction and the Issue of Compensation

The acceptance of the Potsdam Declaration and its timing were both left up to Japan. Emperor Hirohito's decision to surrender at the Imperial Council of August 1945 took place much earlier than had been imagined by the Allied Powers, and that fact was decisive in the appointment of General Douglas MacArthur as Supreme Commander for the Allied Powers. Had the war lasted longer, Admiral Chester W. Nimitz, pushed by the US Navy, might have been named instead. While MacArthur was a politician-style military man who tended to implement political judg-ments based on his personal discretion, Nimitz was more practical, and thus would possibly have been unable to make the sophisticated kind of political judgments that MacArthur made which enabled the postwar constitution to be realized by holding on to the Imperial system, namely, utilizing the Emperor to promote the policies of the Occupation. More-over, had the United States invaded Kyushu in November 1945 as planned, it probably would have dropped several more atomic bombs before then, and may have used chemical weapons as well.

Because Japan had been defeated earlier than expected, the United States overwhelmingly seized the initiative in occupying the country before the Soviet Union could invade the northern island of Hokkaido. On the Chinese mainland,

MacArthur (left) and Nimitz

on the other hand, the United States tacitly recognized the Soviet military occupation of Manchuria and the expansion of influence by the Chinese Communist Party. As China's entire coastal area had been occupied by Japan ever since that country's successful Operation Ichi-Go of 1944, the Kuomintang largely relied on the provision of transportation by the US military to spread from the interior—mainly the capital, Chongqing—to the rest of the country. Meanwhile, in Manchuria, the Soviet Union started to dismantle and transfer facilities from Japanese heavy and chemical industries as war reparations, preventing the Nationalist government from moving into the region. As far as the Nationalists were concerned, Japanese infrastructure in Manchuria was on Chinese territory and therefore belonged to China, but the Soviet Union asserted the right to take them back to its own territory, given that they were Japanese-made.

The US government had assigned Edwin W. Pauley—a political ally of President Truman's—the task of leading a group to investigate German industrial equipment and facilities in Europe and Japanese industrial facilities and equipment in Asia, and draw up a report (the Pauley Report) on reparations to be made by those two countries. It was based on the thinking of the Allies that such equipment and facilities should be transferred to the victorious nations after the war as compensation for the economic damage inflicted on Germany's and Japan's neighbors. Although Morgenthau—who had tried to ram through policies to deindustrialize Germany and turn it into a pastoral nation—was removed from his post owing to the sudden death of Roosevelt in April 1945 and the subsequent promotion of Truman to the presidency, the Allies still did not consent to the revival of heavy and chemical industries in the Axis countries, making it highly probable that such facilities and equipment would be transferred away to other countries. However, the intensifying conflict between the United States and the Soviet Union reduced that probability, and moves to transfer such equipment and facilities generally receded with the announcement of the Marshall Plan by the United States in 1947.

From the conclusion of the war, anti-Communist conservatives in the United States, such as former President Herbert C. Hoover, Secretary of the Navy James Forrestal (who became the first Secretary of Defense in 1947), Undersecretary of War William Henry Draper, Jr., and US Ambassador to the Soviet Union W. Averell Harriman, had hoped to rebuild the West German and Japanese economies in an effort to revitalize the international economy with the United States sitting at the helm.

The political proposals contained in the Pauley Report eventually came to be eviscerated by Hoover, but in the case of Japan, such evisceration only became possible with the collapse of the Republic of China on the Chinese mainland, in addition to the factor of the US-Soviet conflict.

Navy Secretary Forrestal, making a stop in China before his visit to Japan on July 10, 1946, had heard from US special envoy George C. Marshall, the previous Chief of Staff of the US Army, that civil war between the Nationalists and Communists could no longer be avoided. After arriving at Atsugi Air Force Base in Japan, Forrestal conferred with MacArthur, who emphasized to him the need to swiftly resolve the reparations issue in order to rebuild Japan. MacArthur spoke about the use of Japanese machinery as partial settlement toward some of its reparations, pointing out that they had been overvalued on account of their rough manhandling during the war when maintenance had not been taken care of. Perhaps he said that as a way to avoid the outflow of the Japanese machinery to other countries. Both MacArthur and Forrestal believed that postponing Japan's economic reconstruction owing to the failure to resolve the reparations issue would lead to an expansion in Soviet influence in Japan.

Also, regarding the Chinese situation, MacArthur argued that the Nationalist government, despite its multitude of problems such as corruption, ought to continue to receive the support of the United States. Notably, he also told Forrestal that Japan needed to be positioned as the westernmost part of the littoral defense line for freedom in the western Pacific. That view served as the premise to MacArthur's argument the following year for the early signing of a peace treaty with Japan.

Kennan's Containment Policy

In 1948, when the United States announced the shift in its economic policies toward Japan, the Kuomintang army started drastically losing ground in the Chinese Civil War, finally resulting in the creation of the People's Republic of China in October 1949, with the Republic of China being demoted to the status of a regional government on the island of Taiwan. Until the establishment of the Sino-Soviet Alliance in February 1950, the United States had endeavored to "Titoize" the People's Republic of China (i.e., to pry it away from the Soviet Union in the same manner as Yugoslavia). It released the China White Paper in August 1949, arguing for the forsaking of the Republic of China. At the same time, the United States was also conducting diplomatic negotiations with the People's Republic of China behind the scenes, exploring three scenarios concerning the rule of Taiwan if Chiang were forced to step down: (1) placing it under trusteeship of the United Nations, (2) setting up a military administration by the United States, and (3) establishing a government by the Taiwanese people, who had lived under Japanese colonial rule (from 1895 to 1945).

Kennan's proposal of a policy to wrest China away from the Soviets was reviewed by Secretary of State Dean Acheson, and the United States approached the People's Republic of China behind the scenes. However, with the conclusion of the Sino-Soviet Alliance, all those efforts went up in smoke. Nonetheless, the United States continued to work for Chiang's ouster in the Republic of China right up until the outbreak of the Korean War (on June 25, 1950).

The Taiwanese policies of the United States from the summer of 1949 to the outbreak of the Korean War, as mentioned above, were deeply interrelated with the Policy Planning Staff at the State Department, led by Director George Kennan under Secretary of State Acheson, and staffed by such men as John Paton Davies, Jr., who was cited earlier. Kennan had caught the attention of Forrestal, who was groping for a way to contain global communist forces led by the Soviet Union even while the war was still going on, and began to distinguish himself within the State Department starting in 1946.

American conservatives had hoped for an early recovery of the world's economy from an anti-Communist standpoint. They were also wary of emasculating West German and Japanese productive capacity, as not doing so would lighten the fiscal burden of the United States. Amidst the intensifying rivalry between the Americans and the Soviets, the conservatives took control of the security and foreign policies of the United States starting around May 1947. That overlapped with the period in which Kennan's foreign policy began to permeate the government, with the backing of the first-ever secretary of defense, James V. Forrestal.

Out of the five areas worldwide with the proper infrastructure and technology to support the global economy—namely, the United States, Western Europe, Eastern Europe, the Soviet Union, and Japan—Kennan's containment policy was to initially place the Western Hemisphere, Western Europe, and Japan under American influence. Kennan believed that diplomacy and intelligence activities should be used to check the expansion of the Soviet Union and Communism rather than applying military power.

In contrast to Kennan, who was formulating his foreign policy from a position unaffected by American public opinion, Secretary of State Acheson was not immune to its influence, particularly being subject to pressure from the US Congress. The Nationalist government led by Chiang Kai-shek had made inroads into American media and politics since the late 1930s, and the channels between it and the Republican Party grew even more substantial during the war. Truman and Acheson sent a US military assistance advisory group to Taiwan after the publication of the China White Paper not only because they thought that the Nationalist Revolution Army could probably withstand an attack from the People's Liberation Army across the Taiwan (Formosa) Strait, but also because they could no longer ignore the political influence of sympathizers back home in the United States with the Nationalist government's cause.

Shift in US Policies toward Japan and Moves by the Pro-Japanese Faction

Though the conflict between the United States and the Soviet Union was a turning point in postwar Japan, there was also another turning point that has often been overlooked: the chaos and weakening of the Nationalist government in China. Between 1946 and 1948, when the US-Soviet rivalry was becoming more severe, the Chinese Nationalist government, which was to have been the bulwark of US security strategy in the Asia-Pacific region, was thrown into turmoil and became weakened through its civil war with the Communists. For that reason, the United States returned to its earlier emphasis on Japan, which then allowed that country to rebuild its economy in concert with the development of its heavy and chemical industries.

As the civil war increasingly turned against the Nationalists, the early signing of a peace treaty advocated by MacArthur in March 1947 was not realized. The US State Department had formulated an initiative to jump-start the industrialization of East Asia, primarily China, and Southeast Asia by transferring Japanese industrial equipment, but that was retracted once Kennan, the proponent of the containment policy, took charge of policymaking toward Japan within the State Department.

Another proponent of the shift in policy to Japan, along with Kennan, was Major General William Draper, Under Secretary of War from September 1947 to February 1949. Before the war, he had served as a vice president of Dillon, Read & Co., a Wall Street investment bank (the president of which at the time was Forrestal). In 1940, Army Chief of Staff Marshall invited Draper to serve as a member of the President's Advisory Committee for Selective Service, which was under the jurisdiction of the War Department. After Germany's surrender in 1945, he became the chief of the Economics Division in the Allied Control Council in that country. As he was opposed to the policy to deindustrialize Germany—descended from Morgenthau's plan—he instead implemented occupation policies that expedited the recovery of German industry.

Providing indirect support for those moves within the US government were former President Hoover and the domestic pro-Japanese group. Since mid-1946, Hoover, who had called for a reversal of polices toward Japan, was a quiet partner of that group before the American Council of Japan (the so-called Japan Lobby) was formed in June 1948. The council coalesced around such public figures as Joseph Grew (the last prewar American ambassador to Japan, with personal connections with Japanese politicians, businessmen, and bureaucrats), William Richards Castle, Jr. (a confidant to Hoover who had served during the Hoover Administration successively as ambassador to Japan and undersecretary of state), and Eugene H. Dooman (an aide to Grew both during his years as ambassador to Japan and after his return to the United States until the war ended), as well as such private-sector individuals as *Newsweek*'s foreign affairs editor Harry F. Kern and the lawyer James Lee Kauffman.

Another powerful person who coordinated his actions with the American Council of Japan was Army Major General Draper. Former President Hoover, Draper, and the members of the American Council of Japan were critical of MacArthur's economic policies in Japan, as well as the application of the law to purge public officials—especially those from the business world—and the excessive dismantling of the *zaibatsu* financial combines. In particular, Kauffman and Kern, along with the latter's subordinate, *Newsweek* Tokyo correspondent Compton Pakenham, used the media to criticize MacArthur publicly from the perspective of the need for the early rebuilding of the Japanese economy. Kauffman had been a lawyer in Japan before the war, and set up offices after the war both in Japan and the United States as he continued his legal activities.

The San Francisco Peace Treaty and the Postwar Security Framework

While it was the outbreak of the Korean War that enabled Japanese heavy and chemical industries to recover at first, what made possible their sustained development thereafter was the signing of the San Francisco Peace Treaty in 1951, shepherded by the United States, along with the Treaty of Friendship, Commerce and Navigation between the United States and Japan in 1953. Also important was Japan's participation in the Bretton Woods system of international management of trade and finance (comprising the International Monetary Fund, the World Bank, and the General Agreement on Tariffs and Trade). Although Japanese financial and economic interests, particularly those in light industries such as the textile industry, had hoped to normalize relations with the People's Republic of China, Prime Minister Yoshida Shigeru chose instead to establish relations with the Republic of China, on account of interference by the United States. The Republic of China renounced its war claims vis-à-vis Japan when it signed the Sino-Japanese Peace Treaty (officially known as the Peace Treaty between Japan and the Republic of China, or more commonly as the Treaty of Taipei) on April 28, 1952.

The San Francisco Peace Treaty, signed on September 8, 1951, was only a partial or incomplete peace, as the two Chinas and the Soviet Union had failed to sign it. Moreover, he signed the Japan-US Security

Treaty (officially the Treaty of Mutual Cooperation and Security between the United States and Japan) on the same day, while the Korean War was still raging, thereby approving the continuation of a large-scale US military presence and bases in Japan. Prime Minister Yoshida had concluded the treaty without giving prior explanation to either the Diet or the nation. On the other hand, he did not yield to American pressure for massive remilitarization, but instead reorganized the National Police Reserve—set up during the Korean War—into the Self-Defense Forces, which were created in 1954. He thus maintained the policy line of light armament and the posture of a self defense-oriented military. At the outset of the Eisenhower Administration in 1953, new Secretary of State John Foster Dulles had attempted to create a framework of collective security around the United States that also included Japan, but that plan eventually resulted in failure, having been checked by the resistance of the Yoshida government as well as by the suspicion held toward Japan on the part of America's other allies in the Pacific.

At the same time, the United States waited to conclude a security treaty with Taiwan (officially known as the Mutual Defense Treaty between the United States and the Republic of China) only after the ceasefire of the Korean War. While it had feared that the conclusion of such a treaty might let Chiang Kai-shek feel free to invade mainland China, the United States took advantage of the First Taiwan Strait Crisis to force the Chiang government to sign the treaty, making it pledge not to invade the mainland. Thereafter, the Republic of China and the Kuomintang fearing abandonment by the United States, made inroads into American politics and society. The China Lobby (i.e., the Taiwan Lobby) coordinated its efforts with the Japan Lobby in the United States through such channels as the Committee of One Million and *Time* magazine. Although that coordination would not survive Nixon's 1972 visit to China, it contributed until then to the delay in America's normalization of relations with China.

Had the original vision for a postwar world drawn up by the United States during World War II materialized, the Republic of China would have been the leader of East Asia, serving not only as a permanent member of the United Nations Security Council but also as a nation with heft in the World Bank, the International Monetary Fund, and the General Agreement on Tariffs and Trade. Moreover, the Republic of China would have been able to make claims on Japan and interfere in the course of Japan's economic reconstruction in multiple ways.

In reality, Japan was able to access the US market, whose GDP accounted for about half of the world's entire economy at the end of World War II. It was able to borrow dollars from the World Bank, led by the United States, and acquired technology, facilities and equipment, and knowhow related to manufacturing systems from US corporations. Thanks to economic and cultural exchanges promoted by the United States with Japan, Japan's industrial circles, bureaucrats, and academia voraciously devoured American technology and manufacturing systems, which were the most advanced in the world at the time. Japan might have been Finlandized had it carried out equidistant (i.e., evenhanded) diplomacy with the People's Republic of China and the Soviet Union and signed an overall peace treaty. It goes without saying that it would have been impossible in such a case for Japan to have acquired the world's state-of-the-art technology from those two countries.

The determining factor shaping American foreign policy and security policy trends, leading them toward an emphasis on Japan, was the recognition of the utility of the Japanese economy on the part of such men as former President Hoover, as well as Draper and Forrestal among others who were former executives of the Dillon, Read and Co. investment bank. The United States placed priority on Japan's economic stability during the Cold War, tacitly condoning Japan's reluctance toward accepting foreign direct investment from the United States stemming from its neo-mercantilism stance. Also, Japan, fearful of being entangled in America's global strategy, was hesitant as well about deepening ties with the United States throughout the whole society.

Much earlier, in the 1930s, Japan had failed to build a network with US business circles during its headlong march toward war. For the ties of friendship between the United States and Japan to be strengthened in our own day, it thus probably behooves the two nations to engage in deeper economic and cultural exchanges along various levels.

* * *

Recommended Readings for Deeper Understanding

Cumings, Bruce. *The Origins of the Korean War, Vol. 2: The Roaring of the Cataract, 1947–50*. NJ: Princeton University Press, 1992. Japanese translation by Deung Gyeongmo, et al., *Chosen senso no kigen 2 ge—'Kakumeiteki' naisen to Amerika no haken 1947 nen–1950 nen*. Tokyo: Akashi Shoten, 2011.

A detailed study of relations between the United States and the People's Republic of China and the United States and the Republic of China before the outbreak of the Korean War.

Iguchi Haruo. *Ayukawa Yoshisuke to keizaiteki kokusaishugi—Manshu mondai kara sengo Nichibei kankei e* [Ayukawa Yoshisuke and Economic Internationalism—From the Manchurian Issue to Postwar US-Japan Relations]. Nagoya: University of Nagoya Press, 2012.

A more detailed introduction of the facts cited in this article.

Iguchi Haruo. *Kyowato uha to Dagurasu Makkasa daitoryo koho yoritsu undo* [The Republican Party Right Wing and the Movement to Back Douglas MacArthur's Bid as a Presidential Candidate] in *Shirin*, Vol. 92. No. 5. Kyoto: The Society of Historical Research, Kyoto University, September 2009.

The author's latest research on MacArthur.

Iguchi Haruo. *Sengo Nihon no kunshusei to Amerika* [Japan's Monarchy after the War and the United States] in *Nijusseiki Nihon no tenno to kunshusei* [Japan's Emperor and Monarchy in the 20th Century], edited by Ito Yukio and Kawada Minoru. Tokyo: Yoshikawa Kobunkan, 2004.

Focuses on the relationship between MacArthur and Emperor Hirohito.

Schonberger, Howard B. *Nisei Entrepreneur: A Political Biography of Kay Sugahara* (unpublished in English), Japanese translation by Sodei Rinjiro, *Japaniizu konekushon—Kaiun'o K. Sugahara gaiden*. Tokyo: Bungei-

shunju, 1995.
Paints a portrait of a Japanese-American who was active behind the scenes between the United States and Japan during the Occupation period.

Tuchman, Barbara. *Stilwell and the American Experience in China, 1911– 45.* New York: Macmillan Publishers, 1971. Japanese translation by Suginobe Toshihide, *Shippai shita Amerika no Chugoku seisaku—Biruma sensen no Sutiruweru shogun.* Tokyo: Asahi Shimbunsha, 1996.

A Pulitzer Prize–winning book that takes a detailed look at the relationship between the United States and the Chiang Kai-shek government during World War II.

About the Editor and Contributors

The Editor of the Volume

Tsutsui Kiyotada
Born in 1948, Tsutsui is professor and head in the Department of Japanese Culture, also a dean in the Faculty of Literature (Liberal Arts), Teikyo University. He is also a Senior Fellow at the Tokyo Foundation. Tsutsui graduated from the Graduate School of Literature, Kyoto University and holds a Ph.D. in Literature. His area of specialty is modern to contemporary Japanese history and historical sociology. His publications include *Showa senzenki no seito seiji* [Party Politics in Prewar Showa Era], Chikumashobo; *2.26 Jiken to sono jidai* [The February 26 Incident and Its Time], Chikumashobo; *Konoe Fumimaro* [Konoe Fumimaro], Iwanami Shoten; and *2.26 Jiken to seinen shoko* [The February 26 Incident and Young Military Officers], Yoshikawa Kobunkan.

Contributors

Lecture 1:
Watanabe Kota
Born in 1984, Watanabe is a full-time lecturer at the Department of Japanese Culture, Faculty of Liberal Arts, Teikyo University. Graduated from the Graduate School of Law, Kobe University, Watanabe holds a Ph.D. in political science. His area of specialty is modern history of Japan. His publications include *"Senso" de yomu Nichibei kankei 100-nen* [The 100-year History of the Japan-US Relations Surrounding 'War': From the Russo-Japanese War to the War against Terrorism], co-authored, Asahi Shimbunsha and a treatise "Challenging the 'Kasumigaseki Diplomacy': Ishii Kikujiro and Japan's Quest for an Alternative Foreign Policy" in *Teikyo Daigaku Bungakubu Kiyo*, [Journal of the Department of Literature, Teikyo University], No. 46.

Lecture 2:
Koyama Toshiki
Born in 1976, Koyama is associate professor of history, Faculty of Liberal Arts, Teikyo University. Graduated from the Graduate School of Human and Environmental Sciences, Kyoto University, Koyama holds a Ph.D. in human and environmental studies. His area of specialty is modern and contemporary political history of Japan. His publications include *Kensei jodo to seito seiji* [Kensei Jodo and Party Politics], Shibunkaku Shuppan; *Kindai kimitsuhi shiryo shusei* [Aggregation of Historical Documents on Modern Japan's Secret Funds], Yumani Shobo; and *Kuratomi Yuzaburo nikki* [Diary of Kuratomi Yuzaburo], co-authored, Kokusho Kankokai.

Lecture 3:
Iechika Ryoko
Iechika is professor at the Faculty of International Studies, Keiai University and visiting professor, Open University of Japan. Graduated from the Graduate School of Law, Keio University, Iechika holds a Ph.D. in law. Her area of specialty is modern to contemporary history of China and the Sino-Japanese relations. Her publications include *Sho Kaiseki to Nankin kokumin seifu* [Chiang Kai-shek and Nanjing Nationalist Government], Keio University Press; *Nitchu kankei no kihon kozo* [Basic Structure of the Sino-Japanese Relations], Koyo Shobo; and *Sho Kaiseki no gaiko senryaku to Nitchu senso* [Chiang Kai-shek's Diplomatic Strategy and the Second Sino-Japanese War], Iwanami Shoten.

Lecture 4:
Hatano Isamu
Born in 1971, Hatano is a part-time lecturer at Faculty of Law, Seikei University. Graduated from the Graduate School of Law and Political Science, Seikei University, Hatano holds a Ph.D. in political science. His area of specialty is political and diplomatic history of Japan and history of the Japanese navy. His publications include *Kindai Nippon no gun-san-gaku fukugotai* [The Military-Industry-Academia Compound in Modern Japan], Sobunsha.

Lecture 5:
Tohmatsu Haruo
Born in 1962, Tohmatsu is professor at the Department of International Relations, National Defense Academy. Graduated from the Graduate School of Social Studies, University of Oxford, Tohmatsu holds a D.Phil. in political science and international relations. His area of specialty is political and diplomatic history and comparative war history. His publications include *Nippon teikoku to inin tochi* [Japanese Empire and Mandate System], University of Nagoya Press; *Nitchu senso no gunjiteki tenkai* [Military Development of the Second Sino-Japanese War], co-authored, Keio University Press; and *Nichiei koryushi 1600–2000, 3—gunji* [History of Anglo-Japanese Relations 1600–2000 Vol. 3—Military], co-authored, University of Tokyo Press.

Lecture 6:
Shibata Shin'ichi
Born in 1958, Shibata is associate professor at the Department of History of Kokugakuin University. Graduated from Kokugakuin University's Department of History, his area of specialty is modern and contemporary history of Japan. His publications include *Showa-ki no koshitsu to seiji-gaiko* [Imperial Court and Politics/Diplomacy in the Showa Era], Hara Shobo, and *Nippon kindai-shi kenkyu yoroku* [Brief Treatises and Essays on Japan's Modern History], Watanabe Shuppan.

Lecture 7:
Tsutsui Kiyotada
(See above)

Lecture 8:
Iwatani Nobu
Born in 1976, Iwatani is senior fellow at the Center for Military History, National Institute for Defense Studies. Graduated from the Graduate School of Law, Keio University, Iwatani holds a Ph.D. in law. His area of specialty is Sino-Japanese relations and modern/contemporary history of China. His publications include *Tairitsu to kyozon no rekishi ninshiki* [Historical Perceptions of Confrontation and Co-existence], co-authored, University of Tokyo Press, and *Sho Kaiseki kenkyu* [Study of Chaing Kai-shek], co-authored, Toho Shoten.

Lecture 9:
Tobe Ryoichi
Born in 1948, Tobe is professor of history at the Faculty of Liberal Arts, Teikyo Univerity. Graduated from the Graduate School of Law, Kyoto University, Tobe holds a Ph.D. in law. His area of specialty is modern to contemporary history of Japan. His publications include *Pisu Fira* [Peace Feeler], Ronsosha; *Gyakusetsu no guntai* [The Military in Paradox], Chuokoron Shinsha; *Nippon rikugun to Chugoku* [Imperial Japanese Army and China], Kodansha; and *Gaimusho kakushin-ha* [Ministry of Foreign Affairs' Reformist Faction], Chuokoron Shinsha.

Lecture 10:
Hanada Tomoyuki
Born in 1977, Hanada is senior fellow at the Center for Military History, National Institute for Defense Studies. Graduated from the Graduate School of Law, Hokkaido University, Hanada holds a Ph.D. in law. His area of specialty is the military history of Russia and the Soviet Union and the history of Russian Imperialism. His publications include *Nichiro senso heiki/jinbutsu jiten* [Cyclopedia of Weapons and Individuals in the Russo-Japanese War], co-authored, Gakken Publishing, and *Gendai Russia wo shirutameno 60-sho: Dainihan* [60 Chapters to Know Contemporary Russia: 2nd Edition], co-authored, Akashi Shoten.

Lecture 11:
Takeda Tomoki
Born in 1970, Takeda is professor at the Faculty of Law, Daito Bunka University. Graduated from the Graduate School of Social Sciences, Tokyo Metropolitan University, Takeda holds a Ph.D. in political sciences. His area of specialty is the political and diplomatic history of Japan. His publications include *Shigemitsu Mamoru to sengo seiji* [Shigemitsu Mamoru and Postwar Politics], Yoshikawa Kobunkan; *Kindai Nippon no ridashippu* [Leadership in Modern Japan], co-authored, Chikura Shobo; and a treatise "Nippon Gaimusho no taigai senryaku no kyogo to sono kiketsu: 1933–1938" [Competition among External Strategies of Japan's Ministry of Foreign Affairs and Its Outcomes: 1933–38] in *Nenpo Nippon gendaishi*, [Annual Report of History of Contemporary Japan], No. 16.

Lecture 12:
Makino Kuniaki
Born in 1977, Makino is associate professor at the Faculty of Economics, Setsunan University. Graduated from the Graduate School of Economics of Kyoto University, Makino holds a Ph.D. in economics. His area of specialty is modern Japan's history of economic thought. His publications include *Senjika no keizai gakusha* [Economists during the War], Chuokoron Shinsha, and *Shibata Kei*, Nihon Keizai Hyouronsha.

Lecture 13:
Moriyama Atsushi
Born in 1962, Moriyama is associate professor at the School of International Relations, University of Shizuoka. Graduated from the Graduate School of Humanities, Kyushu University, Moriyama holds a Ph.D. in Literature. His area of specialty is modern to contemporary history of Japan. His publications include *Nippon wa naze kaisen ni fumikittaka* [Why Did Japan Decide to Enter the War with the US?], Shinchosha, and *Nichibei kaisen no seiji katei* [Political Process of Japan's Decision Making for US-Japan War], Yoshikawa Kobunkan.

Lecture 14:
Suzuki Tamon
Suzuki Tamon is Associate Professor in the Graduate School of Law and a Member of the Hakubi Project at Kyoto University. He received his Ph.D. in 2006 from the Graduate School of Humanities and Social Sciences at the University of Tokyo. A specialist in modern Japanese history, his publications include *"Shusen" no seiji-shi: 1943–1945* [Japan's Long Road to Surrender: 1943–45], University of Tokyo Press, 2011.

Lecture 15:
Iguchi Haruo
Born in 1964, Iguchi is professor at the School of International Studies, Kwansei Gakuin University. Graduated from tbe Ph.D. program in the History Department, the Division of the Social Sciences, University of Chicago, Iguchi holds a Ph.D. in history. His area of specialty is US-Japan relations and political and diplomatic history of the United States. His publications include *Ayukawa Yoshisuke to keizaiteki kokusai shugi* [Ayukawa Yoshisuke and Economic Internationalism], University of Nagoya Press.

（英文版）昭和史講義──最新研究で見る戦争への道
Fifteen Lectures on Showa Japan:
Road to the Pacific War in Recent Historiography

2016年3月27日　第1刷発行

編　者　筒井清忠
訳　者　野田牧人
　　　　ポール・ネルム
発行所　一般財団法人 出版文化産業振興財団
　　　　〒101-0051 東京都千代田区神田神保町 3-12-3
　　　　電話　03-5211-7282（代）
　　　　ホームページ　http://www.jpic.or.jp/

印刷・製本所　大日本印刷株式会社